Investing for Middle America

John Elliott Tappan and the Origins of American Express Financial Advisors

KENNETH LIPARTITO
AND CAROL HEHER PETERS

palgrave

for St Martin's Press

INVESTING FOR MIDDLE AMERICA: JOHN ELLIOTT TAPPAN AND THE ORIGINS OF
AMERICAN EXPRESS FINANCIAL ADVISORS

© Kenneth Lipartito and Carol Heher Peters, 2001

First published 2001 by
PALGRAVE
175 Fifth Avenue, New York, N.Y.10010.
Companies and representatives throughout the world

PALGRAVE is the new global publishing imprint of St. Martin 's Press LLC
Scholarly and Reference Division and Palgrave Publishers Ltd (formerly
Macmillan Press Ltd).

ISBN 0-312-23398-1 hardback

Library of Congress Cataloging-in-Publication Data

Lipartito, Kenneth, 1957-
Investing for middle america : John Elliott Tappan and the origins of American
Express Financial Advisors /
Kenneth Lipartito, Carol Heher Peters.
     p. cm.
  ISBN 0-312-23398-1
  Includes bibliographical references and index.
  1. Tappan, John Elliott, 1870- . 2. American Express
Financial Advisors. 3. Financial planners-United States.
4. Investment advisors--United States. Financial
services industry--United States.

HG4928.5 .L57 2001
332.6/0973 21 2001-021865

Design by planettheo.com

First edition: September 2001
10 9 8 7 6 5 4 3 2 1

Printed in the United States of America.

Dedications

Carol Peters:
To Ruth Tappan Dowling
Marion Tappan Ryan
Marian Tappan Dowling Heher

Kenneth Lipartito:
To Isabel and Gabriel

Table of Contents

Ten pages of photos appear between pages 146 and 147.

Preface and Acknowledgments

This book has taken a long and winding road from conception to completion. It began in the mind of Carol Heher Peters, who as a child spent hours listening to her grandmother Ruth Tappan Dowling's stories of her Minnesota childhood. Many of Ruth's stories included anecdotes about her father, John Elliott Tappan. Ruth told of John's adventures as a young man on the western frontier, his experiences as a homesteading farmer in northern Minnesota, and his life as a lawyer and businessman.

Public awareness of Tappan's contribution to the history of American financial services evolved slowly. After Ruth died in 1989, Carol decided to complete the genealogical work her grandmother had begun sixty-three years before. At the same time, she also began a search to discover more about her great-grandfather. She uncovered the story of Investors Syndicate in a wealth of primary source material, including a collection of almost 20,000 letters written by Tappan between 1894 and 1919. These were made available through the generosity of Mr. William McKinney, who at the time was vice president of field management at American Express Financial Advisors in Minneapolis. As the mounds of source material grew, and the significance of Tappan's pioneering work emerged, it became clear that his life and the history of his business would be of interest to a wide audience.

After six years of research, Peters produced a draft manuscript that eventually found its way to Kenneth Lipartito, a historian of American business who was looking for interesting material to publish in a book series. It quickly became apparent to Lipartito that here was a unique story, and a rare opportunity to gain insight into the everyday practice of finance during a period for which the historical record was dim. With the help of the descendents of John Elliott Tappan, an agreement was struck. Lipartito would have access to all the letters, research, interviews, and other materials Peters had collected. Taking the original manuscript, he would fashion a broader history, placing Tappan and his achievements in the context of American finance and business history. The task was to complete a work that would bring the very human, personal story of Tappan and his achievements to the public, while also meeting the stringent requirements of high quality professional history. Whether or not he and Peters have succeeded is for readers to judge.

The book could not have been written, though, without generous help from many people. First and foremost the authors express their gratitude to the family of John Elliott Tappan, who provided intellectual, financial, and emotional support to see this project to completion. Marion Tappan Ryan (Mrs. Vincent J. Ryan) has been devoted to it from the beginning, and her words, and those of her late sister, Ruth Tappan Dowling (Mrs. Joseph L. Dowling), make possible the vivid portrayal of Tappan and his wife, children, friends, and business associates.

Other family members were also vital to getting the manuscript out of its box in the attic and into the hands of a publisher. We list their names, in alphabetical order: Professor and Mrs. John Elliott Dowling, Jennifer Ryan Flynn, Doctors Eliot and Katrinka Heher, Mr. and Mrs. Gregory J. Heher, Marian Dowling Heher, Eleanor Dowling Kendrick, and Mr. and Mrs. Vincent J. Ryan, Jr.

Carol Peters expresses special thanks to her mother, Marian Dowling Heher, and brother Eliot Heher. They both spent many hours reading and editing the manuscript, and supported it in countless other ways. Their constant encouragement, faith, and dedication made this book much better than it otherwise would have been. Carol's father, Harry Heher, Jr., gave generously of his time and offered many helpful observations and suggestions. He also provided the key introduction to Mr. Fred Kirby, whose knowledge of the Tappan archives at American Express Financial Advisors eventually led to the Tappan papers.

She also thanks her brother H. Tappan Heher, whose resourcefulness led her to Ken Lipartito; her husband, David, and daughters Emily and Caroline, for their inspiration and constant support; Dr. and Mrs. Joseph L. Dowling, Jr., and Angela Dowling Munro for their encouragement and some very useful archival material.

At an early stage, Susan Moschen and Carol Maki worked as research assistants. They were responsible for finding a wealth of otherwise hidden sources and information. Their dedication and resourcefulness during those years were central to the success of the manuscript. Susan worked in upstate New York and Connecticut and uncovered piles of ancestral information on the Tappans and their relatives. Carol worked in Minneapolis, St. Paul, and elsewhere in Minnesota, in Wisconsin, the state of Washington, and North and South Dakota tracking down every detail she could find on John Elliott Tappan, his family, relatives, friends, and business associates.

Carol Peters also thanks her cousin, Sharon Gallagher Walsh, for a place to stay in Minneapolis during visits to American Express Financial Advisors, and for her extended tours of Minneapolis and St. Paul. These led to every place John Tappan and his family lived and worked. Minerva Balke was equally generous with her time and home in Angora, Minnesota. She graciously extended an invitation to stay while Carol Peters conducted research in northern Minnesota, and drove her to the locations central to Tappan's life in Angora, including other towns in the Mesabi Iron Range where Tappan visited. Her coauthored history of Angora was an invaluable source of insight into early life there.

In addition, Carol Peters thanks her professors at Clark University for their training in history, and her friends Donna and Steven Silvern, who helped locate the house where Tappan was born in Oshkosh, Wisconsin.

Kenneth Lipartito wishes to thank his colleagues at the University of Houston and at Florida International University, and elsewhere, who helped to support his scholarship. The interlibrary loan departments of both universities did exceptional work in locating materials. The Milken Institute of Santa Monica, California, was the first public venue for presentation of this work. Constructive criticisms by members of the Institute and by Naomi Lamoreaux at that meeting were important in getting the project on the right track. Darden Pyron's discussions about the nature of biography provided needed guidance in this fine art. Thomas Castillo was a determined research assistant.

Invaluable were the editing skills of Dr. Elisabeth O'Kane, who overcame the inevitable problems of inconsistency in a jointly written manuscript. She has the sincerest gratitude of both authors. Karen Wolny and Alan Bradshaw at Palgrave handled the publication process smoothly and skillfully. Kenneth Lipartito also thanks Carol Peters' family for tolerating his presence in their home and for the sacrifice of their dining room to mounds of papers and boxes.

Finally, both authors acknowledge the many institutions whose collections provided crucial information and whose staff members were extremely helpful. We list them here, in alphabetical order: Baker Library, Harvard University; Connecticut Historical Society, Hartford, Connecticut; Connecticut River Museum, Essex, Connecticut; Connecticut State Library, Hartford, Connecticut; the collection of papers on Charles Henry Tappan from the Federal Bureau of Investigation, Washington, D.C.; Ironworld Discovery Center, Chisholm, Minnesota; Minnesota Historical Society, Minnesota History Center, St. Paul; Minneapolis Public Library, Minneapolis; Northeast Minnesota Historical Center, University of Minnesota, Duluth; National Archives, Washington, D.C.; Oshkosh Public Library, Oshkosh, Wisconsin; Senate House, Kingston, New York; South Dakota State Archives, Pierre, South Dakota; South Dakota State Historical Society, Pierre, South Dakota; State Historical Society of North Dakota, North Dakota Heritage Center, Bismarck, North Dakota; the University of Minnesota, St. Paul; St. Louis Historical Society, Duluth, Minnesota; the staff historian at the United States Post Office, Washington, D.C.; University of Washington, Seattle; Washington State Archives, Western Washington University, Bellingham; and the Wiltwyck Chapter of the Daughters of the American Revolution, Kingston, New York.

Prologue

An aging figure stood in the doorway to the office. He was neatly dressed in his dark suit and hat. In fact, he was more than neat. He was natty, but in a slightly out of date fashion. He said nothing, but silently looked around as the business of the office continued, uninterrupted. Amid the clattering of typewriters, a young secretary glanced up from the sheaf of papers she was filing. She did not recognize him, though others had seen him before. After a few minutes, he departed, apparently satisfied with what he had observed. Later, the young woman would ask her co-workers, "Who was that old gentleman this morning?" One told her that she did not know his name, but that he used to work here. No, not just work. She thought actually that he had been the owner, or something like that. The young secretary shook her head, with just a touch of pity. Then she went back to work and did not give him another thought.

In 1994, Investors Diversified Services (IDS), a Minneapolis-based financial services firm, ceased to be. It did not disappear due to failure, however, but because of success. Acquired by the American Express Corporation in 1984, IDS was added to that company's travel and credit card operations as a new division. In 1994, IDS was renamed American Express Financial Advisors.

By the time of the 1984 acquisition, IDS had grown into one of the largest financial services companies in America. It managed over $19 billion in assets. It was a fixture in its hometown of Minneapolis, occupying the fifty-seven-story IDS tower in the center of the city. Its new relationship with American Express was built on a foundation of growth that stretched back a century.

IDS sold a wide range of financial products. In the 1940s, it had started one of the first mutual funds, and in the 1950s, it was the nation's leading mutual fund manager. In the financially revolutionary 1980s and 1990s, it would move into banking, property and casualty insurance, individual retirement accounts, and had begun operations overseas. By the time of the American Express acquisition, its divisions included consumer credit, property leasing, life insurance, and brokerage as well.

Particularly strong was IDS's team of field agents, some 5,000 operating throughout the nation, serving 1.2 million customers. Agents were especially strong in what journalists like to call Middle America. This shorthand term embraces both the geographical center of the nation, the middle western states, as well as the more abstract "socioeconomic" center, the middle income groups. IDS agents had close relationships with ordinary Americans who sought to manage their money and savings by using a variety of financial instruments. It was this field force that American Express found especially attractive. It had grown over many years, generations in fact, through contacts, client service, and trust. American Express could not have duplicated such a strategic asset from scratch.

The products that agents sold had a still longer history. The IDS name itself is part of that story. Before it "diversified" into stock funds, insurance, and other financial products, IDS was called simply Investors Syndicate. And it sold one thing only, a certificate designed to reach the ordinary saver at a time when only the rich watched the stock market. Before World War II, banks and savings accounts were about as sophisticated as most middle-class and working men and women ever got. The origin of today's consumer oriented financial markets lies, in part, with Investors Syndicate's pioneering effort. That chain of history connects to the life of the man who founded Investors Syndicate, and hence helped to start the financial services operation that today touches millions of lives. He was that anonymous figure who stood in the door of what had once been his own company. His name was John Elliott Tappan.

John Elliott Tappan was born in 1870, the same year as another figure who would dedicate his life to revolutionizing financial institutions—A. P. Giannini. In many ways, the two could not have been more different. Giannini was the son of Italian immigrants who hawked vegetables along the rough San Francisco waterfront. From those beginnings, he built up the most powerful bank in the nation. Giannini's Bank of America pioneered the use of branches to bring banking services to rural residents and urban immigrants who stood in awe of the granite edifices housing big city banks. Tappan, by contrast, was born on the frontier, to farmer parents. His family had been in the United States for generations. He was of Yankee Protestant stock, and grew up in a far different America than Giannini the vegetable peddler.[1]

Yet the two men shared something. They both believed that financial institutions could be democratized to serve a much larger clientele, particularly Americans of modest means residing outside of the booming urban centers of the nation. Both men lived most of their lives in the city—Giannini in San Francisco, Tappan in Minneapolis. But they identified less with urban ways and people than with those living outside the urban landscape, or those forced to its margins. Giannini focused on struggling but hardworking immigrants and the farmers in California's Central Valley. Tappan targeted aspiring middle-class white-collar workers, usually at the lower end of the managerial and professional scale, and western farmers who felt besieged by the giant financial institutions of the East.

Tappan and Giannini both came to understand the limitations of capitalism for such Americans through their own experiences. This connection to ordinary people linked them to a long tradition of economic reform for the "common man" that stretched back to Thomas Jefferson and his celebration of sturdy yeoman farmers. Both Tappan and Giannini absorbed a deep suspicion of large, incumbent financial institutions located in the centers of power, commerce, and finance on the East Coast. Such fears had first found expression in Jefferson's denunciation of the financial schemes of his rival, Alexander Hamilton. That this debate could transcend the decades and touch a Midwestern Protestant as well as a California immigrant says something about its power in American culture. As John Kenneth Galbraith has observed, only slavery has been more divisive in American politics than money.[2]

Tappan and Giannini shared other features of this "Jeffersonian" economic philosophy. Like Jefferson, they were firmly committed to private property and the promotion of economic growth through individual action. Neither man chose to make his mark on society through the public sector. Both would have run-ins with suspicious regulators of financial institutions, who seemed more comfortable with the large banks and investment operations they supposedly oversaw than with newcomers and innovators challenging those institutions. But both men also felt that capitalism had taken a wrong turn, away from the best interests of society as a whole. Eschewing radical critiques, they decided to reform capitalism from within, through private sector innovation.

The notion that dedicated individuals can, by their own actions, create new models for a better society is a deeply American belief. It is part of a long utopian tradition that was especially strong in the nineteenth-century United States, where fervent commitment to the individual combined with a religious quest for the perfect commonwealth.[3] Although we today often contrast the private and public sectors, in reality the lines separating them are blurred. During moments of high conflict, such as hotly contested elections, opposing interests draw sharper distinctions than can be found in everyday experience. At the turn of the twentieth century, businessmen commonly denounced government interference with the private market, while critics of big business seemed ready to place their faith in government ownership or socialism. But it would be a mistake to apply present-day categories to the past or to take rhetorical language as simply a description of reality. The actual choices people faced in their daily lives were far more complex.

Tappan and Giannini in fact invested their private enterprises with deeply public purposes. They believed that private action could be socially useful, and they sought in the financial system not just a way to riches, but a way to restructure the economy so that more people could lead more secure, happier, productive lives. When necessary, they supported government regulation. At other times, they turned to the market. The point, which they would have stressed, was not some abstract, ideological choice between free market and big government. Rather, it was a pragmatic one—the concerned, private citizen seeking a better society by his or her own actions. In that sense, they were fervent believers in democracy.

Tappan and Giannini also shared one more experience. By the end of their careers, each was living in a nation far different from the one that had nurtured their ideals and given rise to their innovations. In fact, both ironically had helped to usher in a new sort of financial system, whose features and values seemed in many ways to contradict the principles for which they had fought. Tappan promoted individual self-reliance, yet his own creation had become a giant, bureaucratic institution. Giannini had defied the self-satisfied banking elite with his new branch banks, but his old immigrant savings bank had become a powerful, international financial institution. Both men believed that through private initiative, money could be made to serve the people; yet by the time they died, big government held responsibility for the money supply and was the regulator of financial markets. Both Tappan and Giannini in fact saw the institutions they had founded in the interests of the people investigated and chastised for being too big and too powerful.

What follows is Tappan's story. Like any person's life, it is filled with irony and contradiction, as well as its share of triumphs and successes. More important perhaps, it is a representative life. For John Elliott Tappan was one of the many men and women who confronted and sought to resolve a crucial issue that had vexed American capitalism for more than a century. As an economic theory, capitalism promises equal opportunity, equitable treatment, and widespread prosperity, all through a self-regulating marketplace that coordinates individual action. As an economic fact, it has been much less amenable to some people than others. Markets have been far less equitable in their treatment of diverse populations than theory proposes. Not everyone can bend the market to their needs. Not everyone has been able to benefit from money-making opportunities in the private sector. Indeed, at times capitalism has seemed a game only for a small ring of insiders with privileged access to capital and investment opportunities.

John Elliott Tappan puzzled over this issue at the turn of the century, when the first powerful critique of American capitalism and its new large corporate institutions was being launched. He responded as best he could, drawing on beliefs and values transmitted to him from his conservative ancestors, but also from a diverse array of experiences in his own life. His answer may not appeal to those of a more radical persuasion. Tappan was committed to internal reform and private sector action. Nor was he a systematic thinker. But he was a contributor to the salient trend that over the past century has made financial institutions more accessible than ever before. By investigating the life, thought, and achievements of this "ordinary" man of business, we can probe more deeply into fundamental questions that, in a democratic society, are meant to be the concern of all citizens. Can a free market economy also treat all citizens fairly and equitably? Can a healthy economy also be one that opens opportunity for all who wish to seize it? And perhaps most pertinent of all, in a capitalist economy, can everyone be given a chance to find, hold, and use capital, or is it a resource only for the elite and powerful?

CHAPTER ONE

FROM FRONTIER TO FINANCE

Even before he knew it, John Elliott Tappan's life was connected to money. In 1873, when he was three years old, living on his family's farm in Wisconsin, momentous events were taking place around him. America plunged into an economic depression, or "Panic" in the word of the times. But this was not just an ordinary downturn of the business cycle. This economic calamity would reshape the social and political landscape of the nation for years to come. Before it was over, railroad workers would go on strike, paralyzing the country's transportation network in America's first nationwide industrial action. Conflicts between two emerging groups, those who owned factories, banks, and stores, and those who worked in them, would raise the specter of class warfare. Unemployment in the nation's rapidly growing cities would turn "respectable" upper-class members of society inward, away from the poor, bedraggled, and increasingly immigrant masses that made up the bulk of the urban population. In the West, farmers would form new organizations with quaint-sounding names like "The Patrons of Husbandry." They rallied against what they saw as a different sort of social danger—not mobs but monopolists, the rich and powerful who owned the means of transportation, communications, and, increasingly, manufacturing.

The source of all this trouble was obscure. Some pinned blame on the nation's railroads, which grew to enormous size in giant systems stretching across the continent. By the late nineteenth century, railroads were employing thousands, and soon tens of thousands, of laborers. They represented hundreds of millions of dollars in invested capital. Railroad corporations were certainly a force to behold, an economic power the likes of which the nation had never seen. Livelihoods of humble farmers were absolutely dependent upon rail transport. Without it, the cost of shipping to market bulky products such as grain, beef, and cotton quickly exceeded the value of the crop. Shipping costs were crucial to western merchants and storekeepers as well. There was also trouble over another group of behemoths—industrial factories, where working men made more and more of the goods the nation consumed.

The direct cause of misery, though, was traced to something else— money. Money has long been an object of intense curiosity, even worship. It has also long been cursed as the root of evil, the corrupter of morals. But how could something so intangible as money have the power to hold hostage the lives and fortunes of men and women? Here was part of money's mystery and allure. It could roil markets or seal a man's economic fate, even as it did no work itself. In Tappan's Middle West, 1873 saw the start of a divisive debate over money—who had it, who controlled it, and how it should be used. This debate would continue long after the depression abated. It would become the key issue of American politics, deciding several presidential campaigns, not finally put to rest until forty years later, with the formation of the Federal Reserve System in 1913. Money, with its occult power, would be more than John Elliott Tappan's business. It would define the contours of his life.

To untangle the long battle over money that took place in Tappan's world, we have to understand the economy as people in 1873 understood it. Nineteenth-century Americans believed in the labor theory of value, a theory endorsed by both Adam Smith and Karl Marx.[1] In the United States, its most famous exponents included Thomas Jefferson, Alexander Hamilton, and Abraham Lincoln. The theory held that work was the root of all value. Humans gained nothing from raw nature except through their own labor.

Only those who worked by the sweat of their brow created and produced the things necessary for human happiness and progress. Only producers counted in this economy.

Central to conflict in the 1870s was intense debate about the interests of producers against the wealth and power of nonproducers. Producers, those who labored and made useful things, included farmers, but also manufacturers, at least small, local ones. Artisans were producers, as were shopkeepers. So were propertyless workers, who labored with their skills and their hands. Who was not a producer? That was hard to say. Americans tended to have a fairly generous definition of labor, including in this category merchants, professionals, inventors, and to some extent bankers.[2] Still, those who did little more than live off land rents or lend money at high interest seemed to fall beyond the pale. In extreme free labor rhetoric, these nonproducers were condemned as "leeches on the business body," who "produce no wealth, but rather consume it."[3]

In the West in particular, eastern bankers and money men were roundly condemned in such fashion. They profited from their control of the vital supplies of credit and money needed for trade, commerce, agriculture, and manufacturing—the "real" production. But even here it was hard to draw the class line. Capital was entitled to some reward, if a minimal one. Local bankers and moneylenders who provided capital seemed to be performing vital and productive functions. So too did merchants who sold on credit the goods farmers needed. They were often given an exemption from the label "parasite," so long as interest rates were low and money was plentiful.

The notion of value in labor and production had roots stretching back to Protestant and ultimately biblical sources that equated hard work with virtue.[4] However, in nineteenth-century America, the notion also had crucial political implications. More than fairness to the worker, or technical economic theory, was at stake here. In a nation fervently committed to the republican form of government, and with wide aspirations toward democratic citizenship, Americans were keenly aware that liberty and equality were easily threatened by despotic concentrations of wealth and power. It was, after all, the concentration and arbitrary use of power by George III that had touched off the American Revolution. Republics were imperiled by aristocrats, who used wealth and position to gain control of government and manipulate it in their own interests. Aristocrats of finance could pose the same danger.

Equitable wealth distribution countered this danger, by giving every man an equal chance to live the life of a free and independent producer. Free men who owned their own land and property were beholden to no one. They possessed virtue, and virtuous men acted with the public good in mind. Such conditions were considered absolutely essential for democracy.[5] Still, important as equality was, few Americans contemplated radical wealth redistribution or active government intervention to achieve it. There was, in the logic of free labor, no need for activism. Values, of goods or services or even money, in the end reflected, or should reflect, the value of labor put into them. Since labor created value, all those who worked were entitled to the fair and full reward for their efforts. As long as labor received its just reward, as long as no economic parasite siphoned off the value due the laborer, then a fair and equitable distribution of wealth was assured. The Republic might not be a society of exact economic equals, but it should certainly be one of wide property ownership in which each man could support himself and his family without being dependent on another. In a world where labor received the full value of what it created, no one who worked should ever starve or be reduced to a state of charitable dependence.

Implied in this theory was a largely self-regulating market. Labor received its due, unless aristocrats with special connections to the state or monopolists who cornered the market interfered in the distribution of rewards. For this reason, both liberal and conservative Americans generally endorsed a hands-off, laissez-faire policy. Only projects that clearly benefited all classes, such as public works and improvements like roads, canals, bridges, and railroads, or schools, should be actively state supported, and even then in limited fashion, largely by the local rather than the federal government. Far greater danger came when enemies of labor—enemies of the citizen majority, that is—used the state to capture the rewards properly belonging to working men and women.

Even greater than the danger of government corruption, though, was the danger of monetary manipulation. There was no more subtle and nefarious way of siphoning off labor's true reward than by deliberate tampering with the value of currency. The formula for corrupting the Republic by manipulating money worked as follows: The value of labor, determined by work performed, was a constant. But monetary values were infinitely variable. If the quantity (and hence value) of money could somehow be changed, then a clever financial manipulator could line his pockets at the producer's expense. When money changed value, workers' wages and farmers' incomes changed as well, even though the work performed had not changed. Deflation, for example, raised the borrower's burden of debt—and most farmers had to borrow. The moneylender in this case took an unearned increment of value from labor.

Crediting all real value to labor, then, nineteenth-century Americans tended to see changes in money values as unnatural and exploitative. Money had to be tied down, fixed, and tamed so that it stood subordinate to labor. It had to be free from the control of cliques, rings, and insiders. Otherwise, as Andrew Jackson darkly warned in his farewell address, the "money power" would render "property insecure and the wages of labor unsteady or uncertain."[6]

Until 1873, both major parties, Democratic and Republican, agreed that fixing the value of money required an absolute, inviolable standard. Precious metal served as a good standard, and at various times in history gold, silver, or both backed American currency. American farmers, manufacturers, bankers, and workers generally believed that sound money was hard money, as expressed in some metallic standard.[7] Since the supply of metal depended on discoveries of new ore—a rare occurrence—it was impossible to change the value of metal-backed money by arbitrary action.

Although Americans of many persuasions shared this healthy fear of money and gave instinctive support to the "sound" dollar, they did not all share the same self-interest. Increasingly, divergent interests would drive a wedge into the consensus on financial orthodoxy. The first break came during the Civil War, when the Union government was forced to issue paper notes known as Greenbacks to finance the war effort. Most northern Republicans remained hard-money men, however, and they moved quickly to take Greenbacks out of circulation once the fighting ended. Their efforts contracted the money supply, one of the few times in American history that the stock of money actually declined.[8]

In paying off the war debt and taking paper out of circulation, Republicans thought that they were returning the nation to the monetary standards and values existing before the war. But too much had already changed to simply go back to the antebellum status quo. For one thing, northerners had instituted revolutionary changes in economic policy while the South was out of the Union. They supported economic growth through subsidies to railroads and other forms of transportation. They gave land to farmers through the Homestead Act. They founded state-sponsored universities. Most of these measures were uncontroversial, except perhaps to die-hard southern Confederates. Republicans also sought one more thing—to "rationalize" or stabilize the nation's banking industry and monetary system. Banks, the crucial institution of money creation and capital mobilization, became the first battleground in the late-nineteenth-century war over money.

Before the Civil War, there was virtually no federal regulation of banking, and precious little state or local regulation. Under the principles of "free banking," one could simply open a place of deposit, print paper notes, and lend money at interest. Whether these notes actually circulated was another matter, of course. Many traded at a heavy discount, reflecting the shaky reputation of the financial institutions that issued them. But that was the market's problem. Sound institutions would see their notes accepted readily; poor ones would be driven out of business. Serious bankers often sought to enhance their reputation by seeking state charters, but these charters imposed few obligations.

Wide-open banking fit the American ethos of competition and private experimentation. Though disorderly, an open and competitive banking system at least gave all entrepreneurs a fair chance to get capital. Financial openness and bank competition were highly desirable from the point of view of a striving western farmer or merchant, for example, who wanted money cheap and plentiful to develop land and build businesses. Central control of finance, on the other hand, posed a danger to such interests. Centralization might permit a clique or cabal of moneylenders to control the nation's currency, make money scarce, change monetary values, and deprive labor of its just rewards.

Before the Civil War, such fears had largely discouraged central management of the money supply and encouraged a banking system that was decentralized and wide-open compared to that of other nations.[9] Pleasing to agrarians and to those located outside of major cities, this relatively unrestricted financial system was disturbing to more established business interests and financiers in the East. By the end of the Civil War, the dominant view of the Republican party had shifted firmly toward control and financial regulation. The result was the National Banking Act of 1866. It placed restrictions on bank notes, making it all but impossible for state or private banks to issue paper. Although the number of banks grew in the latter half of the nineteenth century, and checks began to supplement currency, the law still had a constraining effect. It raised reserve requirements in a manner that tended to favor banks located in the East. Banks outside of eastern money centers survived by keeping funds on deposit in city banks, which in turn kept funds in the big banks of New York, Philadelphia, and Boston. The guardians of wealth regarded this system as stable and predictable. Increasingly, however, it would be viewed by westerners and southerners as a form of enforced dependence on the lords of capital in the East. The new financial policies were locking down the wide-open financial system that had operated before the Civil War.[10]

Until 1873, monetary conflicts had remained muted. The new banking act was certainly a change, but one grudgingly accepted. The removal of Greenbacks reduced the supply of money, but paper currency like Greenbacks were controversial anyway. When the Panic of 1873 struck, however, simmering monetary conflict suddenly boiled over. Money grew tight, production closed down, and farmers were forced into bankruptcy as banks called loans. Though the contraction eventually ended and the economy recovered strongly after 1879, for many it was a revelatory experience. They now saw a financial system rigged against the West. Stability and rationalization meant tighter money and higher interest rates. In newly settled territory lacking banks or other financial intermediaries, interest rates could be five times as high as they were in eastern cities. Falling supplies of money and the retirement of some $2 billion of war debt fueled deflation, meaning a decrease in prices. Conditions affected different groups in different ways. Agrarian producers experienced low prices for their products, and hence a fall in income, even as overall national income climbed.[11]

Many consequences of Republican monetary policy were unforeseen. Still, taken together, they suggested a pattern to critics. In the West, interest rates were high, banks scarce, and capital hard to find. In the East, there were plenty of banks, money flowed into industry and railroads, and bondholders watched the value of their bonds rise as prices fell. Speculators who had loaded up on Civil War Greenbacks at discounted prices reaped a windfall when they were retired in gold. Power, it seemed, had flowed into the hands of a small group of financial insiders who set monetary policy in their own interest. In 1873, producers were suddenly not in charge of the economy, as the labor theory of value said they should be. Money itself, a mere tool for the honest producer, slipped through the fingers of the producers of real wealth and into the hands of a small clique of bankers and lenders located in the nation's financial centers, New York City especially.

The bankers of New York, of course, did not see things in quite the same way. Supporters of the new national banking and financial order, they argued that the system worked well, regardless of who was hurt. Panics and downturns, though undesirable, were nothing new, either. These natural economic events merely shook out the inefficient and allowed the more competent to pick up the pieces. Modern historians have largely sided with this view of events.

Still, even if the post–Civil War monetary policies worked, they did so in ways bound to create political conflict. By making large, established banks in the East the crucial economic institutions of capital dispensing, the policies created a pyramid structure that moved money into reserve city banks on the East Coast. New York in particular benefited from this arrangement. It had already become the nation's investment banking center, with its sophisticated communications infrastructure and ties to European investors. By the late nineteenth century, it was becoming the domestic financial balance wheel, drawing in funds from the countryside and redistributing them to a variety of uses. To many Americans, this sort of structure violated notions of local autonomy and went outside the old consensus of a self-regulating monetary system based on some intrinsic, unchanging value. No longer was the system self-regulating and fair. Now it was in the hands of one group located in one section.[12]

The telltale sign of this power shift was known as the "Crime of '73." As young John Tappan was celebrating his third birthday, deep in the recesses of Congress a new bill was under debate that would remove silver from the nation's money supply. This seemingly innocuous little bill, which became the Coinage Act of 1873, touched off the great silver controversy that defined the politics of money until the end of the century. The act simply discontinued the coinage of silver dollars. It seemed of little consequence. Few people had even seen silver dollars. In 1836 they had disappeared from circulation.[13] In a classic demonstration of Gresham's law ("bad money drives out good"), silver had been driven from the marketplace. Before 1873, gold was the "bad" money. It was relatively less valuable than silver, pushed down in price by new gold discoveries in the middle nineteenth century, including the famous California Gold Rush. As gold went down in value, silver went up, and relatively lower valued gold coins replaced silver ones.[14] But by 1873, the metals had reversed position. New discoveries of silver ore pushed down silver, making it cheaper than gold. Now, by Gresham's law, gold coins were threatened with elimination.

One might ask, What difference did it make, since U.S. law accepted both silver and gold as backing for money? If silver drove out gold, silver would simply become the new standard. The difference is that by the 1870s, gold had taken on a new, urgent meaning. It was not merely one of several possible standards for money. It was the international medium of exchange. The United States was in fact one of the few bimetallic nations left in the "civilized" world, accepting either gold or silver as lawful money. Most of the world's business, international trade in particular, was conducted in gold. If silver drove gold out of circulation, the United States would be out of kilter with the rest of the commercial world, particularly Europe. Fear in the international financial community over the stability of the gold dollar had already affected America's fiscal health and economic position.[15] With the 1873 law, Republicans moved the United States toward the gold standard, a mechanism for adjusting the balance of payments between nations by expressing different national currencies in the common standard of gold. It was the last piece of the new monetary policy instituted after the Civil War. It would also become the most controversial.

Under the new gold standard, with silver now gone, the amount and value of money in the nation were directly related to the amount of gold in the nation's vaults. Gold, however, was an international medium that followed trade and commerce across borders. The amount of gold in the United States was determined by the nation's balance of payments, or, in other words, by international economic forces far beyond the control or even understanding of most farmers, workers, and small-business people. When American imports exceeded exports (and they usually did at this time), gold flowed out to pay for the deficit. These international economic forces, Republicans argued, meant that gold should have pride of place as the standard of monetary value within the United States. Internationalism also meant, however, that the supply of money in the United States was closely linked to events taking place far from home.[16] Unlike the mid nineteenth century, moreover, there were no big new discoveries of ore to boost the money supply, until the Yukon strike at the end of the century.[17] Decline or slow growth of the money supply, brought on by shifts in America's international position, meant falling prices and periodic depressions, like the one that gripped the nation in 1873.

"Gold" Republicans had freighted seemingly arcane and technical matters of monetary policy with a heavy cultural burden. Without a gold standard, they argued, the United States would lose its international standing, which they wanted to enhance. Without gold, values would be subject to the arbitrary depredations of backwoods bankers and ignorant farmers, who wanted to inflate the currency. Eastern creditors believed that calls for more money and a looser banking structure were mere inflationary ploys by western debtors who wanted to pay off their obligations in currency of lesser value. Such perceived efforts to shirk obligations were denounced in strident moralistic tones.

Opponents of the gold standard were no less self-righteous. They too believed in fundamental values, that money was a "God-given thing," and that metallic currency was "the only real and most perfect medium of exchange," because it had "intrinsic value."[18] A few westerners, called Greenbackers after the Civil War currency, had departed from this tradition by supporting paper money. Most farmers and merchants throughout the West, however, held strong to their belief in bullion, just not gold alone. They sought to protect the nation from the "arbitrary and capricious" changes in value that Gold Republicans were enacting through their experiments in financial reform and internationalism. Westerners believed that prices were being forced down unfairly by bankers more interested in the international economy than in the economic health of the United States. It was not the financial establishment that was suffering from the new monetary policy. Bringing silver back into the game was seen as a corrective move that would restore prices and monetary values to their true and natural levels.

More than narrow economic interest was at stake in denouncing the Crime of '73 and the "gold fetters" in which the nation was now locked. Eastern bankers were seen as sacrificing the people on the altar of international finance, similar to the way the colonies had been sacrificed to the imperial designs of George III. Even more pertinent were comparisons between the banking power and the defunct slave power. Both, said advocates of the producer ethic, subsisted on unearned increments of wealth taken from others. Slave masters did it with the lash; gold masters did it by changing the value of money. Attempting to unite all producers, the founder of the National Labor Union, William H. Sylvis, thundered, "The manufacturer, the farmer, . . . the mechanic, the common laborer" were under the thumb of "a few bankers, brokers and usurers," who set the rate of interest.[19] This highly charged political language of money called for a new political alignment—those who worked and were entitled to the fruits of labor against the remote conspirators of finance.

Young John Tappan hardly had to worry about these weighty issues of political economy, at least not yet. As a three-year-old, his world was being shaped by fate more immediate and personal. The depression, which tore through the farm belt, had hurt his own family's fortunes. But an even more dire family crisis loomed, one that would decisively change the course of his life. Only a few months earlier, John had watched with bewilderment as his father was lowered into the ground, dead from an unknown fever at age forty-two. Elliott Smith Tappan had come West as a homesteader in 1851, settling in Oshkosh, Wisconsin, on a ninety-acre farm. Now John's mother, Adelaide, had to run the farm herself, in the face of a farm belt panic. With hired help, she did so for two years. Then, with the economy still reeling, her father-in-law, John's paternal grandfather, also passed away. These blows, so sudden and in the midst of hard times, were almost more than she could bear.

Weary from work and burdened with grief and worry over money, Adelaide Goodrich Tappan decided it was time to move on. She was nothing if not frugal and resourceful, and had the mind of a businesswoman before such a term existed for female members of the respectable middle class. She put the farm up for sale in February 1875 and took young John and her two other children by train to the small Wisconsin town of Janesville. There they stayed for four years, until 1879. As the depression subsided, Adelaide pulled up stakes once again. She intended to live out her years someplace a bit less isolated than the rural frontier, and brought her family to rest for good in the booming frontier city of Minneapolis. For her other children—Frank, now twenty-two years old, and sixteen-year-old Carrie—urban Minneapolis seemed to offer better prospects than farm life. For nine-year-old John, it meant a sudden and unexpected change from the rural farm life he knew to a challenging engagement with the city. Minneapolis would be John Elliott Tappan's home, a few excursions aside, for the rest of his working life.

Young and vibrant, Minneapolis was still shaking off the last of its frontier settlement dust when the Tappans arrived. Located at the head of the Mississippi River, it was a center of agricultural trade, with profitable lumber and flour mills. Much like Oshkosh, Minneapolis was connected to extraction and farming. Timber and wheat farming drove its growth. Like many optimistic boom town residents, citizens seized on favorable location and plentiful natural resources—such as nearby prime virgin forests and the powerful St. Anthony Falls to drive saw and flour mills—as proof that their town was bound to thrive. They pointed with pride to the symbols of urban progress—the Masonic Temple, the Lumber Exchange. Their crown jewel was a twelve-story-high granite and sandstone edifice, considered, at least locally, as the "first skyscraper west of the Mississippi." This building housed the Metropolitan Life Insurance Company, which provided what was then the largest and most important financial service next to banking—life insurance.

The move to the city had taken the Tappans a long way from their ancestral roots. When Elliott Tappan headed out to Wisconsin thirty years earlier, he left behind several hundred years of family tradition. As the name suggests, the Tappans were Yankee through and through. Or to be more precise, they were Knickerbockers, descendants of New Yorkers whose roots reached back to seventeenth-century Dutch settlers. For 200 years they had made their home in Kingston, New York, up the Hudson River from New York City.

Elliott Tappan's great-grandfather, Christopher Tappen (changed back to the original Dutch spelling Tappan some time later) was an attorney and member of New York's Secret Committee in the American Revolution, a band of patrician patriots. His companions included the wealthy and influential Robert Livingston and George Clinton. Clinton, first governor of New York and vice president under Jefferson and Madison, married Christopher Tappen's sister Cornelia. By the early nineteenth century, the Tappans were well-known figures among the influential residents of the Hudson River communities. Elliott's grandfather worked as an attorney, editor, and publisher of the Ulster Plebian in Kingston. The paper stayed in the family through Elliott's father, John Jansen Tappan, who later sold it and entered the mercantile trade.

Similar strong historical roots linked John Elliott Tappan to the East on his mother's side. Adelaide Goodrich's family had immigrated to America from Britain, likewise in the seventeenth century. They settled in and among the river towns of Connecticut—Hartford, Farmington, and New Britain. One branch made its way to Wethersfield, where for several generations they built sailing ships and made a fortune exporting lumber and trading for rum with the West Indies. Like the Tappans, the Goodrich family had been patriots during the Revolutionary War. One ancestor, Oliver Goodrich, converted the family business to a war footing, sailing as a privateer and raiding British warships from his schooner *Humbird.*

By the time John's father Elliott was born, the Tappan family fortunes may have slipped a bit. The printing and publishing business had been sold to a brother, and family property was losing value as the rural counties of the East emptied out with farmers moving to the rich soils of the West. In the early nineteenth century, the line between respectable tradesman and genteel landowner-patrician was fuzzy, and the Tappans apparently straddled this line. For whatever reason, Elliott also seems to have felt less strongly the long attachment to the ancestral home. Like many ambitious, young, unmarried men, Elliott decided that his future lay in the West. There land was opening up and opportunities for rising through the ranks of society seemed bright in a way they no longer did in the more developed East. Propaganda pamphlets were bursting with good news about Wisconsin's "wonderful climate" and fertile soil. Western boosters implored "the bold young American of the North Eastern States" to choose "a helpmeet, collect some clothing, take up his rifle and hatchet, and trusting entirely to his own prowess, march off in the direction of the setting sun."[20]

It was a westward journey many New Yorkers and New Englanders made in the decades before the Civil War. The "Old Northwest," and the newer frontier states of Michigan and Wisconsin, would be filled with ambitious Yankees, who took much of their culture and their hard-headed business sense with them as they moved. Nature, to be sure, beckoned settlers to "the bosom of the wilderness." But sublime nature could be tamed and developed by men and women who were able to make or raise what they needed with their own hands. Ambitious Yankees saw themselves as just that kind of people. By the mid-nineteenth century, they had already transformed the pristine landscape of the East, lacing it with roads and rails, tying together towns with telegraph lines, and sending smoke up the first factory chimneys. As farming moved to more fertile western soils, New England prospered in industry, commerce, finance, and trade. Similar processes would be repeated in the West as well, which by the time of John Elliott Tappan was beginning to catch up to the industrial East both in overall income and even in manufacturing. But in Elliott's era, the West meant frontier, farming, and a chance to grow up with the country.

The journey from New York to Wisconsin was long and arduous in 1851. To get to his lands in Wisconsin, Elliott stepped onto a train in Kingston that took him upstate to the Erie Canal. A canal boat brought him to a dock on Lake Erie, where he boarded a steamer heading west. After a short stop in Cleveland, the steamer docked at Sheboygan, Wisconsin. There Elliott purchased a cart and ox, loaded his possessions, and made the rest of the way overland. It took him several weeks to finish his trip, alone. His family would arrive by the same route later.

Making a farm on the frontier was no easy task. Hard work was perhaps expected, but the financial commitment and risks required a real spirit of adventure. In the 1850s, upwards of $1,000 were needed to buy sufficient land plus the necessary tools and implements to raise a profitable cash crop.[21] Then there was the backbreaking labor of clearing land of trees and shrubs, turning over virgin soil, building fences, barns, outbuildings, and a house. Even a hardworking farmer had to expect a lean year or two as land was prepared for tillage. Waiting ate up savings.

Under these conditions, most of those who ventured West tended to have backgrounds similar to Elliott Tappan: established Americans with at least a modest amount of capital. However tempting land in the West seemed, few workers were able to muster the resources needed. The average unskilled worker earned little more than a dollar a day in 1850, with unsteady prospects for employment throughout the year.[22] Better paid factory hands still took home less than $350 per year.[23] Landowning on the scale necessary to make a farm profitable was well beyond their reach even if they could save one quarter of what they earned. And few ventured out to raw land in remote communities just to live self-sufficiently. Farming was a commercial enterprise and a competitive one, with farmers closely attuned to the market. It wasn't free and open land so much as fertile and profitable land that attracted westward emigrants.

Some immigrants from Europe were able to make this journey. They were generally Germans and Scandinavians, who sold land in the old country to buy more and better land in the new, settling in Minnesota, Wisconsin, and the Dakotas. Those who disembarked from Atlantic steamers with money in their pockets stood a chance of making it out to the frontier. But most immigrants did not come to America with ready cash. The huge influx of Irish immigrants in the 1840s and '50s arrived virtually penniless, many fleeing the devastating effects of the potato famine. Most quickly settled in Eastern cities, and went to work for wages in textile factories or other manufacturing establishments, though a few made it into farming. The West of Elliott Tappan's time was largely settled by native born Anglo-Saxons, by English-speaking immigrants, and by a smattering of blond-haired, blue-eyed northern Europeans. In language, looks, and culture, the western farm belt would diverge more and more from the increasingly immigrant East, and even from much of the urban Midwest.

Elliott's ox-drawn wagon eventually took him to the borough of Vinland, just outside of Oshkosh, Wisconsin. Oshkosh itself was fairly well settled by the time he arrived. The town had a bank and a school. It was a popular stopping-off point for settlers heading further into open country. Still, it retained the remnants of a raw frontier town. Native Americans lived in the area, and people residing by old trails or working along the rivers saw them frequently.

Elliott had made his journey alone, but his solitude did not last long. He was joined by his parents. The frontier frequently separated families and broke the extended ties of relations common in old and settled eastern towns. But John Jansen and Louisa Goodrich Tappan had no desire to be permanently separated from their only surviving child, and soon joined Elliott in Wisconsin. Then, in 1853, Adelaide Ruth Goodrich, Elliott's first cousin, also moved to Wisconsin. Before leaving New York, Elliott had proposed marriage to Adelaide. The wedding was held the day she arrived.

The Tappan family had prepared well for what they now faced. Elliott owned ninety-three acres of land. By the standards of the great western wheat farms, this was small acreage, though it was enough in Wisconsin to make a decent living. Most farmers in the region grew wheat for market, before the opening up of the Great Plains to hard winter wheat in the next decades. Others in the area had cows for milk, butter, and cheese, as Wisconsin began to build its reputation as the nation's dairy capital. It is not clear if Elliott raised cattle, planted wheat, or sold dairy products. Probably he did all three, and also made extra income selling timber off his land to the nearby sawmills of Oshkosh, which were giving the town its nickname, "Sawdust City."[24]

Building a large, L-shaped farmhouse, Elliott moved his family in. Just beyond his holdings loomed dense, dark woods, and close by stood the majestic Lake Butte Des Morts, at the confluence of the formidable Wolf and Fox Rivers. During long, cold winters, Elliott supplemented the family larder by hunting ducks in the marshes near the lake and by trapping fox, wolf, and rabbit.

For a time, the Tappans were partners in a country store, a small grocery in Oshkosh styled Tappan & Kellett. Each of the partners had about $1,000 in capital backing the enterprise, along with holdings of real estate and intangible assets. They were well enough established to secure a modest line of credit and were reputed to be men of "good character and habits," if of "ordinary ability." The store only lasted for about eighteen months, however, and was out of business by 1859.[25]

Such was the fate of most small commercial enterprises at this time. Few survived beyond a half-dozen years, and going out of business was no sign of shame for an honest merchant. Often, successful entrepreneurs had to try several times before their businesses stuck. It was well understood that even the competent and adventurous faced serious hardship. Accordingly, American commercial law treated debt and bankruptcy leniently, allowing men to start over several times if need be.

The Tappans did not repeat their venture into commerce, however. Instead, they continued to endure the hardships of farm life—long winters, droughts, floods, and insect plagues. Between 1858 and 1864, Elliott and Adelaide lost two children, ages two and three, to childhood illness. Harsh as such losses were, they were not unexpected. In the mid-nineteenth century, child mortality was nearly one hundred times as great as today. The average woman endured five pregnancies, and the odds were better than fifty-fifty that at least one of the children she bore would not live to adulthood. Cold statistics did not, however, make such losses easier to accept. Adelaide would never stop grieving for her dead baby daughters.

By 1872, after twenty years of hard struggle, the farm had grown fairly prosperous. Elliott's holdings were valued at just over $5,000, and he and Adelaide had personal property worth an additional $1,500. That put them almost exactly at the median of wealth for their area.[26] So the pioneer family could feel some measure of security and contentment in what they had accomplished. They had weathered the early years of establishing a homestead. They had three surviving children. All but the baby, John, were old enough to work. During the late summer and early fall of that year, the family diligently gathered the harvest. By September, the crops were in and the hogs had been slaughtered. The air was beginning to turn chilly and the mornings saw the first frosts. Then all turned bleak. On September 13, suddenly and without warning, Elliott died.

The cause of his death is not known. What is clear is that he died of an illness so severe that it claimed his life in a matter of days, perhaps even hours. Oshkosh newspapers reported that an epidemic of unspecified origins was raging. There were stories of townsfolk who seemed healthy one day, but who succumbed the next. Such unspecified, unexpected deaths were common enough in the nineteenth century. Particularly outside of cities, medicine remained primitive. Doctors, if available, were often helpless before illnesses they did not understand. When they were available, they offered treatments that went back to the Middle Ages. Bleeding to "balance the body's humors" remained a popular cure in rural America, even as a more scientific understanding of the body and its functions was being promoted in the nation's advanced seats of medical learning. But infectious diseases, including scarlet fever, yellow fever, diphtheria, and typhoid, were scourges that victims had to face without antibiotics or vaccinations. Cholera epidemics still stalked residents in cities. Yellow fever outbreaks appeared regularly in the fall and spring. Childhood illnesses that today are almost unknown routinely claimed the lives of infants, as the Tappans themselves knew. In matters medical, the hand of Providence remained heavy indeed.

Adelaide buried Elliott in the cemetery on the hill, next to his baby daughters and his mother, who had died the previous March. His obituary read much like that of any farmer who had lived, worked, and died in the common way of life. It noted that he was "among the first to settle in this county and share the trials of frontier life." "His life was the life of the righteous. His death a perfect triumph of faith." "He leaves," the notice ended, "an aged father, wife and three children."[27]

Words to the effect of "a kind husband and father" did not comfort Adelaide. She was so filled with grief and so distraught over the loss that she remained bitter about his death for the rest of her life. Even years later, when asked what had happened to her husband, she would reply, "He deserted the family." Incorrect in fact and filled with anger, her words nonetheless reflected accurately how she felt as a thirty-eight-year-old widow with three children to raise, an infirm father-in-law to care for, and a farm to tend.

Though Elliott had passed away relatively young, Adelaide's situation was not nearly as desperate as that of most widows with small children. She possessed a strong will that did not bend easily to adversity. She also had financial resources from her well-to-do eastern family. Most young widows in the nineteenth century did not. Farm families saved for old age through what historians have called the "family life cycle." They borrowed money to buy a farm, and gradually improved and added to their land, while raising children who would provide labor. When they reached old age, their life's work—their land, tangible assets, and children—were the savings that would see them through the rest of their lives. If a husband died, his widow depended on this accumulation, part of which would be set aside for her maintenance until death, when it would go to the surviving heirs. But if a husband died young and his spouse had children to care for, then it might be too early in the life cycle to survive off the accumulation.

Savings accounts and insurance policies, which were nonexistent for most people a few decades earlier, were beginning to lessen some of the burden of widowhood. Indeed, astute life insurance companies carefully marketed policies at families using just this ploy. They raised the specter of death and dependency. They encouraged husbands to think of life insurance as their way of transcending death and protecting their families when they were gone. Life insurance became *The Proof of Love,* as one popular pamphlet put it. Such marketing efforts were a resounding success. Once disdained as "gambling on a human life," life insurance skyrocketed in popularity.[28]

It is not clear if Elliott Tappan had insurance. Adelaide's later statements about him "deserting" the family suggest that perhaps he did not. Calling his death desertion instead of the hand of Providence indicates that she accepted the notion of death played up by life insurance companies. Responsible husbands should be prepared to transcend death and look after the family, at least financially. Fortunately, Adelaide had moved West with some of her family money. She possessed the skills necessary to make a life. Practical and businesslike, she retained throughout her life a keen grasp of money-making opportunities. Soon after she moved to Minneapolis, she added $6,000 to her nest egg, profit from selling the farm.

In 1877, Adelaide went back to Oshkosh to finish off the sale. After the arrangements were complete and the sale closed, she walked through the house and sat in the kitchen where she had cooked and baked for twenty years. She looked in the bedroom where all of her children had been born, and where two of them had died. She touched the wall moldings she and Elliott had fashioned. Then she walked outside to visit the graves before finally leaving. Adelaide Tappan lived another thirty-seven years, but she never again returned to Oshkosh.

By the time the Tappan family settled in Minneapolis, John was nine years old. He was the youngest child in a single parent household, growing up without a father or elder male presence in his life. Unlike the other children, John was too young to remember his father. He had little in common with his brother Frank, thirteen years John's senior and a much different, more subdued character. With Adelaide busy managing the family on her own, John quickly became an independent, energetic boy with lots of interests. He attended school and held a number of after-school jobs. Though the family had enough money to live comfortably if frugally, John liked to earn his own spending money. He delivered newspapers until he was twelve, then took a position as a shoe store clerk. These occupations were not enough to contain all of his energy, however.

Though living in the city, John retained a healthy interest in nature and the outdoors. Minneapolis was still small enough that the country was only a walk away. John spent his weekends wandering the countryside, watching birds and collecting eggs. Spotting a nest, he would clamber up a tree and cautiously remove one egg. When he returned home, he inserted a straw into the egg and carefully blew out its contents. Then he labeled it and added it to the rest of his collection in a cotton nest in a drawer. He kept adding eggs until he had one from almost every bird in the area, from bald eagles to hummingbirds.

John's life as a boy in the West, his youthful jobs and hobbies, and his pursuit of self-education through direct contact with nature, followed a pattern common among native born males of his generation. His experiences paralleled those of many others who came of age in a rural America growing more urban and industrial. These included the famous, such as Henry Ford and Thomas Edison, as well as numerous other Americans who would see the nation change decisively from what they remembered. Many would look back fondly to idyllic days of studying nature, riding ponies, and learning self-reliance, even as they helped to transform America into something much different from their memories.

Like most middle-class parents, Adelaide encouraged self-reliance and responsibility, in the form of making and managing money. Perhaps because conserving money was now a compelling concern for a widow on a fixed income, Adelaide impressed on John the importance of carefully saving and managing funds. Like his mother, John had a frugal nature. He opened his own bank account with wages from his store job. That did not mean he was miserly, though. He proved capable of the sort of youthful exuberance and material desires that cheerfully upset the moral instructions of the best intentioned parents. When John's bank account had grown sufficiently large, he spent it all on a pony, which became his prized possession and favorite means of transportation.

With their similar personalities, John and his mother were soon at loggerheads. As the teenage years arrived, John's admirable self-reliance turned into less palatable adolescent rebellion. He immersed himself in "boy culture," leaving behind the female world of family, home, and affection to express masculine independence. Nineteenth-century youth commonly followed such a pattern. Boys created a world separate from their mothers, indeed separate from most male authority. In this separate sphere, they learned the characteristics of competitiveness and developed active, even aggressive selves, in contrast to the emphasis on correct deportment and self-control in the female world of the home. In John's case, however, this was more extreme, living in a household without a father figure. John was fourteen before Adelaide was capable of talking about his father. John's only male companionship had been a group of local firemen, with whom he played checkers after school. Within the family, however, he was still the baby, only now with the kind of ambitious and even self-righteous commitment to hard work that invited teasing by his bother and sister, both in their twenties.

One Sunday, the deep emotions stirred up by adolescence and sibling rivalry boiled to the surface and decisively changed the direction of John's life. As the family was preparing for church, John overheard his sister say that she had no money for the collection. Never overly reverent, John saw a chance to get back at his older sister. It was his turn to pass the collection basket that Sunday. When he got to Carrie, he stopped, jiggled the basket, and would not move on. Carrie was mortified as the whole congregation turned to watch the spectacle, while John just smiled.

Later that day, Carrie plotted her revenge. After dinner, John suddenly became violently ill. Adelaide summoned the doctor, who examined John and reported that he had been poisoned. Carrie broke down and confessed that she had laced some cheese he had eaten with camphor. It took John several weeks to recover. When he did, there were no further shots fired in the family feud. Instead, John packed his bags. With little money and no idea where he was going, he knew only one thing for sure: his mother's house was too small for him. In the spring of 1887, seventeen-year-old John Elliott Tappan left home without saying goodbye.

The break with his family was symbolically important for John. A Victorian upbringing, which Adelaide seems to have provided, stressed self-control, but also self-expression in more "manly," physical, competitive, and independent realms. Ideally, proper education, home life, and internalization of values allowed children to grow into self-possessed adults, who kept their passions in check in the interests of social and economic achievement. But for men it was also thought important to part with the maternal world of self-restraint for a time, in order to confront the real, combative outside world. John's abrupt departure and rush to western adventure was an extreme example of such a break, perhaps necessitated by his female-dominated household.[29]

As his father had looked West for opportunity, so John Tappan looked in the same direction, to California. Thin as a rail with a shock of thick blond hair starting to darken, Tappan tramped across the country with a few essentials. He walked, hopped freight cars, and hitched wagon rides. When he arrived on the West Coast, he worked in the mining regions for a year. That experience taught him firsthand what speculative investment meant. "I think it is pretty risky to invest in mining schemes without being on the ground and knowing about things personally . . . " or knowing "somebody that could be trusted" he would later reflect.[30] Tappan also saw the seedier side of life in the mining camps. Miners were an uneducated, rough-hewn lot who spent their hard-earned wages on whisky, women, and gambling. The camps made quite an impression on the genteel Tappan. For example, the violence erupting from the overcrowded saloons reinforced his predilection to abstinence.

After about a year on the road, John contracted tuberculosis. Fortunately he had only a mild case, but a physician recommended a more favorable climate. Washington Territory to the north was reputed to have curative powers for those afflicted with diseases of the lungs, so Tappan moved to Seattle in the summer of 1888. While recuperating, he enrolled in the preparatory department of the University of Washington Territory, to complete the high school education he had left behind in Minnesota. Though he had enough money to cover the $10 per quarter tuition, he did not have funds to pay for room and board, which ranged from $2 to $5 per week. Hearing about a minister who needed a furnace stoker for the church, Tappan accepted free room and board in the church basement as pay for the work. That winter, he huddled near the furnace, reading by its light on cold, damp nights.

At the preparatory department, Tappan studied what he hoped were the requirements for admission to the university. He practiced his penmanship and orthography, and learned geography and arithmetic. In addition, he received instruction in Greek, Latin, geometry, and natural philosophy. Reading Virgil and Caesar were of less interest to him than mathematics, at which he excelled. He particularly enjoyed surveying, and he put his skills to practical use by taking a job as a surveyor later that year. It was the sort of outdoor activity that let him combine his intellectual powers with his love of nature and physical activity.

By May, Tappan completed the curriculum, but he never made it to the next level. In June 1889, Seattle was consumed by a great fire. It engulfed the entire downtown, easily overmatching the human bucket brigade and rudimentary fire fighting equipment sent to combat it. When the last embers died, most of central Seattle was a smoking ruin. Tents sprouted up to shelter the now homeless citizens and businesses.

With Seattle recuperating from the blaze, Tappan decided to put his studies on hold. He took employment as a lumberjack in the Washington wilderness. The industry was booming. Washington lumber production had grown to over a billion board feet per year, ten times its output a decade earlier. Huge timber companies such as Weyerhaeuser were purchasing large quantities of government land and sawmills were going up all over the territory. Some 24,000 men were at work.[31]

As with mining, lumbering was an intensely masculine world of rough-and-tumble living, far from the civilizing influences of domesticity, education, and religion. In the camps, loggers lived dozens, and sometimes hundreds, to a bunkhouse. Without telephones, before radio, and absent any means of fast overland transport, they were about as cut off from civilization as one could be in the continental United States. These conditions encouraged Tappan's natural tendencies of self-reliance. He learned to look after himself, mend his clothes, sew, and cook. Like his mining experiences, lumbering in the wilderness gave Tappan a wealth of adventures to look back on with nostalgia when he reached middle age. He adored the strenuous life outdoors, the early mornings rising to a big cooked breakfast of ham, eggs, hash browns, flapjacks, and coffee. Working along the river, he became friendly with local Native Americans, who sometimes offered him food, usually dog meat. He grew accustomed to sleeping outside at night, on the ground under the stars.

Nostalgia aside, though, logging was no picnic. It was tough work, lasting ten hours a day, sometimes longer. Tappan had arrived before the big logging companies took over the industry, so he was witnessing business under frontier conditions. Many logging operations were small, owner-operator firms, which survived on loans and advances from larger sawmills. The boss logger drove his men hard. Labor was the single largest component of costs, and profits depended on the ability to extract timber from the forest at low cost. Workers might enjoy high wages in boom times, but they were also a cost that stood between the owner and his profit, a resource to be used or discarded depending on the demand for lumber. Workers treated their employers likewise. Independent-minded bush loppers moved in search of better pay at the first chance. Carrying their bedrolls on their shoulders, most bindlestiffs had no permanent address.

One fact about timbering was undeniable: it was dangerous work. The accident rate was the highest of any industry, nearly twice as high as a foundry, itself no cozy spot for the manual worker. Crushed by rolling logs, cut by saws, or literally pounded into the earth by crashing trees, lumberjacks had more ways of dying than most people could count. Wielding huge crosscut saws, men worked nearly beneath logs as they bucked them into forty-foot-long sections. Up above, "widowmakers," thick branches knocked lose by falling timber, dangled hundreds of feet in the air, ready to come down any time and swat a man into the next life. Away from doctors and hospitals, even "minor" injuries, such as hands ripped on the jagged wire ropes loggers handled all day, could lead to serious infections.[32]

Employers strove to keep the cost of accidents down. But in the nineteenth century, this did not mean investing in safety so much as placing responsibility on the shoulders of injured workers themselves. Courts often complied, articulating doctrines that shifted liability from owner to worker. Worker compensation laws would not come into existence for another two decades. The first ones appeared in California, Washington, and Oregon, in part a reaction to the dangerous work of logging that went on there.

Nothing crystallized the reality of this life more vividly than the excitement and danger of a log drive, which Tappan experienced firsthand in the spring of 1890. "River pigs" escorted lumber downstream to sawmills, working continually, grabbing food on the run, with death "a single misstep away."[33] It was harrowing work. Tappan often told his children years later how he and the men feared falling off the logs and being crushed between them.

The drives usually took place during the spring thaw. Timber cut during the winter sat frozen in rivers until it could be moved with the warmer weather. But the mass of logs, waiting for its journey all season, easily became tangled. A few unfortunately placed big pieces could stop the massive drift as surely as a cork in a bottle. A good size jam could send timber thirty feet in the air. Breaking it required horses, mules, steam engines, and explosives. Pressured by more logs moving downstream, the jam became a creaking, groaning mess, emitting a dull roar that every lumber man knew indicated long hard work and, for those who actually had to step out on the pile to get it moving again, a good chance of death or injury.

This sort of work did not encourage a long-term or circumspect outlook on life. Though the pay was good, Tappan noted that most of his co-workers spent it as they got it and saved little or nothing for the future. Logrollers lived hand-to-mouth after the summer, when the good pay ended. They were renowned for their hard drinking, hard living, gambling ways. What was the use of saving money when death was right around the corner and good times could give way to bad in an instant? Collectively, however, loggers had other ways of looking out for themselves. Logging encouraged some of the strongest working-class feelings in the United States. The International Workers of the World found in those Pacific coast logging camps that Tappan had frequented the most fertile ground for their organization. Dedicated to "a universal working class movement," and convinced of "the irrepressible conflict" between capital and labor, the Wobblies sought nothing less than the complete overthrow of capitalism. It was probably the most radical union movement America has ever seen.[34]

Tappan the lumberjack was once again a middle-class man out of place. He remained abstemious among the hard drinking and held personal and political views far removed from working-class syndicalism. He had his prospects set on a white-collar career and higher education, not the life of an itinerant worker or union radical. He saw the harsh realities of the life of a footloose worker whose prospects for the future were uncertain at best and whose hope for upward mobility was subordinate to the simple need to survive and live to the next day. But he saw them one step removed.

John's western adventures finally came to a close in 1890. He had been away from home for nearly three years, during which time he had grown from a callow youth into a self-reliant man. Now nearly six feet tall, his slender frame had filled out somewhat. He had begun to acquire the broad-shouldered, ramrod-straight physique he would maintain through middle age. The return home completed a cycle. Tappan came back to his family, to society, and to the world of work and self-control. It took him some time to shake off the habits of the frontier. He was so used to sleeping on the ground that he ignored his bed and stretched out on the floor, where his mother found him in the morning, curled up in a ball, his head on his arm. But the restlessness had not completely left Tappan's soul. After staying home for a month, he headed out again, this time on a far tamer journey to Duluth. There he got a job, which started him on the road to white-collar respectability. Despite his adventure, Tappan remained a young man of middle-class ambitions. Seeking a career in business, he took classes in stenography during his off hours.

Men aspiring to white-collar careers in the nineteenth century required a host of "secretarial" skills. They had to have neat penmanship and be able to balance account books, take dictation, type letters, and write and answer correspondence. If they worked in banks, the starting position was frequently cashier. Women also began to enter the office labor force at this time, though their numbers would not increase until the second decade of the twentieth century. For men, stenographer and cashier were not dead-end jobs, as they would come to be seen when they were "feminized" some time later. Rather, they were management training positions for ambitious young men who lacked enough capital to enter partnerships or start their own firms. As part of this upwardly mobile world, John Tappan devoted his days to office work and his nights to self-improvement. He continued his education, both formally and informally, taking advantage of the refinements of city life, such as it was in Minnesota.

In the fall of 1891, John heard that Sarah Bernhardt, "The Divine Sarah," was coming to Minneapolis for two performances. He planned a visit home to hear her sing. Lacking the means for a ticket, however, he got into the shows by volunteering as an extra in the production. Afterward, he enjoyed remarking to friends about his and Bernhardt's "appearance together." Though the local papers somehow overlooked Tappan, they gushed over her "superb acting," which "shed a brilliant radiance."[35] In *La Tosca* she showed "how fell the tender tears of love, and the hustling torrents of passion." The theatre of the "Gay '90s" was creating America's first performer celebrities, of which Sarah Bernhardt was the supreme example. Her passionate stage portrayals of classic characters attracted male worshipers from Mark Twain to Sigmund Freud. By flaunting the conventions of restrained Victorian passion and making her own unorthodox private life part of her public persona, she provided unparalleled excitement for otherwise conventional men and women. And by doing so through classical dramatic characters, she conveyed to middle-class audiences the sort of refined, highbrow culture they thought they should absorb.

For Tappan, the ordered calm of professional life and urban refinement had not completely replaced the wildness of the West, or tamed his adventurous side. Forays back to nature, physical activity, and rough-and-tumble competitive activities remained part of his recreational life. In the summer of 1892, he and a friend from Duluth went camping and fishing. Riding bicycles north to a lake, they fished for a few hours and then decided to cool off with a swim. They had only been in the water a few minutes when the blue skies suddenly darkened. Black clouds rolled in, the wind picked up, and in a matter of seconds the sky opened and let loose a furious, blinding rain. Tappan, a strong swimmer, raced out of the water for cover. His friend, further out, was just emerging from the lake when a streak of lightening shot out of the sky and struck him. As he crumpled and fell, Tappan raced to drag him out of the water, but his friend was dead, killed outright. John sat at the edge of the lake, in the pouring rain, his dead friend's head in his lap, screaming for help in the Minnesota wilderness. It was an event that he never forgot, and years later told the story over and over again to his children.

This experience changed Tappan's outlook on life. He became a little hardened after that, unable to forget that death could leap into life at any time and change things in an instant. Over the years, it left him with a kind of resigned acceptance of fate that many people interpreted as a cold or unfeeling attitude. He wasn't insensitive, but he accepted the reality of death, which could overwhelm or upset even the most carefully devised human plans. The tragedy also came at a crucial turning point in Tappan's young career. During the following two years, he completed his preparations and embarked on the path that launched him into the world of financial innovation. By the time he was finished, he had created a new financial product that could, by rational means, tame at least some of the unpredictability that lurked beside human prudence and ambition.

⌇⌇⌇

Events leading up to his innovation exposed Tappan to the changes taking place in American business and industry. Still living in Duluth in 1892, he took a job as a stenographer with the Merritt brothers. It turned out to be a fortuitous move. The Merritts were embarking on a business venture to develop the enormously rich iron ore deposits of the Mesabi Range in northern Minnesota. Like the Tappan family, the Merritts were of Yankee stock, migrants to the frontier a generation earlier from upstate New York and Connecticut. They had prospered in lumber, banking, land development, and prospecting. But the chance for a big score in the untracked wilderness still beckoned this entrepreneurial family.

For years, five Merritt brothers searched through the wilds of remote northern Minnesota, doing the tedious, muscle-fatiguing labor of mapping out iron ore deposits. A decade earlier, miners in the Vermilion mountain range had hit pay dirt with discoveries of broad, rich veins of iron ore. The Merritts were searching a range nearby, which had already been worked over by professional geologists to inconclusive results. Then, in 1890, their quest ended, seventy-five miles northwest of Duluth in the continental watershed that Native Americans called Mesabi, or "Grandmother of All." There, in land scoured by ancient glaciers along ridges barely 1,000 feet above sea level, lay the richest deposits of iron ore in North America, if not the world. All of it stood under just a few shallow feet of fine, gray, crystallized quartz.[36]

Mesabi ore was unusually pure and accessible. Most iron lay deep within the bowels of the earth and had to be mined through a dangerous, expensive process that sent men underground. At Mesabi it was practically lying on the surface, waiting to be scooped up with the swing of a shovel. As Lon Merritt put it, "If we had gotten mad and kicked the ground where we stood we could have thrown up sixty-four percent ore."[37] Two years later, Lon, his brothers, and nephews constructed a railroad through the timberlands and were carting out a million tons of ore. Over the decades, tens of millions of tons of Mesabi iron would go into American steel furnaces, pushing the nation to first place in world steel production.

Through Mesabi ore, the farm- and timberlands of Minnesota connected themselves to the industries growing up around new technologies such as steel. Steel was no ordinary metal in the nineteenth century. It was the building material of industrial culture.[38] In Tappan's own day, a revolution in steel was underway. With the development of the Bessemer process, steel production leapt from a negligible few thousand tons to almost seven million tons by 1890.[39] Plentiful steel, made possible in part by high quality Mesabi ore, provided the cutting edges for prairie plows, the hulls for sailing ships, the rails for trains (and the engines, too), the superstructures for skyscrapers, the casings for explosive shells, the eighteen-inch-thick plate armor for warships, and, later, the bodies for automobiles. Much of what we think of as industry would not have been possible without a metal of such strength, durability, and lightness.

In each of its applications, steel helped to advance a process of social change that would define Tappan's own lifetime. Running on durable steel rails, railroads unified the nation, creating a vast market that brought rural residents and farmers into greater economic proximity with the East. Skyscrapers were one of the urban technologies that moved people from the countryside to cities. They housed the white-collar workers of finance and insurance, workers such as Tappan who left the farm behind in favor of a new sort of intellectual career. Cars became the number-one status symbol of middle-class consumers—both a means of independence and the symbol of achievement as well. In short, steel was a marker for vast changes in the way people lived daily life and defined themselves. Steel, though, had a further significance. It was also one of the new industries changing how America did business, the leading edge of a corporate and financial revolution.

This new world had felt its first growing pains with the Panic of 1873. But by the time Tappan hooked up with the Merritts two decades later, change was spreading to more places and more industries. Giant steelmills, for example, had quickly rendered obsolete most of the small iron forges once run by individual iron masters. In their place came new, giant corporate enterprises led by entrepreneurs such as Andrew Carnegie. Carnegie and his ilk erected huge factories employing tens of thousands of workers, turning out steel and other products at lower and lower prices by using increasingly mechanized methods of production. Along with oil, machinery, electrical equipment, railroads, and telecommunications, steel was big business, and that meant corporations, stockholders, investment banks, lawyers, and full-time, professional managers.

It also meant a new way of doing business. Competition in this new corporate sector was unlike the more genteel and local commerce that still characterized economic life in places such as Oshkosh. In Pittsburgh, industrial titans battled for control of the nation's steel market, as similar corporate giants Pillsbury and Washburn did in Minneapolis' flour milling industry. The battles and machinations of the corporate giants often took on a dark, musty tone to outsiders, who looked askance at "cutthroat" competition and predatory practices that drove the small fry right to the wall. Workers too found themselves no match for the corporate giants. In 1894, Andrew Carnegie's giant Homestead steel works would suffer a crippling strike that did not end until bodies lay dead and the workers' union broken and in ruins.

Though John Elliott Tappan's exposure to the world of big business was limited, he did not like what he saw. He worked in the Merritts' real estate office, learning how to make loans on real property and developing an interest in the value of northern Minnesota land. In his employer, however, he also witnessed a side of the new business life that left him wondering about the nation's future. Machinations of wealth on the scale that the Merritts were operating placed greed well above traditional moral rectitude. So much money was at stake in Mesabi, and so many powerful corporate interests stood to gain or lose, that all else but money itself was of no account. Never overly materialistic, John believed that the pursuit of wealth for its own sake led inevitably to exploitation of the weak at the hands of the strong. Later, he would codify his beliefs about wealth concentration, saying that no man should ever accumulate more than a million dollars in a lifetime.

Perhaps to hide their naked greed, seekers of great wealth continued to pay homage to traditional values of honesty, frugality, and morality. Even as they invoked morality, however, they were striking insider deals and repudiating contracts as served their interests. Men like the Merritt brothers, Tappan soon perceived, showed themselves "as forward in public," but beneath that persona, the man "posing as a saint" was an operator "skinning you the minute your back was turned."[40] Indeed, as it turned out, in the Merritts, Tappan had only seen the tip of the corporate iceberg. Working for the Minnesota brothers, he soon had a front-row seat to one of the legendary corporate struggles of American history.

The Merritts were no more than middling-sized players in the world of big business. To develop Mesabi, they had overextended their capital and borrowed money to acquire land. But when the economy turned sour and steel production fell sharply, Mesabi ore piled up in barges. As debts mounted and income slowed to a trickle, the Merritts faced dire conditions. Armed workers entered the office demanding their pay. At the last minute, a white knight seemed to appear: oil tycoon John D. Rockefeller. He offered to advance the money needed, in exchange for a percentage ownership. Though reluctant to lose their independence, the Merritts struck a deal, hoping that through Rockefeller they would also gain needed connections to the eastern banks and financiers they could not reach on their own.[41] As it turned out, they were sorely mistaken.

Rockefeller, possibly the world's richest man at the time, had little interest in iron or steel. His wealth came from oil. But he knew a bargain when he saw one, and the Merritts' financial straits let him acquire virtual control of their property at what amounted to fire sale prices. Pressed by their obligations, the brothers sold their stock to Rockefeller for a low $10 per share in a depressed market.[42] Under these conditions, it was not surprising that trouble soon arose. Rockefeller the Sunday school teacher and devoted Baptist held the uncouth, backwoods Merritts in low regard. They in turn resented their dependence on Rockefeller's money and contacts in eastern financial markets. Dealing with Rockefeller, Lon Merritt would later remark ruefully, was "the first mistake I made in the whole business . . . the first serious mistake."[43]

Asserting that their property had been taken at an unjustly low price through fraud and misrepresentation, the Merritt brothers brought suit in state court. There they sought to lay claim to an older, deeper principle of ownership than the one Rockefeller exercised with his capital. They had discovered, mapped, and trailblazed their iron claim. They had leased the first steam shovels. They had constructed the railroads and built the docks for shipping ore. By right of conquest, they and not Rockefeller were the true producers of wealth. Only through misrepresentations, false promises, and his own commanding position in the imperial financial order had Rockefeller been able to insert himself into the project of honest entrepreneurs. It was, like the 1873 Panic, a contest between the older principle of producerism, reflecting the labor theory of value, and the new economy, being built on modern finance and corporate structures.

In state court, the Merritts' plea found favor with a Minnesota jury composed largely of farmers and rural residents. They awarded the plaintiffs a $940,000 judgment against Rockefeller, whom local newspapers portrayed as "a financial cannibal who eats men every day."[44] But the triumph was only temporary. An appeals court ordered a new trial. It was, after all, the Merritts who had first approached Rockefeller about money. In the end Rockefeller disposed of the claims against him with a private settlement that included a retraction of all charges of fraud.[45] Ownership and control of vital resources, especially money, were becoming key issues of contention in the new industrial economy. The Merritts had learned how powerful those with privileged access to capital could be.

No branch of the economy, even in the Far West, was out of reach of the largest and most powerful corporations. Mesabi became just another piece of the growing industrial complex of steel and railroads. In the end, Minnesota's mineral wealth did not allow entrepreneurs like the Merritts to enter big businesses such as steel. Rather, it helped to push the steel industry to even greater levels of concentration. In 1901, financier J. P. Morgan combined the Mesabi properties with the steelmills of Andrew Carnegie and a dozen others into the world's first billion-dollar corporation, United States Steel.

Tappan soon had enough of the world of big business. Hypocrisy and disloyalty were apparently the new cherished values of business. Tappan would resist these values all his life. To do so, he needed a position that would enable him to earn a living without having to compromise his integrity or values again. He ended his employment with the Merritts and returned to the education he had abandoned several years earlier. With enough money saved, he enrolled at the University of Minnesota's night law school in the fall of 1893. It was the same grind he had established earlier in Washington, working days to pay for an education that took up most of his nights. During the course of his studies he met the men and women who would form the core of his supporters and partners throughout his life.

It was a good time to stay in school and concentrate on studies. That year, 1893, the nation was plunged into another "panic," or more accurately an economic depression. Even worse than the one twenty years earlier, the 1893 depression touched off riots in the streets, breadlines, bloodshed, and strikes. As though a malevolent giant had snapped the carpet out from under the economy, the depression rolled across the nation, toppling businesses, breaking banks, and busting farmers. Until the Great Depression of the 1930s, it was the greatest economic calamity in the nation's history.

Relatively safe in law school, Tappan saw friends and neighbors lose jobs, homes, and savings. He paid for his education by working part time for the Guaranty Investment Company as a bill collector, wringing out payments on bonds the company had sold to customers now strapped for cash. The job offered clear lessons in how financial crisis and unpredictable economic circumstances could easily turn even frugal men and women into debtors, force respectable workers to leave bills unpaid and accounts past due, and send the bill collector knocking at the front door. It was one thing for "the thriftless who spent as they went" to be in dire straits, but the depression and bank failures were wiping out even those who had saved.

This experience more than any other lead John Tappan to turn financial innovator. "I was a young man of twenty-four attending night school at the

University of Minnesota and working my way through," he would later recount, "when I conceived of the idea of a thrift plan upon a conservative, honest basis that would appeal to people as a means of investing small amounts with the safety and yield that was secured by larger investors."[46] From the bond business, Tappan saw that what small-time investors needed most was a way to consistently put aside a modest amount of money and have it invested for them by someone whom they could trust and who knew the market. Pooling investments would reduce risk by permitting diversification and allow even modest savers access to higher paying securities. Savers needed a financial product that could withstand the periodic downturns of the economy, or at least give them a fighting chance at stability. Tappan set out to provide it.

~~~~~

Tappan's ideas of diversification, pooling, and risk reduction were of course basic to the concept of financial intermediation. Financial institutions, or, more precisely, financial intermediaries, stand between the individual saver, with his or her funds, and the users of those funds. They mediate between the two halves of the savings/investment equation, presumably for the good of both parties. Intermediaries collect funds from the saving public, giving back some return or interest payment. Those funds are then placed in income-earning assets. If the intermediary is good, he or she can profit from the "spread," the difference between the income earned on assets and the money that has to be paid to savers to surrender their money. An intermediary who possesses superior expertise, knowledge, or access to information about risks and returns can invest the public's money better, safer, and at a higher return than the public can do by itself.

The theory is simple, but deceptively so. Connections that bring savings together with investment do not appear automatically. New, untried forms of investment carry unknown risks. Smart savers also know that some companies promising to multiply their money may well be hideouts for con artists. Money invested in land or in one's own business offered the sort of direct, hands-on control that believers in hard work and personal autonomy valued.[47] Even the high-flying industrial tycoon Andrew Carnegie once defined his investment strategy as "putting all your eggs into one basket, and then watching the basket carefully." So financial institutions that moved savings to distant capital markets were a radical departure from traditional wisdom for most middle-class Americans.

For the majority of people, banks were the most important financial intermediary in the nineteenth century. Commercial banks took deposits and directed them into a variety of commercial loans. Their portfolio of assets was limited by law and custom, however. Deposit-accepting, nationally chartered banks could not lend on real estate, and before the twentieth century, did not generally hold stocks or other corporate securities. Few commercial banks were interested in the small accounts of workers and farmers in any case. Savings banks and building and loans, organized for the mutual benefit of their members, accepted deposits with the intent of lending money out as mortgages for their depositors. But they only operated in restricted areas, mostly in large cities, and were not as successful at mobilizing capital across geographic boundaries.[48] In any case, banks paid relatively low interest rates, about 3 percent in the late nineteenth century. In contrast to today, moreover, banks catering to small savers actually paid lower rates on larger deposits.[49]

It was in fact difficult for the poor or working class to save much money. Despite individual examples of frugality, overall savings was negative in the bottom end of the income distribution. Most saving was done at the upper end of the scale. In 1890, for example, families earning between $400 and $1,000 per year, the range approximately from unskilled to semiskilled worker, saved around 8 to 10 percent of income. Those earning $2,000 and over saved close to 40 percent of income. Workers earning less than $400 saved virtually nothing.[50] So banks and other existing intermediaries saw little reason to cater to the working poor.

The logic of diversification and pooled capital had largely appealed to those at the upper end of the wealth scale. In the mid-nineteenth century, Scottish and English investment companies collected funds from British savers and directed these monies into overseas investments in the Americas. The funds of these so-called investment trusts went into land mortgages, then, later, railroad and industrial stocks. These institutions served middle- and upper-class Britons at a time when Britain was the center of global finance and had plenty of savings that needed a secure outlet. Somewhat as in a modern mutual fund, investors did not risk their money directly on individual company stocks, but purchased instead securities issued by the trusts. Generally, the trusts paid dividends in the 5 to 7 percent range.[51]

On the American side of the Atlantic, investment trusts were much less common in the nineteenth century. The earliest precedent was the Massachusetts Hospital Life Trust. Originally a life insurance company, it branched out into investment operations in 1823. Accepting contributions of $500 or more, it paid a return equal to the average received on its diversified portfolio of assets, minus a .5 percent management fee. In 1894, just as Tappan was contemplating the limits of American financial services, the old Massachusetts company abandoned life insurance entirely and became strictly a trust and investment company. A year earlier another organization, the Boston Personal Property Trust, had replicated the pattern of the older Scottish and English land investment companies. Over time, several more intermediaries of this sort would come and go. In 1904, a specialized securities investment operation opened in Boston to pool savers' money for investment in railroads and utilities. A few banks also formed their own securities affiliates in the early twentieth century.

Although proponents of investment trusts and similar ideas believed that these institutions could "give the investor of moderate means the same advantage as the large capitalist," their reach was in fact quite limited.[52] None of them accepted small deposits, or operated extensively beyond the nation's largest cities. Most behaved like closed-end funds or like investment clubs for a small group of friends and insiders.[53] The "moderate investor" they targeted was still relatively high on the scale of wealth and financial sophistication. The minimum stake for an investor was at least $100 and often considerably more. Also, the trusts were not always secure. British investment trusts enjoyed a boom in the 1880s and 1890s, but when the economy turned down in 1893, many were wiped out. With them went investor confidence.

Trusts and mutual funds would not become widely popular in the United States or England until the 1920s. Meanwhile, those who made use of these early forms of pooled investment had to be wary. Unscrupulous promoters, for example, tried to lure participants with vague promises of outstanding rewards from investments in captivating locales such as Latin America, which went through a boom in the 1880s followed by a bust a few years later. Others promoted "blind pools," which revealed nothing about where one's money actually went. Presumably the attraction was the insinuation of some sort of inside deal available only to a select few who got in early on the opportunity and asked no questions. Blind pools could easily be manipulated into swindles, with operators pocketing the money after paying a few attractive dividends. Even honest trusts held dangers. Managers could speculate with clients' money in risky ventures, such as underwriting the stock offerings of unknown companies. Such activity could produce high underwriting fees, and returns well beyond normal dividends promised to the trust clients. Extraordinary profits, however, ended up as bonuses to the trust management. So, in effect, managers risked their clients' money on speculative ventures, but took most of the profit for themselves. Such problems of agency and information would plague the British trusts in the downturn of the late nineteenth century. In an age of limited regulation, with a public inexperienced in the subtleties of variable investments, new financial products faced an uphill struggle to establish a track record of probity and performance.

What other choices did the saver of modest means have? The New York Stock Exchange had been in existence since 1817. In the 1890s, common stocks of industrial corporations were just starting to be listed on the exchange. But it was foolhardy for people with limited funds to consider plunging their money into stocks. Trading volume was far too low to provide the sort of liquidity that most people needed. So volatile were returns, moreover, that before 1900, stocks on average yielded less than bonds, which were far more secure.[54]

Tappan, it turns out, had formed his ideas during what in retrospect was a dawning moment of financial revolution. For the vast majority of the population, savings options were limited, and in many cases insecure. Yet new, higher yielding instruments beckoned those with substantial funds and knowledge of emerging financial markets. Tappan was one of a number of innovators who would develop new institutions to bring some of those advantages and opportunities from the elite into the hands of the average citizens, helping to change the way Americans saved money. During his lifetime Americans would move money out of cash and other liquid assets into pensions, government bonds, and eventually corporate securities. They would save less in banks and other old-style financial intermediaries and depend more on new financial instruments. Less of their motivation for savings would be the desire to buy a farm or start a business. More would come from the desire to own a home or retire from work. Behind these changes stood growing incomes and other broad macroeconomic changes. But there was something else as well—a change in the culture of saving and in the way institutions handled money.[55]

Before the Civil War, Americans had used a variety of financial institutions to manage money. Among them were commercial and investment banks; savings and loans and savings banks; property, casualty, and life insurance (both commercial and mutual); and private trust funds. These intermediaries helped to collect savings and direct those funds to profitable investments. The most innovative and fastest growing of the lot, life insurance, grew dramatically in the decades around the Civil War, making contact with the scattered American population through commissioned agents.[56] Despite a strong Jeffersonian distrust of concentrated financial power, despite President Andrew Jackson's attack on eastern banks, the truth is most Americans made use of all financial means available to serve their interests and manage their money. What was most controversial was not financial institutions per se, but those that were perceived as too powerful, too remote, and controlled by an elite.

After the Civil War, a whole host of new financial intermediaries of various shapes and sizes emerged, and these would begin to open opportunities for investment to a wider range of users. Credit unions, mortgage companies, personal and sales finance companies, pension funds, land banks, common trust funds, and, beginning in the 1920s, investment firms handling collections of financial assets supplemented the services of traditional financial intermediaries. Even commercial banks that once disdained small accounts began seeking them out, a move that A. P. Giannini would later dramatically advance. Consumers began paying bills with checks instead of cash, or with government paper instead of specie. They financed retirement (itself a new word) with pension funds instead of relying on children's support. They gave over their inheritance to be managed by trust departments instead of family members. They even began to finance purchases instead of paying cold, hard cash. By the end of this long period of change, more and more people were putting their money in the stock market, or giving it to professionals who ran mutual funds.

On a per capita basis, the years between 1850 and 1900 saw the fastest rate of increase in assets held by financial organizations in the nation's history. That rate was nearly matched again in the period from 1900 to 1929. Not only did institutions increase in number, size, and diversity, they also increased geographically, spreading throughout the nation, penetrating formerly remote, closed-off towns and markets. Thousands of small operations sprang up (and unfortunately died off) quickly. Large, traditional institutions, such as commercial banks and even life insurance companies, became less important in this period of innovation. New ways of mobilizing capital, holding assets, and earning a return on an investment became more important.[57]

It was, in short, a heady time for financial innovation, before the calamitous stock market crash and depression of the 1930s, before government would step in to regulate practices and supplant private savings with public entitlements. But all that opportunity stretched out into an uncertain future. What was certain, and amazing, was that at age twenty-four, John Elliott Tappan was embarking on a bold new financial journey while staring right into the teeth of a howling economic tempest.

CHAPTER TWO

THE MONEY QUESTION

Eighteen-ninety-four seemed like anything but the right time to get into finance. The last great depression of the nineteenth century was in full swing and no place was immune. The crisis turned one-fifth of the nation's labor force onto the streets. Eastern factories went silent, thousands of businesses shut down, 500 banks closed their doors.[1] Tappan could see in his own backyard that people were suffering terribly. Up in the iron district, mines were still, shrouded in a blanket of snow. Penniless old men wandered the streets in working-class St. Paul. Across the river in Minneapolis, railroad baron James J. Hill wrote, "very few farmers have any money, and the local banks are unable to aid them. The banks themselves, including many which had been considered entirely strong, are terribly pinched."[2]

Hill's railroad, the Great Northern, was itself devastated by a tremendous strike led by the socialist leader of the American Railway Union, Eugene Debs. In this age of laissez-faire, unions were generally small, weak, and poorly regarded by the professional and middle classes. Nonetheless, the Great Northern strike sharply divided the Minneapolis community. Debs, a forceful speaker with a broad vision of social improvement, came to nearby St. Paul to plead the case for the workers.[3] Facing a hostile audience at the local chamber of commerce, he spoke movingly about the plight of men trying to support families on a dollar a day. In the city itself, the poor had become suddenly visible, with women picking through garbage dumps for food, while unemployed industrial workers or bankrupt farmers rode the rails searching for work.

Dispiriting conditions indeed, but the depression was having an odd impact in the West, brewing up a new mix of economic ideas, many of them aimed at reforming or changing the nation's financial system. Returning to themes first articulated during the depression of the 1870s, these ideas culminated in a broad critique of American capitalism. Long-standing grievances about money welled up into full-scale class conflict, pitting workers and farmers of the West against the new industrial economy and its financial handmaidens located in the East.

Westerners had long been suspicious of the East, though this conflict had never prompted division akin to the North-South split of the Civil War. After all, many who had ventured out West, like the Tappan family, had come from the Yankee East, and shared with the merchants and bankers of New York and Boston a common culture. But by the late nineteenth century, ties that united East and West were under severe strain. The western farm economy was diverging markedly from the more industrial economy of the North.

The depression of the 1890s revealed just how far apart the sections had grown. Agricultural prices tumbled faster and further than did the general price index. Wheat that sold for 85 cents a bushel in New York brought the Minnesota farmer only 50 cents.[4] Relative to what they were paying for tools, supplies, machinery, and humble rural luxuries like lamps, sewing machines, furniture, even overalls, farmers were getting less and less for their crops. At the same time, farm debt was going up in real terms. As prices tumbled, farmers had to pay back loans with money worth more than the money they had borrowed. Under this crushing burden, once proud landowners were dispossessed, turned into mere renters and tenants.[5]

Those who could borrow money were actually the fortunate ones, however. For too many farmers, simply securing capital and credit enough to run their farms was a problem. The nation's financial system was highly segmented, and newly settled western states like Minnesota had far fewer financial institutions than did the cash rich East. Interest rates in a western city such as Omaha were twice as high as the prime rate in Boston.[6] It was particularly galling to Americans who believed that "the soil" was the source of all wealth and prosperity to find tillers of the soil under the financial thumb of eastern bankers once again.

Like the Panic of 1873, this depression too gave rise to competing theories of what was wrong with the nation. For those in the West, responsibility lay with eastern industrial and financial interests. Railroads had monopolized the means of transportation, cutting into the slim profit margins of sodbusters who had to sell their products hundreds of miles from home. Grain elevators and warehouses in Chicago and Minneapolis had a lock on the market, charging farmers exorbitant rates for storing, sorting, and selling their goods. Dealers in "futures" contracts bought and sold pieces of paper that represented wheat or corn, making fortunes on these trades, though no actual wheat or corn ever changed hands.[7] Urban consumers were paying more for bread, milk, cheese, and meat, but farmers got a smaller cut of the profit, the surplus skimmed off by clever middlemen. Worst of all, eastern financiers had monopolized the money supply. This "money trust" was the mother of all trusts according to angry rural critics. It denied farmers and western urbanites the funds they needed for improvement. It concentrated capital in the East. It fed a speculative frenzy in industrial securities that destabilized the "real" economy.[8]

Out of the depression of the 1890s, a new political party emerged as the best voice of this financial critique that America had ever heard. Started in Lampasas County, Texas, the Populists, or People's party, recruited a membership over two million strong, and won several state and many local elections. In 1892, they made their bid for national attention, articulating their beliefs in the Omaha Platform at the party's convention. Their list of demands contained much that was familiar. They wanted to discipline monopolistic corporations and end concentration of land ownership. Their proposals for monetary and financial reform expressed the heart of the antimonopolist sentiment. America had to democratize its financial system. Populist programs included government backed, farmer oriented financial intermediaries, and "free silver," or the reintroduction of this metal into the money supply. Money had to be brought back under the control of the people, and wrestled from the clutches of money masters. Better "the people," through their elected representatives, control the money supply, than private banks and "money kings."[9] Capitalism, they held, could and should remain on a human scale, within the grasp and understanding of any competent individual.

Debates over money and economy in the 1890s formed the immediate context in which John Elliott Tappan turned innovator. Living in Minnesota, he could not help but be aware of the controversies that were dividing farmers from industrialists, controversies that had been in existence since he was born. The Populist attack on financial practices is a window on a now lost moral economy. It was this moral economy that would remain a vital part of what Tappan believed he was trying to support in his own business ventures.

Populists ascribed to the basic principles of producerism and its attendant labor theory of value. However much frayed by financial innovation and economic change, producerism continued to attract a surprisingly wide range of Americans. In Minneapolis, for example, Charles Pillsbury, founder of the giant Pillsbury Flour Mills, believed futures trading destabilized prices and was unnecessary. He proclaimed solidarity with the wheat-growing farmers of his state, and supported laws to ban futures contracts.[10] More generally, those reared in the nineteenth century still believed that production was virtuous, an end itself. Its purpose was not merely to provide wealth for consumption, but was rather a test of moral fiber, with accumulated wealth the outward sign of character. Money that came in easily and without work, it was believed, inevitably went out easily and for purely indulgent purposes. Consumption, especially conspicuous displays of wealth, represented greed, an endless desire that could never be satiated. Money, cut free from real production, fed such desire. It promoted a desire for wealth with no natural limits.[11] The results could only be a society of concentrated wealth, and the end of the sort of producerist equality on which democracy rested. At stake in the controversy over who controlled the money supply and how money was used were not simply issues of class interest. The American traditions of a self-governing citizenry rooted in property ownership and independence were at stake.

How valid were these complaints about money? Under the gold standard, it is true, monetary growth had failed to keep pace with output, causing deflation. Other claims about financial inequity, however, find little credence with modern economists. Despite laws prejudiced against banks in the South and West, the amount of currency in circulation increased toward the end of the nineteenth century. Checks supplanted coin and paper money. The number of banks also grew, despite the strictures of the National Banking Act. Financial intermediaries increased their presence, both in terms of sheer numbers and also in terms of new functions.[12] New gold discoveries such as the great Yukon strike of 1898 eventually relieved even the monetary shortage, though only after several decades of deflation. Indeed, despite periodic crises, overall the economy did grow, if not as fast as before or as fast as some economies in Europe were growing.[13] Productivity continued to increase, as did real wages. If prices and rates of return on capital fell, this only indicated how abundant and fruitful production had become, particularly in agriculture. American grain and other agricultural commodities led the way in exports. Meanwhile, American industrial output increased dramatically, surpassing agriculture as the chief source of wealth in the nation after 1880.[14] Improvements in technology lowered prices for transportation, machinery, steel, and oil over the long haul. Even transportation charges—as measured by railroad freight rates—were far lower than they had been a generation earlier, despite what farmers believed.[15]

Applying our own understanding of the economy to conditions a century ago, however, is a recipe for missing the point. The debates of the late nineteenth century were about more than the technical issue of how fast the supply of money should grow, or if interest rates were too high. Those issues were important, but they do not explain the intense political acrimony of the times. They do not account for the formation of new national political parties dedicated to financial reform in every presidential election between 1872 and 1896, not to mention the dozens of new state and local political organizations.[16] They cannot account for the reorientation of both the Democrats and the Republicans around the issue of money, or the publication of literally hundreds of financial tracts, in rough, miniscule print, devoured by weary farmers at the end of a long working day. One of these, written by "Coin" Harvey, an unknown, self-taught economist with less than a high school education, sold more than a million copies.[17]

To those who remembered the "Crime of '73" and who had lived through lean years, the 1890s depression was the final straw. It was the proof that confirmed their theories about money, conspiracy, and the erosion of the position of the virtuous producer in a new, hostile economy. When citizens a century ago spoke in these terms, or debated improbable schemes for financial reform, they were expressing beliefs about how the economy should operate. When they invented or sought to invent new economic institutions, they were trying to reconstruct the economy in line with their ideals. It is into this tradition that John Elliott Tappan and his financial innovation fits. He, along with many others of various political persuasions, was responding to the dispiriting economic conditions found in western states like Minnesota.

Like other farm belt reformers, Tappan was seeking through financial innovation a way of reconciling economic institutions with social and political ideals. If the financial system eventually responded to criticism and became more attuned to the needs of the average person, in part the efforts of financial innovators like John Tappan were the reason.[18]

The issues for America's future were never more sharply framed than in the great monetary debates of the 1890s, which culminated in the presidential election of 1896. On one side stood private, national institutions imbued with the aura of expertise—banks, commodities exchanges, investment houses. The other side was represented by a new party, the Populists, who dreamed of democratic control by ordinary individuals of key financial institutions. Both sides believed the other had broken faith with tradition. Both sides used a language of monetary naturalism to wrap their financial programs in the cloth of fundamental values. Seen this way, the great money debate was not over markets versus government, industry versus agriculture, capitalism versus socialism, or gold versus silver. It was really a debate over which institutions could best achieve social harmony and support an economy consistent with notions of individualism, freedom, democracy, and capitalism. What neither side fully saw was that, despite their defense of tradition, they were actually promoting new ideas and institutions for managing and using money that would lead the nation further and further away from traditional economic ideas.

Sitting in Minneapolis, John Elliott Tappan was anything but a wild-eyed Populist. Though capable of assessing the merits of political platforms without the blinders of pure partisanship, he generally voted Republican. In the upcoming 1896 election he supported Republican William McKinley against William Jennings Bryan, the Democrat and Populist candidate. Tappan believed firmly in "honest money." To him, that meant gold, and he thought Populist rhetoric was only playing havoc with commerce. The triumph of fundamental values, he believed, would restore business confidence and pull the nation out of its doldrums.

Tappan's commitment to Gold Republicanism, however, was tempered by his deep belief in the need for reform. He was never a purely conventional thinker on monetary matters. Over the course of his life, he would support candidates of different parties and accept a measure of government regulation in his business. He believed that wealth, though important, was a means, not an end. He believed there were or should be limits to accumulation, and that the desire for wealth was not unbounded but tied to the rhythms and span of a natural human life. Though unprepared to accept the radical challenge Populists posed to the economic status quo, Tappan did not dismiss the feelings and frustrations that had given rise to it.

More important than partisanship to Tappan was his firsthand understanding that something needed to be done, particularly in his home state of Minnesota. These events deepened his appreciation of the problems of money and economic instability. When working as a bill collector during the depression, one of Tappan's assignments was repossessing a piano from an elderly woman. He wrote asking her to make at least some payment on the delinquent account or else he would be forced to take action. Hearing no word, he reluctantly went to her home, a third-floor walkup in an old downtown apartment building. Before he reached the top of the stairs, a door opened, followed by a violent crashing sound. Looking up, Tappan was able to leap aside just in time as a piano came careening down the stairs, smashing into a pile of kindling on the second-floor landing. Rather than give up her prized possession, the woman had reduced it to rubbish. This experience reinforced Tappan's belief that if even honest, hardworking men and women were being forced into dire straits, perhaps something really needed to be done.

He was not alone. In fact, beneath the political rhetoric about money, the debates over the gold standard, and rallying cries such as "free silver," changes in financial institutions were beginning to take place, though ones perhaps different than either party advocated. This widespread financial innovation would contribute to the late-nineteenth-century boom in financial services.[19] Even the heart of the corporate economy, the stock market, underwent a modest degree of opening, as unlisted securities began to appear before the public.[20]

It would be easy and conventional to separate this sort of financial innovation from the high ideals of the Populists. But as the case of John Elliott Tappan shows, this hard and fast distinction does not hold up very well. Through his own business, Tappan believed, he could help reconcile differences dividing the West and East, promote financial independence for ordinary citizens, assist farmers in their quest for money and capital, and start up new financial institutions outside of the eastern dominated ones that would serve the needs of those with modest incomes and aspirations. Where he differed was in rejecting the old labor theory of value, the notion that capital's reward was to be extremely limited and given grudgingly. He was not a Populist, but not quite a full-blooded Gold Republican, either. Rather, in his life and work he would seek an extraordinary marriage of western financial reform with eastern financial orthodoxy.

In 1894, John Tappan and local Minneapolis attorney Henry Farnham submitted articles of incorporation for a new firm, Investors Syndicate. After receiving approval from the state commissioner of insurance, the company was organized under the general incorporation statute of Minnesota in July 1894 with $50,000 in capital. As expressed in the charter, its purpose was extremely broad. Investors Syndicate was authorized to deal in government and corporate bonds, stocks, mortgages, notes, and all kinds of personal property, to buy and sell such instruments for other persons, and to issue its own notes and obligations of debt. But the real purpose was much simpler. From his experiences in business and finance, and from a keen appreciation of the financial needs of the small investor, John Tappan had conceived of a new investment instrument, which he called a "face amount certificate."

In modern parlance, a face amount certificate worked much like a zero coupon bond. Buyers purchased certificates at a discount, and then held them until they matured to a face value of $1,000. The holder thus received an implicit rate of interest, which varied depending on the amount paid and the time to maturity. Most customers, though, bought them on installments, originally $6.00 per month. Generally, Tappan's certificates paid around 6 percent, which was several points above what banks could offer and well above the 2 percent on government bonds or 3 percent on bonds of railroads. The higher yield made them attractive to investors who were looking to increase the earning power of their savings without taking the risks of corporate stocks.[21]

"Its object," Tappan wrote, "is to encourage frugality and to assist and encourage its patrons in saving systematically small sums monthly."[22] Banks and other investment options promised similar things. But for the most part, the average person had only limited opportunities for using such savings vehicles. Either they were too speculative, or, if safer and more traditional like banks, they paid low rates of interest. Only the rich really had a chance to take advantage of higher rates of return, since they could afford greater risk and they had accumulations large enough to buy bonds, stocks, or land in sufficient quantity to diversify their portfolios. By contrast, Investors Syndicate planned "to take the earnings of the many," and "treat the earnings of . . . the rich and poor alike, on the same basis." "All classes," Tappan maintained, would have "a safe place to invest their money."[23]

Tappan linked his financial innovation to traditional values. He believed in thrift, hard work, and self-reliance. These were exactly the sort of values that Populists and other believers in the labor theory of value claimed were being subverted by the monopolization of money. The corporate economy was turning once-proud producers into dependents of the big operators, and making workers into factory robots. Though Tappan discounted the effectiveness of the wholesale change proposed by the Populists, he still believed he could "encourage frugality," which would assist the average producer in steering clear of trouble in an unstable economy. Tappan recognized, however, that self-reliance in the modern world required ingenious and often unprecedented organizational innovation.

In this regard, the plan partook of the Republican party faith in expertise and private economic leadership. As a response to the social crisis, it sidestepped government and politics and rested on a belief in experts, well trained in finance and insurance and capable of making rational investments. In their belief that "the people" should have direct access to credit, that farmers should cooperatively market products and buy what they needed, Populists rejected large-scale organization, particularly corporate organization. They denied that efficiency demanded a division of labor whereby specialists in finance, insurance, banking, and marketing made crucial decisions in the chain of production. Tappan, by contrast, was thoroughly part of the white-collar world, and experienced in the ways of modern finance. His expertise would be key to making his new venture fly.

Past experience was crucial in Tappan's claim that he knew what he was doing, that the average person should trust in his knowledge. Working with the Merritt brothers, for example, he had gained a firsthand knowledge of real estate investment, as well as a sharp lesson in the dangers of tangling with the wealth and power of eastern corporate and financial giants. As an insurance agent, Tappan had learned the actuarial techniques needed to predict the behavior of populations of customers. He had also held down a job for the Colombian Investment Company, which had offices in Minneapolis. Among other things, Colombian sold contracts similar to those Tappan would promote. Investors could put in small amounts of money and wait until the contract matured, also to $1,000. Like insurance, these bonds were marketed by networks of agents. Populists and others in the producerist tradition believed that institutions such as banks and futures markets stood between the producer and capital or credit. Their reforms were actually designed to eliminate intermediary organizations and give everyone the same connection to the market. Tappan was building an intermediary institution, but one steeped in experience and expertise and designed to mediate more directly between the producer and capital. It was a subtle but crucial distinction.

The mainstream nature of Tappan's ideas can also be seen in his commitment to professionalism. Despite his western adventures, Tappan's pursuit of a university education and white-collar career showed that his primary allegiance was with the professional class. Like others whose future could no longer be found in agriculture, he had turned to the professions as a sort of haven. Professionalism offered the responsibility and respectability that came from independence impossible in working for a large corporation. Tappan already knew from his venture with the Merritts that he had no liking for big business and the heedless pursuit of wealth on the grand scale. And being a small cog in a corporate machine was not appealing to someone with the individualism and self-reliance Tappan had already shown. But his family had left farming behind a generation before. Tappan turned to law, a profession where one could hone expertise, run an independent office, and have the local respect that came with both.

By venturing into finance as an independent businessman, Tappan was not really breaking with this pattern. He continued to practice law, and for much of his life lawyering would be his main source of income. He organized Investors Syndicate as a corporation, but ran it like a partnership, depending on friends and family for initial support. It would always remain a highly personal business for Tappan, who drew no income out of the firm until 1915. Every cent of profit was ploughed back in.

Tappan's belief in professional expertise and experience, rather than common-man democracy, set him off from the more radical critics of American capitalism. He did not believe individuals on their own could effectively handle the gyrations of the modern economy, or that simple, cooperative solutions would suffice. As corporatists had forcefully argued, experts, scientifically trained, were the proper managers of the people's welfare. True believers in modern organization, such as big business industrialist Andrew Carnegie, claimed that such expertise was best housed in big, national organizations. In *The Gospel of Wealth,* Carnegie's famous answer to Populist critics, the steel titan wrote that prosperity required the concentration of wealth in the hands of the few. This wealth, however, became "the property of the many," as the wealthy man acted as "agent and trustee for his poorer brethren, bringing to their service his superior wisdom, experience, and ability to administer."[24] Tappan would have agreed, to a point. The Syndicate proposed to make wise, safe investment choices for its clients. On the other hand, the sort of institution Tappan was proposing was both national *and* decentralized. It did not embrace the sort of concentration of wealth in the hands of the few Carnegie thought inevitable. The nature of the face amount certificate, as well as the small size and cooperative structure and atmosphere of Investors Syndicate, set it off from a typical insurance or bond company located in New York or Chicago. For much of its early life, the Syndicate would be resolutely local in orientation. Its investments, its personnel, and its center of operations would all remain largely in Minneapolis, firmly under the eyes of Tappan and his partners.

Throughout his career, Tappan would find himself in tension with these two sets of values. He targeted the broad public, rather than the elite. He appealed to the reason and common sense of his customers, avoiding inflated claims that appealed to avarice and exploited ignorance. He kept his firm small, and invested much of his personality and values in its image and operations. Yet he was playing with the sort of tools that were building the corporate economy of remote experts lodged in powerful national institutions who made the active decisions of the economy. Such institutions tended to reduce the public to mere consumers of products and services. Particularly over the organizational issues, as to how big Investors Syndicate could grow and how impersonal and bureaucratic it could become, Tappan would feel this tension.

All those were concerns for the future, however. More immediate was the question, Would it work? Would anyone buy this new product, the face amount certificate? Marketing financial products to small investors was no easy task. Others who had tried had failed in the unstable nineteenth-century American economy. A precedent for what Tappan proposed to do had been established during the Civil War by merchant banker Jay Cooke. Cooke successfully marketed $500 million worth of Union securities to a broad group of subscribers across the North. A relative newcomer to investment underwriting, Cooke broke with tradition and set up a network of 2,500 agents around the country to take his business directly to the people. In contrast to established banking houses, he used colorful, direct sales tactics, the sort of thing that would appeal to less sophisticated clients. Newspaper advertising plus a blizzard of handbills, circulars, pamphlets, and broadsides caught the eye and appealed to deeply patriotic sentiments.[25]

This promising start unraveled after the war, however. When the innovative banker tried to market the bonds of the Northern Pacific, a railroad that aimed to open up the rich timber reserves of northern Minnesota and prime farmlands of the Red River Valley, he ran into trouble. Railroad bonds evoked no patriotic sentiments. The extensive system of correspondent banks and subagents to do retail selling cut into profits. Cooke's advertising provoked withering satire from the Wall Street press. Apply to your nearest "Banker, Butcher, Baker, Apple-woman, Peanut-Man, Paper-vender, or Bill-poster," one derisive article laughed, a direct shot at Cooke's dream of selling the railroad securities to the financially uninitiated, as he had the Civil War bonds. The attack proved all too prophetic. Unable to gather up a head of marketing steam, Northern Pacific bonds languished on the market, and the House of Cooke was spun into bankruptcy by the Panic of 1873.[26] After this disaster, few others were willing to follow in Cooke's footsteps.

By Tappan's time, some firms were beginning to seek out the public more aggressively with new financial products. Some, like the Colombian for which Tappan had worked, sold bonds this way. Corporate bonds, however, remained an option largely for the well-to-do. They were too chancy for those with little cash to spare. When companies slid into receivership or went bankrupt in the unstable late-nineteenth-century economy, bondholders were lucky to get cents on the dollar. More directly comparable to Tappan's plan was the "Iron Hall," which sold certificates for $40 per year. Aimed at a somewhat wealthier market than Tappan's, the Iron Hall plan blew up spectacularly, leading to investigations and accusations of fraud.[27]

In all, the best existing option for long-term investment for most people in the nineteenth century remained life insurance. Collecting money from small investors all over the nation, insurance companies placed it in higher yielding investments than the individual would chance on his own. By pooling funds and diversifying, insurance companies were able to reap attractive returns, which soon made them extremely large and wealthy.

Customers saw only a part of this wealth, however, since the main benefit insurance provided was payment in event of death. For those who, lamentably, died young, the contracts paid quite well. In an unstable economy in which life spans could be cut short by infectious disease, poor health and nutrition, or high rates of industrial accidents, insurance was a wise choice for many of modest means. Indeed, at a time before social security or significant state welfare, it was often the only source of protection the families of miners, industrial workers, and farmers had.

Insurance, however, was not money for investment so much as protection against tragedy. It was, as John Tappan noted, money for death, not "money while you lived." There were "two great things," wrote Tappan in his advertisements: "money and life." His syndicate applied "life insurance principles to business" to pay clients "while living, that which life Insurance Companies pay your heirs at death." Insurance companies scrutinized policy applications, looking to weed out those who might die young and thus collect before they had paid many premiums. By contrast, "HEALTH! AGE! SEX! have nothing to do with the COST of the face amount certificate."[28] It was available to all who could make the payments.

Tappan's experiences in the insurance industry clearly gave him part of his model. Like insurance, face amount certificates were sold through agents to the general public. They allowed individuals of modest means to make small payments each month, rather than lay out a substantial up-front sum for a bond or security. They pooled capital, which was invested at higher yields than small savers could realize themselves. Like an insurance contract, Tappan's contract matured over time. That is, after the contract holder had made a number of payments, there was a guarantee of a return. So long as payments were maintained, the contract would, over time, pay full value. Those who could not keep up payments eventually forfeited their investment. But there were ways of avoiding this outcome. For those who wanted their money back sooner, the contracts had surrender features, which paid back what was put in, plus a smaller return. Or one could take out a loan against the cash value accumulated in the certificates.

In all, the face amount certificates were designed to take into account the precious conditions of those who had limited resources and a strong aversion to high risk. For example, monthly payments were small. Tappan lowered the monthly minimum payment from $6.00 to $2.00. Provisions for forfeiture were extremely lenient. Payments were due on the first of the month but there was no penalty for twenty more days. If the holder could not pay, the company carried him or her for several months, the cost being born by lengthening the time to maturity. In more extreme cases, Investors Syndicate would lend contract holders the money to keep paying. Though these features gave Tappan free use of the investor's money during the time he or she was behind payment, they also assured that temporary insolvency or personal financial crisis did not mean total loss.

In these features, Tappan was clearly following in the footsteps of the insurance precedent. Insurance companies, responding to public criticism, had begun incorporating into contracts safety features designed to make it more difficult to forfeit policies for failure to keep up payments. They included cash surrender values and loan features. Still, even by the 1890s, several large insurers had yet to make these features standard on all policies.[29] Tappan, by contrast, offered such protections from the start.

In contrast to bond schemes, such as those of the Colombian or Iron Hall, Tappan's contracts also had advantages. The maturity date when customers would see their money back was fixed and definite. Tappan could take, if needed, up to twenty years to pay out the $1,000, a feature that was later relaxed to a ten year maximum. Longer maturities, of course, made contracts less attractive to customers. But they made the product safer as well. The Colombian, for example, had grown rapidly by maturing contracts fast, so fast that it found itself caught short when the crunch came.[30] Tappan avoided this enticing, though dangerous, practice in favor of a long-term perspective.

Collecting the public's money was one thing. But where did the money go, what generated income to pay off investors? Here too Tappan merged innovation with tradition. Land was the source of wealth for Tappan, a position he never articulated but one that seems implicit in his own life. From frontier adventures through his days as a Minneapolis businessman, he would continue to make nature a major part of his leisure time activity. He would also continue to invest in land, both for his own account and his company's. The face amount certificates made their money by putting clients' funds into first mortgages on improved land. Initially, the money was invested nearby, in and around Minneapolis, where Tappan could keep an eye on borrowers and their collateral. Minnesota, Tappan reported, was "in the center of [a] fine agricultural district where total crop failures are never known."[31] By investing funds "at home where we are familiar with values and can personally inspect and look after each loan," he minimized the difficulties of lending money on land, which were considerable in the nineteenth century. In this way, Tappan wrote, he could "net ten percent interest on farm loans," and with such funds "mature every obligation."[32] Ten percent simple interest yielded over 7 percent compound interest, which was more than enough to pay off the 6 percent certificates and retain a profit for the company.

It was the financial conflict dividing the nation that gave Tappan this opportunity. Precisely because interest rates were different in different places, and precisely because some regions, like Tappan's own West North Central, were highly dependent on capital from elsewhere, the plan stood a chance of working.[33] Mortgages, or loans made to purchase real property secured by that property, presented special problems in the nineteenth century. Borrowers were asking for money well beyond what they earned each year, offering as their main security the land they sought to purchase with the loan. If the borrower defaulted, the lender could take possession of the land, but to get his money back, he had to turn around and sell the land. Selling land was no easy matter, especially from a distance. Titles had to be checked and secured, liens removed, lawyers had to write up contracts and conveyances in accord with local property laws that varied state to state. Although land was a hard, fixed asset—it could not walk away—it was also an illiquid one. No two pieces of land were the same, and the value of land could change sharply. Foreclosed property depreciated as it sat waiting for sale. Lenders did not want to be saddled with these burdens. They were in the financial business, not farming or real estate.

Land mortgages presented other problems as well, especially as lenders and borrowers of capital grew further apart. Since land is fixed in place, distant lenders needed local agents who could inspect the land offered as collateral. Agents had to find borrowers, take applications, and, if necessary, handle the messy business of foreclosure. Quality agents were hard to come by. Even knowledgeable agents had incentive to make questionable loans when they were being paid by the amount of business they wrote. Together, the information, transaction, and monitoring costs made it difficult and expensive to move funds from capital rich areas like the East to the farm belt towns and cities of the West.

Newly settled agricultural regions suffered especially hard from the mortgage shortage. Although the late nineteenth century is thought of as a time of rapid industrialization, in fact America was growing by expanding its land and natural resource base, even while building industry.[34] Encouraged by the Homestead Act, western farm acreage tripled after the Civil War. In lands west of the Mississippi, the increase was sevenfold. It was this situation that gave rise to the competing claims of farmers and industrialists over control of the nation's financial system.

Conditions in Tappan's home state were typical of the western mortgage experience. Minnesota's population increased from 600,000 to 1.1 million between 1875 and 1885.[35] Much of it went to the Twin Cities, which in turn needed funds for commercial structures and houses. But many new farms opened up in the surrounding wheat belt, too. There, farmers needed money for land, equipment, seed, and supplies. The existing banking system, as Populists complained, seemed structured to move funds into growing urban areas and into industry, rather than into remote, newly settled farmland. Northwestern states such as Minnesota paid a high premium for capital, and had to import substantial amounts of it from elsewhere, more so than most other regions of the nation.[36]

The business of farming not only required capital, it required sympathetic lenders who understood the particular constraints of farming. Even successful farmers faced crop prices that went up and down like a roller coaster. When prices were high, farmers had little choice but to expand, taking on debt and mortgages to produce crops for the market while the market was hot. Then they crossed their fingers and hoped that they made enough money on the market upswing to pay down that debt before the inevitable slump came.[37] Those who were caught short in a falling market faced looming mortgage payments and lowered incomes. It did not help that the most common form of mortgage was not the long-term, self-liquidating one that most home-owners use today. Instead, mortgages were short-term, unamortized loans with a balloon payment of principle at the end. Those whose big payment coincided with a low price year were caught between a rock and a hard place. These were just the sort of conditions that made Minnesota a hotbed of Populism. Indeed, Populist proposals included two plans that dealt directly with this credit crunch. One would have allowed farmers to borrow money on their crops, instead of just land. Another called for government aid to support land loans to farmers.[38]

Mortgage problems in the West had grown especially acute just as Tappan opened for business. National banks were prohibited from lending money on land, and most state and private banks followed suit.[39] Mortgage companies filled this void for a time. But overlending in the 1880s had knocked many mortgage companies out of the market in the hard-pressed 1890s. In part, this collapse stemmed from exactly the sorts of problems Tappan was seeking to solve. Agents of mortgage lenders extended funds to marginal properties in order to secure commissions. Overlending contributed to the great swoon in the mortgage market in 1896. Large mortgage banks continued to operate after the debacle, but they held only 2 percent of bank capital, and their bonds were not listed or traded on New York markets. In all, less than a third of mortgage debt was held by intermediaries. Most funds were still provided through private loans, from estates, trusts, families, and business firms.[40]

Despite risks and problems, there was good reason to invest capital in the West. Though farm commodity prices were volatile, the rich soils of Minnesota were extremely attractive to ambitious farmers. Hard winter wheat fetched a premium in good times. Tappan, like most nineteenth-century businessmen, was sanguine about the future. By investing locally but borrowing nationally, Investors Syndicate could become an interregional capital mobilizer, if it succeeded as Tappan hoped. It would market its contracts across state lines, while avoiding the high transaction and monitoring costs that plagued even large interregional investors. Tappan lent only on real, improved property and required borrowers to make monthly payments of principle and interest. As the first mortgage lender, he held title to the property. These provisions gave the Syndicate collateral in case of hardship, while reassuring certificate holders that their money was backed by something more solid than faith in one man. The depression of the 1890s underscored the dangers of such unsecured financial arrangements, with the collapse of speculative banks and bond companies like the Colombian.

Through several innovative features, face amount certificates were able to reach the difficult-to-serve mortgage market. Banks and other intermediaries often had trouble making long-term loans on real property because the funds they used were subject to immediate withdrawal at the whim of the depositor. Institutions with access to long-term capital could get around this problem, which is why insurance companies entered the mortgage market in a big way at the turn of the century. Most insurance policyholders did not get their money back until they died. Death was a predictable statistical regularity, which insurance firms could easily plan for in their financial strategies. Like insurance firms, Tappan had structured the certificates with the long-term in mind. All the incentives were for clients not to ask for money back until the contracts matured. Lenient provisions against default also encouraged people to keep their capital with Investors Syndicate. Such provisions helped savers save, but also allowed Tappan to enter the otherwise pitfall-ridden mortgage market and take advantage of higher interest rates on long-term mortgages.

The repayment method on loans served a similar purpose. Borrowers were attracted to Tappan's mortgages because they allowed payments to be made in small monthly amounts over a long period of time. Only 1 percent repayment was required each month, or $10 on each $1,000 borrowed. Added flexibility came from provisions that permitted early payment of principle or even double payments one month in order to skip a future month. Small, marginal borrowers with uncertain cash flows would likely have found these features attractive. Traditional short-term, renewable loans presented special dangers to them. First, there was usually an additional charge each time the loan was rolled over. Each renewal also invited scrutiny into the condition of the property and borrower. There was always danger that the lender would decide to call the note, placing the borrower in the unenviable position of liquidating assets—most likely his land and homestead—or defaulting.

The longer term of the loan attracted borrowers, but benefited Tappan and his company as well. Each month he received payments on loans, some of which could be reinvested. Only after the borrower had paid $100 in a calendar year did loan principle decrease. With this leverage, Tappan was able to reap higher rates of return. By relending payments, his actual return on capital was closer to a 9 percent compound rate, if all monies were reinvested at all times.[41] And Tappan consistently found more borrowers than he could serve. With these returns, Investors Syndicate could well afford to pay certificate holders the promised interest rate.

Initially at least, Tappan did not have to worry about the difficulty of making and supervising mortgage investments through agents. He could supervise and inspect the properties he directed funds toward. This cut transaction costs. The costs of foreclosure, in fact, gave him the incentive to create lenient default features for both his loans and his certificates. It was a brilliant confluence of interests at work. Tappan was able to appeal both to savers and borrowers with uncertain cash flows by reassuring them that total loss or foreclosure was the last thing he wanted. And it *was* the last thing he wanted, because it was cheaper to keep the loan on the books than to take possession of defaulted property. This policy was made possible by the corresponding policy of keeping certificates active at all costs, even when the investor fell behind. So long as he had use of the investor's money, he could keep it out in loans, repaying matured contracts with new money coming in. In the future, the defaulters, encouraged by this lenience, might even restart their payments, an option kept open for them.

In theory, then, Tappan had created a structure of incentives much different from those of other financial products. Too often, financial innovators had sought the fast buck, a quick profit, using exaggerated promises to snare the unwary. Once snared, investors in these schemes often found it difficult to maintain payments or extricate themselves from their "investment." The result was default and a loss of all the investor had paid in. Even insurance companies had not fully shed these tendencies. Based on how he structured both his assets and liabilities, though, John Elliott Tappan seemed intent on avoiding the road of financial chicanery from the very start.

Of course, Tappan was not the only innovator thinking about ways of meeting the needs of small savers and borrowers. Other financial institutions emerged at this time to take up the slack where large financial institutions had failed. Building and loans, first established in 1831, operated as credit cooperatives for would-be home buyers. They collected funds from their members and gave those funds to other members who needed them to buy or build a home. By the end of the nineteenth century, more than five thousand building or savings and loans were in existence. Most were located in cities, to lend money on urban property, and only a handful lent to more than a hundred different borrowers. Their membership was heavily drawn from male blue-collar workers, lower level white-collar wage earners, and working women. The average account was a few hundred dollars.[42]

Savings and loans operated most effectively when they mobilized local capital for local purposes among members who shared something in common—religion, ethnicity, or occupation. Community sanctions, local knowledge, and strong personal ties among members were vital to their success. Cultural connections between lender and borrower discouraged cheating or default, but it was not possible to impose such discipline on just anyone.[43] Efforts by S&Ls to reach a broader public foundered, as national institutions fell apart in the devastating 1893 depression. Overall, the membership and assets in building and loans declined for the next decade. So these institutions offered little aid to the problem of capital shortages in areas like Minnesota.[44]

In all, then, Tappan merged precedents based on the emerging world of modern financial institutions in a corporate economy, with older traditions of cooperation found in the fraternal savings and loans and in Populist proposals. By casting a widening net to middle-class savers, he could tap into funds from surplus areas in the East, moving them to the capital short West. He did not depend on the personal ties that older, traditional intermediaries used to handle transactions and inculcate fiduciary discipline. His was, in this sense, a modern financial product, based on objective information and clear, contractual obligations. Yet those who borrowed money from Investors Syndicate were borrowing from a local, independent business, not some agent of a faraway eastern financier or even a bank caught in the web of correspondent relations spun by the national banking system. This was just the sort of local or regionally based economic institution that antimonopolists favored. Populists were big on such institutions, and indeed for all their fiery rhetoric, farmers often sought nothing more than a level playing field with corporations and eastern financiers.[45] Savers who provided the funds, of course, were still concerned about their security. As we shall see, Tappan had an answer to that problem, the potential conflict between the "principals" who actually supplied the money and Tappan himself as their agent. This too merged aspects of traditional business culture with modern financial structures and methods.

The idea was sound, and the need obvious to Tappan. But only experience would tell if people would buy the contracts. Tappan was out on his own. His former employer, the Colombian Bond Company, was in bankruptcy, a victim of the depression. Now he needed his own organization to push his idea.

Investors Syndicate formed its first board of directors in 1894. It consisted of David Judson, whom Tappan had met while employed as a bill collector, and Carrie Cragin and Herbert Herd, friends from his university days. Cragin, who worked as a manager in a local mill, stepped in as the company's first president, before she was replaced by Judson three days later. Tappan did not seek the top post, but instead took on the duties of secretary-treasurer. It was common practice in other financial institutions that the secretary did most of the crucial work of investing. He would never officially head the company he founded, but nonetheless would be its guiding spirit.

With the board installed and the letters of incorporation safely filed, Investors Syndicate opened for business at 204 Lumber Exchange Building. One of Minneapolis' first "skyscrapers," the Lumber Exchange soared twelve stories into the air, tall enough to use the new machines called elevators. It was a well-known landmark that harkened back to Minnesota's nineteenth-century heritage in lumber and mining. The address, however, could not disguise the fact that Tappan and his small entourage had no money, no staff, and little more than a lease on an office and a typewriter. Only later would he admit that he did not even have enough cash on hand to pay the printer's bill of $18 for a small supply of certificates and a prospectus.

An early cash flow crisis was quickly averted when Tappan sold his first policy. Following the lessons he had learned selling insurance, John approached J. L. Ludwig, superintendent of one of Pillsbury's flourmills, most likely introduced by Carrie Cragin. Ludwig was exactly the sort of customer the Syndicate needed. Employed by the largest and most respected company in town, he was well-off, though not rich, and his example would be watched closely by others of small means, including the better paid workers under his charge at the mill. This was the broader base of middle- and working-class savers Tappan sought. "Salaried people," Tappan soon realized, were the best prospects, because they had reliable incomes. Members of the new white-collar and managerial class were thus Tappan's target market. Early customers would include lawyers, dentists, teachers, painters, coopers, druggists, and proprietors of groceries, lodging houses, and dairies.[46] Laying out his prospectus, Tappan waited while Ludwig thought it over. A good salesman, Tappan knew, did not say too much before the customer replied. Finally the mill superintendent gave his response. Asking only if Tappan was "connected" to the company whose products he was offering and if it was "all right," he handed over $30 in gold for three contracts. "I don't believe" Tappan wrote, "that any money I ever received looked quite as good as that did." Investors Syndicate was in the marketplace.[47]

The sale came none too soon. Not only was the printer's bill due, but the next day a representative of R. G. Dun, the nation's largest and most influential credit reporting bureau, stopped by. The Dun Company (today

Dun & Bradstreet) traced its origins back to before the Civil War. It had been started, ironically, by a Yankee abolitionist named Lewis Tappan, who came out of the same part of New York State as John Tappan's family, though was no relation. Dun's provided eastern merchants and financiers with vital information about the credit worthiness of retailers, wholesalers, and other businessmen and women operating throughout the United States. So a report from a Dun agent weighed heavily in determining the reputation of any new enterprise. Information was becoming increasingly important in an economy of national proportions with rapid development taking place in once-remote frontier regions. Though telegraph lines connected all of the major cities and most of the towns and hamlets of the nation by 1894, long-distance telephone lines were in their infancy, only reaching as far west as Chicago. Visits from agents and personal opinions, more than faceless or seemingly objective information, counted when it came to determining which businesses got capital and credit.

Credit agents visited new businesses as they opened, and returned periodically thereafter to check on the character of the proprietor and the scale and profitability of operations. Particularly for the hundreds of thousands of small partnerships and proprietorships of western towns and cities, this information was extremely hard to gather and highly subjective. Agents took note of stock on hand and checked with banks for records of liquid assets. Mostly, though, they investigated reputations, and made personal evaluations of the owners. Comments on appearance, religion, drinking habits, family background, race, and ethnicity were not only common, but expected, and used by lenders in determining how much credit to extend.

There remains no record of the Dun Company evaluation of Investors Syndicate, but Tappan wrote about the visit. "He [the Dun agent] called on me for the purpose of procuring some information concerning the company and a copy of its financial statement. It was, of course, impossible for me to comply with this latter request, but I did sit down and frankly and clearly explain our proposed plan of business." Explaining "frankly and clearly," and winning over skeptics by force of character and reputation, would turn out to be Tappan's major preoccupation in the early days. In this case, his efforts were a success, for the agent offered his opinion that the company, though new, had a plan that should be deemed "reasonably safe." For Tappan the experience reinforced his belief that much depended on his ability "to meet every obligation . . . on its due date and to conserve and protect the investor's money with every safeguard possible." Success was going to hinge on overcoming the natural fear and reluctance of these investors to jump into a new and unknown market.[48]

It was hardly surprising that a new money-making scheme raised some eyebrows. To overcome skeptics, Tappan had to build his own reputation as much as that of the plan and the company. Early customers provided references and referrals to friends, who became customers as well. Even so, a number of burdens weighed the Syndicate down. Tappan's former connection with the Colombian Bond and Investment Company, a company now bankrupt with clients stranded, did him no credit. It tarnished his worthiness in the eyes of cautious clients. There was little to do but meet this challenge head-on. Turning misfortune into potential business, Tappan contacted each of the old Colombian bondholders. "I was connected with the Colombian," he wrote, "and although I am not personally liable, yet on account of the fizzle of that company . . . I am going to give all the old bond holders a chance to transfer whether they are in good standing or not." The old Colombian clientele, Tappan hoped, would sign on with his venture, giving him a head start in forming a client list.[49]

It was crucial to distinguish what Investors Syndicate was trying to do from the Colombian plan. "We do not use the objectionable system and have the benefit of the various bond companies' experience, and never have been nor will be interfered with as we comply with the law in *every* way." The objectionable system Tappan referred to was the practice of maturing on the basis of a lottery or a random drawing. The idea was to appeal to investors by offering a chance at a fast payout, although this also made the "investment" something like a game of chance. Chance and risk, highly subjective and unpredictable matters from the perspective of the average investor, would be among the most important issues Tappan confronted in his early years. Much of his work in this regard consisted of defining for investors what constituted an "acceptable" risk and differentiating acceptable market risk from mere "chance."

Competing investment schemes often sought to skirt this issue by hiding risks, only to have the hidden dangers come out when the company failed. Others deliberately conflated risk with chance, and used chance as a marketing ploy. The Colombian lottery plan did just that. Usually, the first person to take out a contract stood first in line to have their investment matured—paid off at the full interest rate. Since all investment plans were risky, those who signed up early generally had greater assurance that the company would survive long enough to pay out the promised return. As the number of policyholders grew, new income provided funds for maturing older contracts. But those who came aboard late might well worry if anything would be left for them when their number turned up. In an unstable economy, bankruptcy was commonplace. To relieve this worry and stimulate sales, some investment companies turned to the lottery system. It was an effective marketing ploy, but also one that caused many to see the whole operation as little more than a thinly disguised gambling den. Tappan made it clear that he would never introduce elements of chance into his contracts. It was a position that marked him as a believer in the moral economy, the economy based on real values, not flights of fancy, fictitious paper wealth, or manipulation.

In November 1895, Investors Syndicate moved offices to the Guaranty Loan Building. The new building offered lower rent, probably courtesy of the depression. It also had a large law library, free to tenants. Tappan was trying to complete his night school law courses by June. He was so busy, he neglected his personal correspondence, apologizing in later replies that he barely had time to sleep. So a convenient library was a major attraction. The new building also advertised the Syndicate in a rather more modern style than before. With an exterior of Lake Superior sandstone, and just five years old, it was one of the most spectacular buildings in Minneapolis. The interior made effective use of glass and iron, with a giant skylight, giving the whole inside a light, delicate aspect. It had been the tallest building in the city when built in 1890, and its rooftop garden restaurant afforded spectacular city vistas. It was a fine way to end the first full year of business.

Still, the hectic pace of life was pulling Tappan in several directions. While starting his duties as secretary-treasurer of the Syndicate, he continued to work elsewhere, as a bill collector and at the Union Freight Agency. Meanwhile, finishing up his law school work, he studied nights for the bar exam. Tappan's situation kept him in touch with those struggling to stay above water in the lingering depression. Though his mother was financially independent, he did not want her to support him. Instead he moved in with his sister and her husband. Books, classes, clothes, and transportation were the necessary items of life. He rode a bicycle to and from work and school, until it was stolen. Then he walked, for he had no money for a replacement. The only breaks in the routine of work and study were occasional trips to see friends in Duluth and time out for hunting and fishing.

At least his social life took a turn for the better. In 1895 he met Winnie Gallagher, a young "office girl" who worked nearby as a secretary. It was not love at first sight, though John did remark to a friend, "she has the whitest teeth I ever saw." About 5 feet, 5 inches tall, neat and attractive with thick, curly auburn hair and big green eyes, Winnie Gallagher took good care of herself. She could afford to. With a good salary from her job, she was one of a small but growing number of white-collar working women who were starting to fill up the offices of insurance companies, banks, and large corporations that relied more and more on information to manage far-flung affairs. Winnie's origins, though, were somewhat atypical.

About the same age as Tappan, she had arrived in Minneapolis from western Ireland. One of thirteen children, her mother had died when Winnie was ten. So, like Tappan, she had been raised by a single parent, and had experienced the difficulties and conflicts with older siblings who also acted as substitute parents. Her father, a cattle and horse trader, was relatively successful, which enabled Winnie to get a good education. Despite his success, however, Winnie's siblings gradually left for better opportunities in America.

Older bother Thomas landed in New York and made his way to Cincinnati. Once he was established, he welcomed other family members to join him, functioning as their "way station," a common pattern of immigration. A few years later, Winnie decided to take up his offer. She packed up her possessions in a small trunk and went by wagon to Sligo, one of the larger towns in rural western Ireland. She arrived to see a large boat filled with passengers like herself. Hugging her father, whom she would never see again, she boarded the boat for America. Like the brothers and sisters who preceded her, she arrived at Tom's doorstep in Cincinnati after landing in New York and taking the train overland. Taking some courses in stenography and typing, she put her education to good use. Then she moved on to the West.

Not many Irish immigrants off the boat had the training to do office work, certainly not many young women from western Ireland. Nor did most of them end up, as Winnie would, out in the rural West. Industrial cities such as Chicago and Pittsburgh, ports such as Boston, Baltimore, and Cleveland, or booming metropolises, especially New York, were the favored destinations. In two years, however, Winnie had left Cincinnati for the small town of Red Wing, Minnesota, where another brother, Patrick, lived. In Red Wing, Winnie worked for a prominent local firm, Charles Betcher & Co., manufacturers of iron, steel, heavy hardware, and wagon, carriage, and sleigh stock.

Before long, she attracted the attention of Fred Busch, son of a prominent local banker. It seemed a good match.

Though from a somewhat higher social class, Busch was Catholic, as was Winnie. They were in the planning stages for a wedding when Winnie's baby sister Anna wrote saying she too was coming to America. Feeling obligated to help Anna get established, Winnie postponed the wedding, which angered her fiancé. He accused her of waiting to see if she could find a better suitor with more money and called her a gold digger. Apparently the class differences were not so easily smoothed over. Winnie became furious, removed the diamond ring from her finger, and flung it at him. The engagement was off, and Winnie had a reason to leave Red Wing.

A few months later, Winnie and Anna relocated to Minneapolis. It offered better prospects for two young, single women, and a fresh start in a bigger town for Winnie. Moving into a respectable boardinghouse, Winnie found a job as a clerk for an insurance firm, earning enough to pay Anna's room and board while putting her through stenography school. When her courses were finished, Anna went to work as well, giving the two sufficient income to pay for their rooms, with plenty left over for clothes, theater, and other entertainment.

Young immigrant women working and living in the cities at this time were objects of some suspicion from middle-class matrons, who feared that they would fall prey to moral dangers as "women adrift." Certainly the life of a pioneering white-collar employee presented dangers, from unwanted male attention or sexual harassment on the job. Men and women working side by side in offices was a new thing, as the formerly all male world of clerks, stenographers, and cashiers became more feminized. But the opportunities for an independent life and income for unmarried women were hardly the dangers upper-crust, native born Protestants made them out to be. Winnie and her sister seem to have managed their lives in the city quite well.

In the spring of 1896, as Tappan was pushing Investors Syndicate, working at other day jobs, and completing law school, he and Winnie Gallagher began to date. They took long walks, rode bicycles, and occasionally went to the theater. It must have been more difficult for John than Winnie, for she had a good income and more free time than her suitor. But the relationship soon turned serious, and John announced his intention to marry Winnie. Neither his mother Adelaide nor his sister Carrie approved of the union with a Catholic and Irish immigrant. But John had come out from under the thumb of his family years ago when he left for the West Coast. He ignored their criticism and proposed anyway.

His impending wedding corresponded to other passages in his life. On June 6, 1896, Tappan graduated from the University of Minnesota College of Law. His graduation picture shows the profile of a young man with a set jaw and a long, aquiline nose, looking into the distance. These features were accented by his clean-shaven face, uncommon at a time when men wore beards and mustaches to add character and maturity to their appearance. Those who knew Tappan, though, would remark especially on his deep, penetrating blue eyes, his most striking feature. The color was unusual enough to be slightly unnerving at first glance. Three years of independent living in the West erased any suggestion of baby-faced immaturity in the twenty-six-year-old.

Completing the sporadic education he had begun a decade ago in front of a furnace in a Seattle church basement, Tappan had finished law school with a respectable B average. Little stands out on his transcript to indicate a future financial innovator. In fact, Tappan did not elect to take courses in trusts, mortgages, or real property. His best grade was in partnerships. Allowing himself a short celebration, he rode to Duluth and spent a week with friends. Getting back, he found things in Minneapolis quite well. "Crops are fine here," he wrote, "and the wheat men are expecting one of the best crops we have ever had."[50] It was a cool summer, but for one thing: politics. They were, Tappan noted, "red hot."

The money issue had finally come to the fore of American politics. In the 1896 election, William McKinley, the Republican, wrapped himself in the flag and stood firmly behind the gold standard. He was opposed by William Jennings Bryan, a Nebraska Democrat who favored an expanded money supply. Harkening back to the "Crime of '73," Bryan and his supporters campaigned on the platform of "Free Silver" and the reintroduction of silver into the money supply. Though not exactly endorsing the Populist agenda, Bryan was able to capture support from this third party as well.[51] The election was closely fought down to the last day. McKinley had plenty of help from business, especially corporate business, building up a huge campaign war chest with the help of men like John D. Rockefeller and banker J. P. Morgan. His political strategist, Ohio industrialist Mark Hanna, even invented a new holiday, Flag Day. Every patriotic American carried a flag on that day, making the national symbol also an implicit endorsement of McKinley and sound money. Bryan, however, had youth and energy on his side, and a gift for oratory. He rode the long tide of discontent that had created the Populist party and monetary unorthodoxy. In the end, though, it wasn't enough. Sound money triumphed in a contest that brought out 80 percent of the eligible voters. McKinley and gold defeated Bryan and silver, 51 percent to 49 percent.

With the defeat in 1896, the Populist challenge was over. However, the questions raised, even men like Tappan acknowledged, were legitimate ones. Certainly any man living in the West should be able to see that money and access to money was not equally distributed. But to Tappan, the debate over gold and silver was a false, even pernicious debate. Money was tight enough without throwing the entire monetary system into turmoil. A better answer, he might have said, lay in supporting new institutions like his own Investors Syndicate.

As if to pronounce his faith in hard money, John Tappan scheduled the most important day of his private life for November 3, 1896. "To celebrate McKinley's election," he and Winnie Gallagher were married that day in St. Stephen's Church in Minneapolis.[52] The ceremony was performed by a Catholic priest, but in the church vestibule because John was not Catholic. The small ceremony was attended only by Anna Gallagher and John's immediate family. In fact, the whole courtship was such a whirlwind that John did not tell his friends about the marriage until after his honeymoon. The honeymoon itself though had been planned by John—a hunting trip with his bride, whose wedding present from her new partner was a hunting rifle. Winnie would never go hunting again, but for John, the return to nature was a pattern he would follow his whole life.

By the end of 1896, Investors Syndicate, like John Elliott Tappan, had embarked on a hopeful but still uncertain course. He had assets of $2,500 and a handful of subscribers. Back from his honeymoon in November and settled into the new offices, Tappan was ready to "push" the company. "I think we have the best plan in existence today and one that is bound to succeed and it will succeed."[53] There was a sense that the financial fate of the nation had been in the balance. "Hope now that McKinley is in, you will be able to sell some business and make something," Tappan wrote optimistically to a friend. He responded to the return of financial orthodoxy with a new contract, one for half the former amount, so that investors need only pay a dollar each month. These contracts were not as profitable, given the cost of paperwork, but he offered them nonetheless, out of his firm belief that "the only way to get ahead and make anything is to save so much each month."[54] Though the "hard times" had hampered business, Investors Syndicate was prepared to "strike out vigorously after the election." Not free silver, but the Syndicate plan was Tappan's answer to the money question. In the firm's first annual report he proclaimed, "We have built upon the rock and laid the foundation broad and deep and are sure of getting the enormous business which our plan and system so richly deserve."[55]

As always, of course, faith in the future had to be tempered by reality. Investors Syndicate was a tiny new company. Bigger and stronger firms than this had fallen like houses of cards in the depression. Still, as Tappan would show, his flowery words were more than catchy advertising copy. The founder of Investors Syndicate truly believed he had developed a revolutionary financial product. Now he set out to prove it.

CHAPTER THREE

A FOUNDATION OF TRUST

As Tappan wound up business for 1896, the depression was bottoming out. Months earlier, the eye of the maelstrom had passed right over Minneapolis. An army of unemployed workers tramped through the city, heading east for a showdown with the Republican administration in Washington, D.C. Dubbed "Coxey's Army," this stream of discontent had its origins in the summer of 1894, when 500 men on foot, led by Jacob Coxey and his family, marched out of Massillon, Ohio. Making fifteen miles per day, they invited others to join them in the nation's capital, where they would petition Congress to alleviate the economic suffering.

For several summers, similar "armies" followed, departing from Chicago, Los Angeles, and San Francisco. They went on foot, hopped freight, and in a few cases commandeered engines and cars from railroads. The group that passed through Minneapolis was most likely "Jumbo" Cantwell's group from Seattle. This band of unshaven, rough-hewn lumbermen and miners no doubt frightened the respectable citizens of the city. But Tappan would have recognized the type from his days out West. More disturbing were their ideas. The handsome Cantwell, a former saloon bouncer, frontier gambler, and prizefighter, mounted a stage in the Twin Cities to address a crowd of supporters and well-wishers. He offered that it was no worse to hang a few congressmen than to let Congress steal from the people what was theirs.[1] Political corruption, brought on by concentrated wealth and monopoly power, was overshadowing American institutions of democracy, in Cantwell's opinion.

With their martial organization and occasional outrageous statements, the Coxeyites gave the threat of impending violence to an already tense moment in American history. But the tumultuous end of the nineteenth century was marked by real violence elsewhere. In the Homestead steel works of Pittsburgh, striking workers were fired upon by company-employed Pinkerton agents, and returned fire. State militias were called out, bayonets fixed on rifles, to end labor disputes. A bomb exploded in the middle of a march by Chicago anarchists, killing several policemen. Two presidents were assassinated. Anyone who thought the 1896 election had settled the nation's conflicts was mistaken.

Though the industrial armies of the unemployed hanged no one, Cantwell's threat aside, they did converge as promised in Coxey's camp outside of Washington. Boasting that a half-million men would join him, the march's leader settled for several thousand and carried his "petition in boots" directly to Congress. Coxey supported an agenda of expanded currency to pay for public works, which would be undertaken by unemployed industrial workers. For a moment, he merged in one program the answers to the two main sore points of the economy: the shrinking money supply and the insecurity of industrial employment. Generally these were distinct concerns of different classes, farmers and workers, who rarely saw their interests in common. Indeed, in the 1896 election, Bryan had lost precisely because too few industrial workers supported his plans to raise farm prices and deal with problems of credit and capital that bedeviled producers. Coxey momentarily bridged this rift, by emphasizing the weakness of traditional notions of independence and self-reliance in a modern economy. Neither workers nor farmers would be able to support themselves, his petition implied, without intervening organizations and programs designed to deal with periodic instability.

Tappan's view of Coxey and his protest movement is revealing of the young Minnesotan's mind and his mixture of social values and business. While stumping for his program around the country, Coxey visited Minneapolis. There he and Tappan met. A representative from Investors Syndicate arranged the meeting, suggesting, perhaps half in jest, that the charismatic Coxey would make a good salesman. Much to Tappan's surprise, Coxey walked into the office a few days later. On the surface, it was an improbable encounter—a respectable young lawyer with ambitions in finance, and a soldier fighting for the poor and unemployed. But after Tappan explained the face amount certificates, Coxey only responded that he "had his hands full with some zinc mines in Missouri." The Syndicate agent had been right. Short and bespectacled, Coxey was an Ohio businessman, not a flaming revolutionary.[2]

Indeed, Coxey's background was quite similar to Tappan's. Born in rural Pennsylvania, Coxey had moved to Ohio as a youth. For ten years he worked in a rolling mill, before acquiring enough capital to buy a quarry, which he still operated while leading his protest. Reputed to be worth some $200,000 and a fancier of fine Kentucky thoroughbreds, Coxey the Buckeye business-man should have been a staunch supporter of the Republican party. But then, the "mob" he led was composed less of zealous radicals than of ordinary men and women who had lost their farms or jobs.[3]

Tappan and Coxey, close in background and experience, had different philosophies, but these differences reflected the same fundamental ideal. Both were middle-class men whose work and life experiences had sensitized them to the economic problems faced by the average worker. Coxey organized his march in disgust over having to lay off workers at his quarry. Both infused their business lives with a larger sense of social responsibility, mixing business and reform. Supporting his political ventures with sales of a patent medicine he dubbed "Cox-E-Lax," Coxey appeared again and again on the American political stage, especially in moments of economic crisis. He ran on the Populist ticket for Congress; he led marches to Washington in 1914 and again in 1928, on the eve of the Great Depression. In 1932 and 1936 the Farmer-Labor party, whose roots were deep in Minnesota, nominated him for president.

Though Coxey and Tappan diverged in their approaches to the money issue, they swam in the same stream of thought. Coxey supported soft money, money made cheaper and more freely available to producers. His public works plan was to be financed by "interest free bonds" issued by state or local governments. The bonds would be deposited with the United States Treasury in return for legal tender notes to pay workers on public works projects. Ingeniously, his scheme would expand the money supply and alleviate unemployment, while improving the nation's infrastructure—roads in particular—to the benefit of all.

Tappan, of course, remained a hard-money Republican. But he also sought a safe, simple, moderate means of giving the average citizen control over money, by providing outlets for earning interest. Over time, their ideas saw some convergence.[4] In 1914, Coxey shifted his emphasis to federally sponsored banks set up in each and every town, like post offices. These small-scale financial institutions were to accept real property as collateral and make loans that could be repaid on installments over twenty-five years. The idea was to help farmers buy land and workers secure home ownership. Both goals were part of Tappan's plan, too.

Where they fundamentally differed was on tactics. Coxey, like Tappan, was less performer than persuader. Both were quiet men who won converts through absolute conviction rather than fancy oratory. Coxey, however, also believed in direct political action. Rolling across the country with his 500 men, trailed by commissary, band, and panorama wagons, he sought change by mobilizing people politically, through symbolic actions and by illustrated public lectures. At his side were his wife and his newborn son, whom he named Legal Tender Coxey, "as a pertinent reminder of the sovereign right of the government to use its own full legal tender as money."[5] Coxey looked largely to politics for reform, using his business ventures to support his political ones. Tappan stuck to his own private venture.

Still, the leap from business entrepreneur to reformer was shorter in the nineteenth century than today. One of the most powerful Populist spokesmen in Tappan's state, for example, was the congressman and tract writer Ignatius Donnelly. Donnelly began his career as a lawyer and successful land speculator. At one time, he worked as lobbyist for the banker Jay Cooke, during his failed Northern Pacific bond marketing effort.[6] But Donnelly also had a strong social conscience. He organized savings societies to help immigrants acquire homes and established cooperative stores for farmers. He attacked insurance firms for investing their premiums out of state and he supported an alternative mutual insurance association sponsored by Minnesota Populists.[7] A political firebrand who knew little party loyalty, he switched from the Democratic to the Republican and back to the Democratic party again. All the while he edited a Populist newspaper across the river from Tappan in St. Paul and wrote some of the most compelling words on Populism, the preamble to the organization's Omaha Platform of 1892.[8]

In both his politics and business ventures, Donnelly sought to rescue the individual from what he saw as the dangers of modern mass society—a mechanistic, conformist, authoritarian future. His dystopian novel, *Caesar's Column,* warned of a coming war between robotlike workers and corporate leaders. It was as much a condemnation of the individual's loss of political and economic independence as it was a plea for social justice between classes. Despite his radical political course, Donnelly displayed a deep phobia toward the faceless urban mob created by industrial capitalism. Concentrated power, including money power, was for Donnelly at the root of the problem. The alternative he advocated was not collectivism, but a nation of free independent producers, farmers, and small artisans.[9]

For Tappan, individualism and autonomy were important values as well. He still believed that independence from large, bureaucratic institutions remained an option. Yet he also depended on bureaucratic systems of organization and expert knowledge to make his financial product work. This was one of the thorny ideological issues of turn-of-the-century American politics. Conservatives viewed the Populists and labor radicals as malcontents who wanted only a handout. Calls for government intervention were dismissed as cries for the dole, a paternalism corrosive of fundamental American values. The response to such charges was that the poor sought a hand up, not a handout. The system was broken and needed fixing. Even successful businessmen like Coxey and Donnelly could see this. By the 1890s, in fact, the staunch Republican former president Benjamin Harrison was shaken enough by the depths of misery to advocate a public works program, against the policy of his own party.[10] No longer was it possible to go West and seek opportunity. Busted and out of work westerners were following Jumbo Cantwell east to seek answers. As Tappan too would discover, creating institutions that could liberate people as free and independent producers was increasingly difficult in an economy of large-scale corporate institutions.

⚓

In the meantime, new concerns loomed at the young Investors Syndicate. Despite hopes that the end of monetary controversy would return business to a normal footing, several more Minneapolis banks had gone under. The predicted upsurge in orders for face amount certificates failed to arrive.[11]

Fortunately, the small size of Investors Syndicate, its low overhead, and modest early goals offered some protection from unsettled conditions. Tappan had never promised get-rich-quick schemes. "If you expect to get $1,000 from us for a few dollars, and get it in a few months," he told his customers, "you will be disappointed, as we never pretended to be capable of performing miracles." The certificates remained "safe and profitable." No one should hesitate in recommending them to their "best friends."[12] But Tappan's philosophy of saving was "all good things come to those who wait."[13]

At least Investors Syndicate did not have legal worries, as did some similar firms. Tappan had already seen what happened when financiers ran afoul of the law. While he was in law school, the need for income had driven him to take on a number of jobs. One was with the local office of Guaranty Investment Bond Company, based in Chicago. Almost immediately, the company ran into trouble. First, it came under investigation by the Post Office. In the days before the Securities and Exchange Commission (SEC), the Post Office was practically the only enforcement arm of the federal government on financial matters. The numerous investment schemes that arose and then fell in the 1890s had motivated Congress to increase these investigatory powers, especially regarding matters of money. The Post Office's mandate to prevent fraud allowed it to stop the mail of any company or individual using it for illicit purposes. In the days before computers, faxes, or even much long-distance telephone service, that was a powerful weapon to check abuse by information-based financial companies.

Guaranty eventually prevailed in the courts, but then it was struck by a second blow. George MacDonald, the company's president and Tappan's employer, was thrown in jail for "swindling." He was convicted of selling bonds by making false claims, a common if underhanded practice among investment company sales agents trying to work up business in the field. Unable to run his company from jail, MacDonald had begged Tappan to go to Chicago and take over. Tappan agreed. Though only twenty-four years old, he was proud to be asked to serve as conservator of the Guaranty. He arrived in a city still reeling from a violent strike at the Pullman Palace Car Company works. With the nation's economy slowly reviving, Tappan had his hands full trying to rescue the company. It was the sort of obligation that he felt was almost a public service, however. If the crisis caused Guaranty to fold, many investors would be stranded, adding to the already shaky reputation of investment companies.[14]

The experience with Guaranty gave Tappan pause to reflect. Many financial innovators were trying to find ways of tapping into the nation's vast horde of savings, particularly from middle- and lower-middle-class households. It was easy enough to promise higher returns than banks or more traditional intermediaries could offer. It was much harder to convince people to hand over their money and make such schemes work. MacDonald's troubles showed just how tricky it was to establish a reputation for running a safe, legitimate business, especially an innovative business.

This issue of "legitimacy" would vex Tappan during the early years. It went right to the core of the issue of intermediation. Standing between the public and investments, intermediaries have a fiduciary obligation to conserve and protect investors' capital, while also competing for funds by offering the highest returns possible. What, however, separated an honest, legitimate investment product from a mere con game? Many schemes came and went in the late nineteenth century. They all faced this same question. What persuaded the public to send in their funds? Legitimacy meant convincing investors, and watchful legal authorities, that an investment plan really did intend to give clients a fair return for their money—that it was something more than a way of bilking the gullible.

Many investment companies spoke, and continue to speak, of offering the public a "fair" return. But all investment carries some risk, and a fair return is really nothing more than the payout discounted by that risk. In the nineteenth century, it was well understood and accepted that investors took their chances. There were no guarantees or bailouts should things go bad. Yet absent government oversight, investment companies could promise the moon. Investors often had no way of determining whether their hard-earned dollars were being carefully tended, wasted on frills, or simply pocketed by officers of the company. The market itself did not resolve such questions, since even the best planned investments could turn sour through no one's fault. How could the public distinguish between an honest, competent fiduciary who lost money simply due to normal market risk, and a cheat, charlatan, or incompetent who never had a chance of making money for anyone, except perhaps himself?

Particularly in periods of innovation, determining what was legal and legitimate, as opposed to what was fraudulent and immoral, was impossible to set down by hard and fast rules or by a simple application of reason. Indeed, the answer to this question depended crucially on what entrepreneurs such as Tappan did and how well they did it. So a good part of the pioneering days at Investors Syndicate was spent trying to convince the public that the face amount certificate was in fact an honest, legitimate innovation. Tappan had many questionable precedents to overcome. The Colombian and Guaranty had failed because they did not, as Tappan put it, maintain the relation of debtor and creditor.[15] That is, they had not paid investors from the earnings generated by the investors' own money, but rather from the sales of new contracts. At worst, such operations were like giant pyramid or Ponzi schemes. They kept afloat as long as new money came in faster than payments went out to existing subscribers. Eventually, though, the base of new investors was too small to support the growing edifice. Tappan's certificates clearly spelled out that each investor had a separate contract, as with "a bank and a depositor." One's return came from investments actually made.

Still, plenty of other investment firms sought ways to cut corners and increase the marketability of their products. One of the leaders of the new big business economy, sugar magnate H. O. Havemeyer, voiced the common wisdom when he said, "Let the buyer beware; that covers the whole of people," including those who invested their hard-earned dollars in financial assets. If the ignorant or unfortunate lost their savings, so be it. "You cannot wet nurse people," Havemeyer declared, "they have to wade in and get stuck and that is the way men are educated."[16] It was a hard way to learn the lessons of saving and investment, if the cost was all that one owned.

Fears of "getting stuck" sometimes urged even careful investors to throw prudence to the wind and take a flyer. Safe, slow investment sounded fine, but if all of one's savings could be wiped out in an unexpected bankruptcy or sudden economic downturn, what was the sense in being patient? These fears made lottery type systems of investment, in essence games of chance, more popular than logic or prudence otherwise dictated. As noted earlier, for example, some of Tappan's competitors used the "multiple" system for maturing contracts. They paid off investors not on the basis of who bought the first contract, but on the basis of a random drawing. However dubious such systems seemed, they often proved quite popular with the public.

Lack of information was the reason. Investors often had no way of knowing whether the financial underpinnings of an investment company were strong and sound or weak and rotting. Early contract holders might get their money out with interest, but latecomers might be buying into something that was teetering on the brink of collapse. Financial disclosure and reporting laws were practically nonexistent and varied widely from state to state in these years before the SEC. Standard accounting principles had yet to be set down firmly, and even large corporations rarely issued annual statements audited by professional accountants.[17] With a dearth of good information, many investors looked skeptically at companies that had already written a substantial volume of business. Normally, a solid track record should have assuaged fears. Instead, growth made it harder to attract new business. Potential investors worried that by the time their number turned up, it would be too late, the company would have gone under. An unstable national economy that had experienced two major depressions in twenty-five years made such fears credible. With the lottery-like features of the multiple system, however, even latecomers stood a chance of seeing a return on their investment. The company might not be wholly sound, but one could turn up a low number and leap the line ahead of earlier subscribers. Enticing because of the possibility of large returns fast, such plans also made investment into a form of gambling. And in the nineteenth century, gambling was a huge social controversy.

Americans had trouble making up their minds if investment and gambling were the same thing, or if they were distinct. The experience of insurance companies is instructive here. By the late nineteenth century, life insurance was big business, growing fast from humble beginnings a half-century earlier. In America in particular, life insurance had soared, successfully negotiating an early, shaky reputation as immoral and irreligious. The assets of insurance companies increased 12,000 percent in America between 1850 and 1900, and the number of policies in force surpassed that of the rest of the world combined.[18] In Europe, insurance still retained connotations of illicit blood money and gambling on human life, but in America life insurance had successfully cleansed its murky reputation. Popular preachers such as Henry Ward Beecher "sacrilized" insurance by proclaiming it a useful, rational, and godly way of protecting loved ones from harm when the family breadwinner died. The father of modern actuarial science was an American named Elizur Wright, a fiery abolitionist before the Civil War who brought the same zeal to the cause of insurance reform. Wright believed that rational, mathematical principles of risk management made insurance into something scientific, removing the connotations of gambling.[19]

Though life insurance made the transition from gambling to investment, its troubles were not over. After the Civil War, life insurance firms faced a much more competitive marketplace. Agents took advantage of improved rail and telegraph connections, combing the countryside in search of business. On the road it was tempting to make false or misleading claims to unsophisticated rural or blue-collar clients, plunging insurance back into controversy. Searching for new, attractive products to sell, one company, The Equitable Life Assurance Society, began offering in 1868 a dubious type of policy called a tontine. Tontines dated back centuries. They had been used in France, England, and the Netherlands at the dawn of the commercial age in the seventeenth century. Their inventor, an Italian physician and banker named Lorenzo Tonti, had devised the idea of mixing insurance and gambling as a way of raising revenue for King Louis XIV of France.[20] Subscribers paid a fixed amount each year, and received both insurance on their life and a chance at taking away a large pot of money. Those who died early benefited from the insurance aspect, getting out more than they put in. Those who died later, or in extreme cases the last survivor, walked away with the money and interest left in the common purse. Those who could not maintain all the payments over the years were the big losers, for they received nothing for the money they put in.

By combining a death benefit with a chance at a huge return, tontine schemes proved extremely popular in nineteenth-century America as well. They fueled an enormous expansion in life insurance, which had been starting to look like a slow-growing, mature industry. By 1905, over two-thirds of policies in force were tontines.[21] Their immense appeal indicates the opportunities available to those who could figure out how to reach the growing savings needs of the public. Nonetheless, tontines soon came under attack and were finally outlawed as a result of the 1905 Armstrong Committee insurance investigations.

Despite condemnations, tontines were in fact neither inherently risky nor conceptually flawed. Used properly, they could be effective tools of asset management. Offering both insurance and investment, they worked quite well for those with little cash who wanted protection from catastrophe. In effect, the "investment" portion of the tontine was like Tappan's plan, and was also a precursor of mutual funds and other broadly aimed investment pools that combined monies to make large-scale investments. Where tontines failed was in running over the blurry line separating sound, rational tools of management from risky, unsavory games of chance. Investigators condemned the "additional benefit" that survivors derived from the death of earlier participants as "appeal[ing] to the gambling instinct."[22]

Why did it matter so much whether an investment plan fell into the "gambling" category or not? All investment is chancy to some degree. And what exactly did people mean when they condemned something as gambling? The moral economy of Victorian America sought to link investment with virtue, reward with work. Tontines and other lottery-like investment plans ran afoul of this moral economy. Some tontine plans, for example, provided no benefits in case of death but merely paid out to the last remaining policyholders the remains of the money collected. Since only survivors received the proceeds of the investment, it was all too easy, critics charged, to promise the sky, knowing that most people would underestimate their own risk.[23] High returns depended on "the other guy" not keeping up payments or dying early, which sounded appealing to those who were convinced they would survive to the end. Since high returns primarily depended on lapses, tontines appeared like a con game ready to sucker the overconfident. To boost the payout track record, agents of tontine insurance companies also had incentive to oversell the policies or to attract those in financially weak positions, knowing that such customers would be likely to default and increase the pot for the rest.[24]

Because chance was linked to human life span, tontines also recalled the moral issues that insurance companies had confronted decades earlier. In fact, for these reasons tontines had been regulated out of existence in Europe by the nineteenth century. Before they were outlawed, insurance companies were allowing people to take out policies on the lives of others without their knowledge. People bet on how long the king would live, how long a government would stay in power, on births, deaths, even on the loss of virginity. Anonymous policies raised the unseemly thought that the policyholder might just make sure to collect by bumping off the insured. The rebirth of the tontine in America signaled that gambling with a chance of high payoff remained a popular if questionable way of pursuing wealth. But as in Europe earlier, the conflation of chance and risk, gambling and rational investment, proved impossible to accept in a society that believed in a beneficent, rational marketplace.

From our perspective it would be all too easy to dismiss these "moral" concerns as out of step with economic reality. But economic reality, as understood by nineteenth-century men and women, was exactly the point. They were still steeped in notions of a "real" economy, where values did not change at a whim but were tied to things of natural value such as precious metal and hard work. Economic sense and moral sense were assumed consistent. "Commerce cannot exist without the controlling presence of moral obligation," wrote the president of a prestigious university. Economics was nothing more than the "application of the Ten Commandments."[25]

These notions of the market, grounded in the producerist idea of virtue, accepted as legitimate some level of chance in all business operations. But as with fluctuations in the value of money, risk was assumed to be governed by "real" forces or natural laws that could not be manipulated arbitrarily or used to the detriment of one class in the interest of another. Chance and risk, in other words, were parts of the moral framework of market society, not beyond it. Gambling, on the other hand, was beyond the pale of virtue and morality. It redistributed wealth on the basis of unearned reward. It promoted unproductive consumption, which was frivolous and wasteful.[26] Hitting it big in a game of chance was like making money as a speculator—it undermined the commitment to labor.[27]

The modern justification of gambling, as a leisure pursuit no worse than any other, had no credit in the late nineteenth century. The reduction of work and reward to mere leisure and consumption was exactly what producerists feared. It detached consumption from its moorings, letting it float above character or morality.[28] When lines separating real investment from gambling broke down, chicanery and manipulation had free reign. Card sharps, mountebanks, and lottery hustlers threatened the fabric of market society by using people's natural self-interest for unproductive ends, in pursuit of the ever-elusive pot of gold at the end of the rainbow. Appearance, once more, threatened to substitute for reality.[29]

In an age of financial innovation, grasping the real was proving no easier than nailing down a blob of mercury. Old assurances kept slipping away as new consumer financial products appeared. Yet it was still important to keep trying to make those distinctions. Americans were not ready to abandon wholesale the moral and scientific certainties of the nineteenth century. Shutting down lotteries and jailing suspected frauds like George MacDonald seemed protective of this crucial line between the real and the artificial.

Even pro-market conservatives such as John Elliott Tappan lauded investment and exchange while simultaneously condemning gambling or the appearance of gambling. Tappan's free market was also a rational and moral one. His appeals to the public were always couched in the uninflected language of mathematics and plain speaking, as when he sold his first contract to the Pillsbury mill superintendent. In the early years, Tappan worked hard to distinguish the face amount certificate from tontines and lotteries. He noted how one tontine plan charged $3 per month, or $500 in a lump sum, both of which Tappan believed were too high for "the poorer classes." In addition, tontines paid out large lump sums to only a few parties, the lucky survivors. These plans, Tappan understood, would have done better had they "not paid so much to one person but have divided the money up among several."[30]

Lottery-like systems depended on being able to write new business, to keep the cash flowing to pay off policies whose numbers came up. "We don't blame you for being disgusted at the way the Colombian did [business]," Tappan acknowledged, "but our plan is different. We have done away with the multiple system as the courts decided there was where the element of chance came in, as one person might get a multiple (or lucky number as the Court termed it) and another would get a numerical which would take five times as long to mature."[31] Tappan emphasized that returns to the investor depended less on writing new business than on solid investments in land and real property. So it did not matter when one took out a policy. In all cases, the oldest would always be matured first.

As insurance regulators and state attorneys turned a skeptical eye to policies with gambling features, Tappan hoped this would provide him with a competitive edge. "We had one of the best attorneys in the Northwest look up carefully all the lottery laws and the briefs in the cases against the various bond companies and our plan is the result and he says we are absolutely invulnerable and more legal than almost any of the insurance companies." Whether or not his plan was deemed legal and gained public acceptance would be determined in practice, as Investors Syndicate grew. For now, Tappan hoped he had avoided the sort of features that tarnished the reputation of his predecessors.

The gambling question was one of two issues of "moral strategy" that Tappan had to confront. The other concerned power, the power that investment companies and handlers of "other people's money" possessed when they pooled funds and made investments on behalf of clients. The problem of power reflected the unequal knowledge possessed by investors vis-à-vis their customers. Such inequality was an inevitable feature of financial intermediation. After all, if the average person understood the market and could invest as well and as easily as the professional, there would be no need for intermediaries. But such difference in information and knowledge could easily lead to unscrupulous operators taking advantage of clients. Successful financial innovators had to overcome this problem. Here too, Tappan could watch and follow the precedent of insurance companies, which were wrestling with these very issues as he was launching his new company. This debate over power and accountability in the insurance industry spoke to concerns over money, power, and public responsibility that also affected Tappan's Investors Syndicate.

In the 1840s, when life insurance was just taking off, most companies sold term policies designed to provide financial protection against unexpected death. But after the Civil War, life insurance evolved into a true financial product. Companies introduced the "level premium," whereby the insured paid the same yearly amount regardless of age. With age, of course, the risk of death increased, which meant premiums should have risen. Rising premiums would have made life insurance less attractive over time. To eliminate the problem of rising premiums, insurance companies "overcharged" clients when they were young, so that they could "undercharge" them as they aged. The money paid in early, far more than necessary to insure a young healthy adult, went into a reserve fund, where it was invested with the expectation that eventually this fund would be needed to meet the extra cost of aged subscribers.

In accumulating reserve funds, insurance companies were following sound actuarial procedures, but they were also taking on the responsibility of investing the client's money. Some firms began offering dividends, paid back to subscribers each year. The dividends reflected the extra money insurance companies earned on investment of subscribers' premiums, over and above what was needed for death benefits. But even with dividends, insurance companies still accumulated huge reserves of the public's capital, which a handful of corporate executives were able to use or invest as they pleased. Tontines in particular accrued giant reserves, since all premiums were held until the policies matured and the profits could be divided among the survivors.[32] Indeed, the preferred name was deferred dividend policy. Once again, in theory, this was perfectly acceptable. Policyholders turned over their money to insurance company experts who made wise decisions. But, capital concentration in the hands of a few New York–based corporations rekindled the old debate over economic democracy that had played out in the Populist era.

How well were the companies looking after the public's funds? Exactly what rate of return was promised in an insurance contract? With tontines in particular, in the long wait to maturity anything could happen. Unsophisticated policyholders could easily be fobbed off with a modest return, leaving the insurance company considerable profit on the difference between what it gave out and what it earned in its investments. Critics of insurance companies noted the huge bonuses paid to soliciting agents, the high salaries of insurance executives, and the plush New York offices in which many firms ensconced themselves. Some insurance firms used their access to the public's savings to become major players in corporate finance, funneling investment into stocks, purchasing banks and trust companies, and disguising their more speculative investments behind affiliates and subsidiaries. Companies that made high profits on stock investments but could satisfy policyholders with modest dividends had a lot of cash left over, some of which simply went to high salaries and sumptuous perks for officers.[33]

Though people appreciated the protection life insurance offered, they also sought ways of bringing these financial behemoths to heel. Many voted with their dollars, moving out of dividend policies into new "assessment" policies offered by fraternal societies. Declaring that "the reserve fund is a crime," assessment firms accumulated no reserve and offered no dividends. It was strictly "pay as you go." Among poor and immigrant workers, this sort of term policy proved immensely popular. Although lacking an investment feature, assessment insurance had low premiums—at least when the subscriber was young—and could be dropped at any time without losing money. Assessment companies proclaimed that they sold "insurance rather than future dividends," or offered "dividends in advance," a sentiment that Tappan echoed later with his phrase "money while you live." By "keeping the dividend in your pocket," the subscriber was assured of getting the full value of the money he paid in.[34] It was a rather blunt rejection of the smooth talk and proclaimed expertise of the professional money manager.

For people at the lower end of the socioeconomic scale, the returns of investment schemes, even dividend insurance, looked risky and uncertain. Even with the protection features of cash surrender, many risked forfeiture. Unsophisticated in the ways of finance, they had no way of knowing if their dividend represented the full value of their money. Indeed, who really knew where the money went once it left for insurance company headquarters in New York or Boston? By contrast, assessment insurance seemed connected to older, cooperative values based on trust and mutuality. It was often sold through working-class fraternal organizations, such as the Ancient Order of

United Workmen or lodges and secret societies such as the Masons. They used no agents or salesmen, made no promises of great returns, and placed on the subscriber no pressure to take out more than was needed.

By 1896, fraternal and assessment insurance had surpassed commercial insurance in value of policies in force.[35] The sudden and startling success of the new companies suggested that dividend-based policies accumulating reserves raised serious questions in the minds of the public about cost, trust, and fiduciary responsibility. Critics of commercial insurance noted how much cheaper the assessment companies could write policies, without all the fancy apparatus of salesmanship. Reformer Louis Brandeis proposed an even simpler and safer expedient—Savings Bank Insurance. Customers would receive a life insurance policy as part of the interest on their savings accounts. Here there was no question that the money one paid in was definitely one's own, and not in the hands of insurance executives.

By questioning the value of the dividend policy, assessment insurance had raised an important point. What protected the customer from the company's superior knowledge of the market? So long as dividend policy was at the discretion of insurance executives, it served mainly as a marketing device. Companies paid dividends when they wanted to attract more clients, but reduced or even eliminated them at will if they had all the business they needed. There was nothing like a definite "account" for the subscriber's money, even though the reserve technically was the property of those who had paid into it. Assessment companies had their own problems. By not accumulating a reserve, they often had to dun customers for additional assessments whenever claims unexpectedly rose above company income. As the population of policyholders aged (and hence the rate of payout increased with rising deaths), it was necessary to expand the client base with fresh young blood. So assessment companies worked something like pyramid schemes, collapsing when they could no longer add new subscribers fast enough to pay out mounting claims. But apparently these features did not dissuade the public, which was more concerned about the loss of money placed in the reserve fund of dividend insurance firms. A collapsed assessment company cost the subscriber nothing in a "pay as you go" scheme. One merely bought a new policy from another firm.

All of these issues eventually came to a head in 1905, in a massive investigation of life insurance before the Armstrong Committee.[36] It was the final act of a growing movement for regulation that had already seen several states create insurance commissioners to punish insurers for questionable financial practices and deceptive advertising. The investigation brought to light what people had long suspected. Insurance companies had tremendous latitude in their use of the public's funds, and those monies were frequently employed for matters only distantly related to insurance—lobbying, high finance, office perks. The investigation was so damning that one newspaper advised insurance firms to hoist the black flag and stop pretending they were sailing a missionary ship.[37] In the end, insurance firms were required to scale back the executive salaries, cut waste, provide a more definite accounting of the use of subscribers' money, pay annual dividends at a higher rate, and eliminate risky underwriting ventures using customers' money. The reforms were designed to make the managers of the reserve fund act more like the fiduciaries of other people's money, and to connect the money paid in by clients to a clear payout.

For Tappan, the experiences of life insurance foreshadowed problems he would face. Investment had to be kept separate from gambling and speculation. Using other people's money carried special obligations, a public trust, recognized by the courts and legislatures. It was not sufficient to simply pay a decent return. It had to be clear to contract holders that they were giving to the company a "definite sum for a definite time." The method of determining the return had to be clear to customers also. Investments themselves would be carefully scrutinized, to be sure that management fees were kept low and funds were going into prudent assets.

Yet there was also reason to be optimistic from the insurance experience. Despite embarrassing revelations from insurance company chiefs, the Armstrong investigations would actually help insurance companies, which survived, even thrived. They scaled back their investments in stocks, eliminated some of their subsidiary trust and investment banking affiliates, and reduced their active participation in new corporate finance. But they continued to grow and prosper as their policies reached further down the socioeconomic scale. Tontines disappeared, but, in their place, whole life policies combining death benefits and investment proved very popular. For all the fulminations against the financial power wielded by insurance executives, the fact remained that experts and professionals would be key actors directing the pooled funds of the public into a wider variety of investments.

Convinced that he had avoided the pitfalls of his predecessors, Tappan believed neither law nor government would present major obstacles. He was happy to see that investment companies in general were growing, despite the blow to their reputation in the 1890s depression. A growing market and a more sophisticated public would open up more opportunities for his own modest operations. "It is only a matter of time when they [the certificates] will be recognized as being all right, that is the good ones." The main problem with competitors like the tontines was their questionable legality and the embarrassing investigations they sparked. Like most businessmen, Tappan sought predictability from the law, especially in something so touchy as handling other people's money. The investigations and allegations "make people suspicious, and make it hard for us to get agents and do business."[38]

For example, Tappan's old employer George MacDonald was back in the news. An article in the *Chicago Daily Tribune* described his new Diamond Investment Company as another "Brilliant Scheme, by a man just released from eleven months' imprisonment for swindling." MacDonald had taken offices in the Dexter Building of Chicago for his coupon plan, a thinly disguised lottery. "Investors" bought coupons, which were redeemed for prizes, in this case "diamonds, watches, and bicycles." The object, Mac-Donald declared, was to "get rich by short, easy stages," while vindicating him and "proving the United States wrong in declaring him a swindler."[39]

These schemes pained Tappan, for they seemed on the surface similar to what he was proposing. MacDonald had hired agents to canvass downtown Chicago with $100 certificates, sold for a $5 deposit and weekly payments of $1.25. When retired, the coupons could be redeemed for prizes said to be worth $100. As the skeptical reporter noted, it all depended on how and when the obligations were retired. The system did not guarantee the holder any specific reward, but required additional participants to provide the cash to redeem the coupons of the existing members. To keep players in the game, the prizes rotated. When one's certificate came up for redemption, the prize desired might or might not be available. Those who sought a gold watch but came up with a bicycle would have to wait, and keep paying. "I was a martyr to a brilliant business idea," MacDonald claimed, "and I am showing my faith in it by pushing it again with only slight changes as my lawyers said were needed to make it technically legal." No doubt Tappan would have preferred his friend spare himself the martyrdom, for the superficial similarities of their plans could well threaten Tappan's own claims to legality.

The soundness of Tappan's plan was largely theoretical at the early stages. Many would-be innovators dreamed up investment schemes, but these perpetual-motion money machines quickly confronted the inexorable laws of mathematics when they tried to grow. They could not take in enough money to make promised payments. They withered at the first sign of an ill economic wind. Tappan had built in safeguards, with a contract that gave him up to twenty years to mature a policy. But such a long date into the future also made the certificates less attractive. It was important to build up cash fast and begin maturing policies, to show the public it could be done. Then, too, the margin between what the investments took in and what the investor expected as a return was thin. Efficiency demanded a larger client base over which to spread the operating and management costs, particularly the high costs associated with tricky land mortgages.

Some of the costs faced by Investors Syndicate were offset by lapses. When contract holders failed to keep up payments, their money reverted to the company, a standard feature of insurance policies and bonds bought on installment. As payments were made, contracts accumulated cash value, so generally clients did not simply lose all they had paid if they failed to complete a contract. Still, they would not break even until the fifth year. Tappan had figured his plan on a 2 percent lapsation rate. If 98 percent of his clients made all payments, he could still fulfill his obligations and earn a profit. This placed him in a strong position. In practice, more than 2 percent would default. That was a simple, statistical fact long demonstrated by insurance practice. Those additional funds would be pure profit to Investors Syndicate.

The issue of lapses and surrenders proved to be a vexing one, however. It showed how difficult it could be to establish public trust in a new investment enterprise. Bond and insurance companies were raked over the coals for encouraging subscribers to bite off more than they could chew, and then watch them fall behind on payments. The controversy over tontines had arisen in part because these policies had a very high rate of lapsation.[40] Many investment companies exploited to its fullest Havemeyer's dictum that in finance, as in all else, "let the buyer beware." They enticed subscribers with low up-front fees and small weekly or monthly payments, knowing that some would never be able to hold on to the end. They pounced on the earliest opportunity to forfeit the contracts of their clients.

From a moral point of view, one could argue that those who failed to keep up their payments got what they deserved. "The man who falls by the wayside loses," Tappan himself had written, "and the persevering person reaps the reward."[41] Like other investment companies, Investors Syndicate could benefit from lapses by those who did "not have the steadfastness of purpose enough to carry their contracts through to maturity."[42] Indeed, it was tempting to exploit this source of profit. One early Syndicate contract, for example, paid a lower 4 percent rate of interest, but also split with the customer all profits derived from "excess interest earnings, fines, transfer fees, forfeitures, surrenders and lapses."[43]

Simply taking the public's money was not what Tappan had in mind. In fact, he wanted to encourage investors to stay for the long term. The contracts "fully and carefully" spelled out the terms for lapse and surrender. "We do not aim to deceive anyone," regarding these features of the contract, he wrote.[44] The contracts were so plain, in fact, that Tappan maintained "there is absolutely no excuse for a person lapsing his certificate, unless he is determined to do so."[45] More substantially, he backed up words with action. The controversial 4 percent interest rate contract with its profit sharing features was dropped. Investors Syndicate was to be a new type of investment company. It was "no experiment," he confidently wrote, plainly ignoring its experimental status. "The plan is so conservative and safe that we can fulfill every obligation without a single lapse, and even if we should stop getting new business at any time."[46]

The last sentence was a slight exaggeration, but only slight. In figuring a low lapsation rate, Tappan was clearly not thinking of lapses as a major source of income. Insurance companies had lapsation rates ranging from 25 to 30 percent. In reality, only about 5 percent of Tappan's clients who took out a twenty-year endowment policy ever completed all payments to the end.[47] Not all lapsed, of course. Some took early cash surrenders, others sold their contracts in secondary markets. Most likely, though, a bit more than 2 percent actually failed and had to forfeit their contracts. Still, a careful look at the face amount certificate would show that Tappan could genuinely claim no special interest in encouraging excessive lapses. Experience indicated that the vast majority of forfeitures occurred early, within the first few months, before the investor had made many payments. As Tappan emphasized, "the Syndicate derives no benefit" from these early lapses. Most of the initial payments went to cover sales, marketing, and overhead costs, producing no profit for the company.[48]

It was important to establish in the public's mind a high degree of trust. Features designed to minimize the dangers of total loss through lapse or forfeiture helped here. Customers could dispense with monthly payments and simply buy a contract from Tappan for an up-front lump sum. Almost all of the company's clients were too poor for this option, however. In years of economic instability—frequent before World War II—many would be caught short of cash at one time or another. In recession years, lapsation rates would be far higher than the 2 percent minimum, sometimes as high as 40 to 50 percent. To convince the public that he did not relish pocketing their money, Tappan made the rules of lapsation extremely lenient. Even when a subscriber missed payments, he could be reinstated, either by renewing his old policy or by having previous payments credited to a new one.[49]

Tappan personally was forbearing with those who owed him money. Many times he wrote directly to investors who had stopped making payments, asking them to start up again before they lost all they had put in. When one subscriber could not complete his payments, Tappan offered to help sell his contract to another investor. "Write to us the lowest cash value you will take for it," he suggested, "we will, if it is reasonable, take the matter up with some of our other members, and I have no doubt but that we can dispose of it for you."[50] To those who were out of work, Tappan penned reassuring letters. "If you do not get work and it is hard for you to get the dues, and you run behind for a month or so, I will protect you and see that it is not lapsed." When the investor requested more time to pay, Tappan replied, "Postal from your wife stating that you were ill and could not get in to pay your dues duly received, and we will protect you in the matter."[51]

Failing to pay on time was a common problem in an unstable economy with no central banking system or macroeconomic management. Merchants waited on overdue accounts, doctors and lawyers treated their clients with leniency, checks were slow to arrive in a postal system that still used horses and carts, employers did not always meet weekly payrolls. The fact was, most people would be late with at least a payment or two over the life of a contract. Rather than simply pocketing the money of late payers or charging them a stiff penalty, Tappan took a different approach. He added extra time to the end of the contract. Those who were late a week had to wait an extra week until the contract matured. By giving the Syndicate "free" use of clients' money, this extension increased total returns to the company, which made sure it had the money "out" in interest-earning assets all the time. Though

Tappan profited from this policy, it also provided for his clients great flexibility and liquidity, two major concerns for small investors with little spare cash. "Even where they can make their payments on time," Tappan found, some simply "wish[ed] to do something else with their money." They were free to do so, without worrying that they would suffer a lapsed contract or late fee.[52]

Tappan was following the sort of long-term outlook for his company that insurance expert and industry critic Elizur Wright had advocated a generation before. Convinced that insurance companies were doing themselves and the public damage by taking advantage of those who failed to make payments, Wright admonished, "profits caught by the trap of forfeitures frighten away ten times the amount" of new business.[53] It took thirty years and some prodding from government to convince insurance companies of the wisdom of this insight. For Tappan it was the starting point of establishing a bond of trust with the client.

Tappan was seeking business among men and women who lacked a sufficient margin of wealth to protect themselves against sudden illness or an unexpected reversal of fortune. For this reason, customers who fell behind due to unforeseen circumstances were granted special protections, over and above the terms of the contract. Policy was to write at least two letters to be sure the subscriber was not ill or incapacitated before moving to cancel. It was both sensible and just not to exploit the situation. "If a man gets out of work or gets sick and cannot pay his dues," Tappan assured his contract holders, "we will loan him enough money on it to carry it for a year or longer." That did not mean charity. The loan had to be repaid in full, and during the time of the debt the contract did not move toward maturity, giving Investors Syndicate free use of the funds. Nor were these provisions intended to forgive the improvident or encourage freeloaders. After the year was up, the individual could "die, get well or get a job." A man's first duty, Tappan steadfastly maintained, was to repay all debts. Those who took advantage of his leniency he dismissed as chiselers who lacked "manliness" or personal integrity.[54]

The category of "unmanly" included all who fell behind for no good reason. They failed the test of success by letting down their end of the bargain. For them, more time and forbearance were not matters of decency, but mere charity. And Tappan was not in the charity business. When one subscriber prevaricated over the $100 he owed in back payments, Tappan cut him short. "You have been so awfully slow in this matter, and have made so many promises, that . . . I cannot depend upon what you tell me. These payments must be made now as you promised," Tappan concluded, "or I shall absolutely give you no further time whatever. This is final."[55]

An important part of the Syndicate's success depended on these notions of virtue and character. When one of the first certificate holders, an old friend, refused to pay and tried to repudiate the agreement, Tappan had no hesitancy about suing and garnishing his bank account "in order to maintain our rights."[56] To another he wrote, "regarding the small balance due." "Now Mr. Borncamp, this matter of yours has been running for five or six years. We have simply let you go your own gait and we must say that when you are getting the good salary that you are and then for you to ignore our letters, that is pretty shabby treatment."[57] To critics who responded that this was too harsh, Tappan had an answer. "Bring up any man whom we have not treated squarely," he challenged, "and if anyone says we have not, they say what is untrue. I will venture to say that our reputation for squareness and honesty is as much above that person's standard as the sky is above the earth, and we would thank you to tell us of anyone who makes such charges, as we will take steps to shut them up in short order."[58] Defending the company's reputation was only good business sense in a business involving money, but for Tappan the issues were also personal. It involved his own integrity and reputation for manliness.

Manliness and integrity remained powerful words in Tappan's world. They were the gendered side of the producer tradition. They referred not only to traditional male characteristics such as strength, bravery, and honor, important as these were. The defining feature of manliness was the ability to support oneself and family independently. Manly men were respected because of their "competency," which meant not only individual prowess and skill, but the property or capital needed to earn a living. "Almost everyone wishes to obtain a competency," Tappan would write to prospective investors.[59] With such property, real or personal, one could live a life of dignity and autonomy, free from the will of others, without dependence on charity or handouts.[60]

These notions of manliness had been bandied about in the great political debates over money in the nineteenth century. To farmer-producers, competency not only meant economic independence, but was the basis of political democracy as well. Only those who were free and autonomous could exercise the necessary virtue to govern themselves and the nation. Before the Civil

War, northerners like Tappan had accepted a powerful ideology of "free labor" built around such notions of manliness and self-governance. Dignity and independence were accorded to freeborn men, which excluded most women and many others. Slaves were perceived clearly to lack manliness, and for northerners the spread of slavery into the western territories during the 1850s was a frightening prospect. After the Civil War and defeat of slavery, threats to manliness came from elsewhere. Manliness meant resisting other powers that threatened to ensnare free producers—the money power conspiracy and its corporate monopolies, most notably.

In launching his new financial product on the wings of this older tradition, Tappan was subtly altering meanings embedded in the language of manliness. By the early twentieth century, manliness took on different connotations. For example, as America became more industrial, more and more workers spent their entire lives earning a living as employees of others. There was nothing wrong with paid labor, but work for others had once been seen as only a stepping-stone to manly independence. As one of the most eloquent spokesmen for free labor ideals, Abraham Lincoln, stated, "I am not ashamed to confess that twenty five years ago I was a hired laborer, mauling rails, at work on a flat-boat—just what might happen to any poor man's son." But, Lincoln believed, a free man could "better his condition." For a free man, he wrote, "there is no fixed condition of labor, for his whole life."[61]

By Tappan's time, independence was becoming impossible for many workers. Among the middle class, the proportion of self-employed in the labor force dropped precipitously between 1870 and 1910, from 67 to 37 percent.[62] In the East and urban Midwest, a true working class toiled in mills and factories. These permanent employees were often immigrants from southern and eastern Europe. As slavery had given the issue of manliness and independence a racial tinge, immigration raised fears of cheap labor from "backward" countries flooding the states. Even in Minnesota, the values of a more industrial society with a highly specialized division of labor were beginning to make themselves felt. Employees of Pillsbury's mills were not and would largely never be independent owners. Some of them were also immigrants from strange lands with strange ways.

These were the very people to whom Tappan hoped to sell financial independence: wage workers and lower-middle-class, white-collar employees. Many of his clients were women, widows trying to protect their savings. Still, Tappan would continue to draw on traditional notions of manliness and independence all his life. He stressed the values of entrepreneurship, integrity, fulfillment of obligations, and the trust that went with a man's word. He also repeated his offer to the public again and again. Wise investment could give one a "competency," or, in today's advertising parlance, help them achieve that elusive yet fervently sought after state, "financial freedom."

⁓

Even as Tappan played on powerful old symbols and words, he was helping usher in a new sort of economy. People's financial independence depended on products sold to them by professional money managers offering invest- ment counsel. Success, even for men, had less to do with independence and property ownership, and more with hard, constant work for a wage. Middle- class Americans more and more made their livings as employees of bureau- cratic corporations. Traditional patriarchal notions of the family, in which the male breadwinner made all financial decisions, were being challenged by women who were entering the workforce. Tappan's notion of success reflected these changes. Success and getting ahead, he wrote to clients, meant "stick- to-it-ivness" and "pluck," and "keep everlastingly at it." It did not necessarily imply physical labor or toil over one's own business.[63] The way toward a competency now was "by putting aside a small monthly amount, which you would otherwise spend and get nothing permanent from"—something possible for men and women alike.[64] Investments were good only if "you will stick to it and keep up the dues," he reminded clients. Persistence was a virtue, more so in a world where fewer men owned their own enterprise or engaged directly in physical labor. If men were no longer literally defined by their physical ability to wrest a living from nature, they still had to show the masculine virtues of persistence and pluck.

Changes in the meanings of manhood and independence were reflected most clearly in the changing lifecycle of work. Male workers were beginning to save up for and plan "retirements," when they would no longer operate their own businesses or even work for a living, but live off of accrued earnings. This notion of retiring from active labor and consuming one's life savings was just emerging as Tappan was starting Investors Syndicate.[65] In 1880, nearly 80 percent of men aged sixty-five or over were still in the labor force, compared to less than 20 percent today. Shorter life spans, insufficient income, and a lack of financial assets had once made retirement either unnecessary or impossible. Work might slow down and wages fall as toil took its toll on aging bodies. But neither farmers nor factory workers could expect to enjoy a long period of leisure resting on accumulated savings. Those who did withdraw from work, partially or wholly, voluntarily or because they were disabled or fired, found it a much less pleasant experience than today. Many lived in poverty, and almost all were forced to rely on help from children and family members. Few could afford to remain independent or live alone.

Between 1880 and 1900, however, possibilities for a life after work improved substantially. A big decrease in older workers took place over those twenty years. In part the change was due to rising incomes, in part to generous Civil War pensions for veterans. Important causes of the change, however, resided in the private sector. Corporations began offering privately financed pension plans, which virtually required workers to leave the company at age sixty-five, or face a financial penalty. American Express was the first company to offer its employees a pension, in 1875. Other big firms in growing industries followed suit, and by the 1920s this benefit was common in many industries for white- and blue-collar workers alike.

Together, growing use of corporate pensions and government support for old age helped to construct retirement as an accepted, viable stage of life. Corporate pensions, for example, were used to ease workers through the door when they were no longer productive. Thus pensions assumed that work was only one phase of life, and that the worker would be an employee throughout this phase, rather than a temporary worker on the way to independent ownership. In the 1930s, Social Security payments—a response to the image of aged, unemployed men, useless to society, living out their days scrounging for food in garbage heaps—only reinforced this definition of work as but one stage of life.[66] Both corporate pensions and government transfers encouraged workers to think of age sixty-five as the end of working life. They built up in younger workers the expectation that they should and could finally retire from labor. The growing trend toward retirement would have been just perceptible to John Elliott Tappan when he started Investors Syndicate. By the early twentieth century, however, social engineers, policymakers, and commentators were noting the reality of a life after work, and many were committed to encouraging a comfortable period of retirement as an alternative to old age poverty or working to physical exhaustion.

As retirement became an accepted social concept, the way people saved and their reasons for saving changed as well. Once, people had protected themselves against old age disability through their families or by improving their chief asset, land. Traditional savings instruments—land and children—gave way to paper ones. In place of family members, the aged would turn to financial professionals for assistance. These changes would help Tappan's own business grow.

As with other trends in savings and investment, though, these too pointed to a much different world than the one John Tappan had grown up in. Money for retirement was not exactly what he first had in mind. The notion of retirement as a distinct phase of life is closely connected with leisure and consumption. One "dissaves" during retirement, or consumes one's savings. In setting aside money for retirement, people save in order to enjoy a certain level of consumption after they cease to work. Beyond a certain point, more wealth has little effect on either their decision to retire or how they live after they retire. This sort of saving is not about building productive wealth and passing it down to heirs, at least not primarily. It is about achieving and maintaining a certain lifestyle for a certain time. Tappan generally encouraged people to save in order to build a "competence," or a comfortable and independent life rooted in production. He did not necessarily see himself contributing to "leisure" or a retirement lifestyle rooted in consumption. Yet retirement of just this sort has helped to fuel the consumer financial services industry.

Retirement and saving for retirement subtly altered the meaning of words like "independence" and "autonomy." One of the most striking trends in the lives of retirees, for example, is the steady growth of independent living. Far from a recent development, living alone was something retired people sought almost from the beginnings of retirement. Those who could afford to, quickly left the households of relatives and offspring. Even if more money could be accumulated or greater wealth obtained by living with family members, most retirees chose to spend their income on independence. Independence meant having sufficient financial freedom to live by themselves, to not depend on their children. In a sense, it took on a meaning almost opposite to what it had had in the nineteenth century, when the independent producer carefully accumulated property to be passed down to later generations, in return for living out the final years as part of his or her extended family. This was the pattern Tappan's grandparents had followed when they moved to Oshkosh.

Independence in the modern era, by contrast, has became a consumption choice, a matter of personal lifestyle rather than a political bulwark of democracy or a part of the family economy of independent producers.

As is often the case, fundamental social and economic change was being explained by use of an older vocabulary. Manly independence, words that Tappan understood and used, were being given new connotations. He spoke to his clients about persistence, saving a small amount each month, eschewing the temptations of easy money and luxuries to put money aside. This seemed something like owning and improving one's own land. But independence had become a different sort of value, made not by the sweat of the brow so much as careful, rational investment in paper securities. It did not necessarily imply saving one's wages in the hope, as Lincoln put it, of moving from dependent toiler to independent producer. Indeed, the savings were really being used not for virtuous production but for consumption, in the form of leisure and retirement.

Changing attitudes toward work, leisure, and wealth opened Tappan's window of opportunity. These trends would also make it harder for him to see how ideas of integrity, trust, and a man's word could remain as vital as they had once been. A world of dependent workers, housewives, widows, and wage-earning women saving for retirement or consumption was not in accord with traditional notions of manly independence and virtuous production. A world of easy money in loose finance and big corporate gain was a far cry from the narrow road between tradition and innovation Tappan was trying to walk.

The tension between traditional values and the way business was being practiced hit home to Tappan in 1895. His relationship with his friend George MacDonald had grown strained. MacDonald was busy cooking up new financial schemes, but still had not paid Tappan money owed for wages during his earlier stint in Chicago, or for contracts Tappan had sold for MacDonald's old company. Then in May, to great embarrassment, Tappan received an overdue bill from a Chicago clothier. He had purchased a new suit on the promise that MacDonald would pay for it as partial compensation for the work he had done. Chagrined, Tappan wrote to the haberdasher, explaining what had happened. "I wish to do whatever is right in the matter," he stated, "and I think I can get him [MacDonald] to make up the back payments . . . but he has had rather bad luck as you doubtless know."[67] Then Tappan wrote to MacDonald. His letter was temperate, and merely reminded his old friend that he had been promised the suit and the rest of his due. "I did not mention it before as you were having trouble and would probably send me some as soon as you could, but I need it now as I lost more money than my salary came to this winter by not being here, as things in the office were in terrible shape, as some of our agents had got the best of us, and I have had to make it good and will need every cent that I can get."[68] The letter was to no avail, and by August, Tappan still had not been paid. Convinced that his old employer was thoroughly dishonest, he filed in court for what he was owed, and never spoke to George MacDonald again.

Tappan soon found that he had to defend his own integrity in an even more important way. As he had witnessed, less scrupulous competitors had run afoul of the law. Though his legal mind told him that Investors Syndicate conformed to the rules on the books, it had yet to be tested in court. On January 29, 1897, it got its first test. A letter arrived from the postmaster general in Washington, accusing Tappan of "being engaged in a lottery for the distribution of money." It was a terrible blow, after so many letters to friends and clients assuring them that the certificates were both safe and legal. Tappan had proudly answered inquiries about his product by declaiming, "of four companies which are located in this city ours is the only one which has never been notified that the plan must be changed or the mails will be stopped."[69] He had tried to design his certificates to avoid just these legal complications, and, more than that, to be true investments rather than ill-concealed games of chance. Now he would have to convince the federal government.

There was, Tappan believed, no way the face amount certificates could be outside the law. If they were outlawed, he confidently wrote, "the government would have to pull down the whole fabric of commercial law."[70] The basis for Tappan's confidence was what he saw as a clear contractual obligation that ran from the company to its certificate holders. The certificates were in essence promissory notes to repay money plus interest by a certain time. The only question was how soon Investors Syndicate paid back the money. The faster it redeemed notes and paid out interest, the better for the investor. There was no promise that money would be paid back any sooner than twenty years, but clearly Tappan's strategy was to pay it back faster, using new money as it came in, funds from lapsed contracts and returns from investments. But his plan, unlike tontines, was not linked so closely to lapses and surrenders. "We do not depend upon any certain number of lapses, but can fulfill without any lapses," he wrote.[71] Nor did Investors Syndicate employ the lottery-like multiple system, whereby contracts came up for renewal on the basis of some random or chance factor. Those who took out the first contracts saw their contracts matured first.

The legal footing of the certificates seemed strong, but, until the postal investigation, it was only theoretical. In his letters, Tappan himself exaggerated certain features, while playing down others. For example, there was the still hotly contested issue of lapses. Only under ideal circumstances could Tappan fulfill each and every contract. He himself reckoned that with the costs associated with the mortgage market, he would still need about a 2 to 3 percent lapsation rate to mature the contracts as he had hoped and stay in business. In any case, if it was really going to take twenty years to pay off each contract, then the certificates were not going to be very appealing. In practice, about 15 percent of investors thus far had failed to keep up their payments.[72] That may have been better than many insurance companies. It was certainly better than pyramid schemes, which depended on an increasing percentage of investors falling by the wayside and often had very severe penalties for failing to meet a payment on time. Still, the role that lapsed policies played in Investors Syndicate's profits was the sort of feature that tended to conflate what Tappan was calling "real" investments with gambling enterprises and other financial products under suspicion.

As an innovative new form of security, the face amount certificate raised questions of contract and commercial law. Though invested in real property, they constituted a promise to pay funds that Investors Syndicate did not actually have on hand when the contract was made. Perfectly honest investment plans worked in just such a manner, promising a return based on what the investor believed he or she could earn in the market. Futures contracts did likewise. They were a promise to deliver commodities that one did not actually possess at the time of signing the contract. Commercial law allowed for transactions based on promises and good faith. But the courts had to review these new forms of paper property. They eventually declared that futures contracts were legal, even though the parties to the contract did not actually deliver physical commodities to each other, but only settled on the change in price when the contract came due. On this issue, the Supreme

Court's reasoning was revealing. Futures contracts were legal precisely because the parties *could* make delivery of actual goods.[73] Intentions mattered. In 1895, the Supreme Court had also ruled, in the *Durland* case, that when a company "entered in good faith upon that business, believing that out of monies received, they could by investment or otherwise, make enough to justify the promised returns, no conviction could be sustained, no matter how visionary might be the scheme."[74] In other words, so long as the investment company acted in good faith with the client's funds, it could not be held liable if the investment collapsed.

Investors Syndicate, Tappan argued, certainly met this criterion. It took money with the promise and intent of earning returns to make the payments advertised. It actually made investments. By maturing several of its early contracts, it had also demonstrated that it could fulfill obligations. Still, past success was no guarantee that the plan was sound enough to sustain further growth. If Investors Syndicate enjoyed some success merely due to its small size, then it was little different than a pyramid scheme, in which early investors reaped rewards, but only because later ones could not. Determining the soundness of the certificates was necessarily an imperfect science, since there was no empirical evidence that could definitely show the plan would always work as promised.

Given these uncertainties, postal inspectors had reason to be skeptical. Other operators had made similar promises using comparable terminology. Men such as George MacDonald lurked about, ever at the ready with still another get-rich-quick scheme. Postal inspectors had first become suspicious when one of Tappan's former agents had started a competing enterprise across the river in St. Paul. His plan included several obvious lottery features, which led to his being shut down. Unable to understand why he was put out of business while Investors Syndicate was allowed to continue, the competitor wrote to the Post Office for explanation.

Tappan and his lawyer Henry Farnham quickly mounted a response. It was a tricky situation. If the Post Office was not persuaded by their legal reasoning, there would be no other recourse. The Supreme Court had ruled that postal decisions could not be reviewed by the federal courts. And in any case, a long, expensive court proceeding would do more harm than good by frightening away investors. With the company's fate in the hands of faraway federal authority, the only safe course was to make any and all alterations necessary to satisfy these parties. "We would gladly change our literature, if the department objected to any part of it, and would point out what was objectionable," Tappan wrote.[75] The promise was to no avail. The reply from Washington was worse than Tappan and Farnham had feared. Investors Syndicate was accused of fraud and lost its mailing privileges. Worse, word of the decision was sent out over the Associated Press for publication throughout the nation. Appeals to the postmaster general and Justice Department went unanswered. Only three years old, Investors Syndicate was suddenly at death's door.

Tappan was fuming. He suspected that he was the victim of a conspiracy. "Thomas [the assistant attorney general on the case] is undoubtedly paid by the insurance companies," he wrote angrily.[76] Insurance companies were making enormous amounts of money while paying out a very small rate of return on policies. Undoubtedly, they perceived new financial intermediaries paying higher returns directly to small investors as competitors. Dollars that went into Tappan's certificates were dollars that could have otherwise ended up in insurance corporations' coffers. It was a double bind for new firms like Investors Syndicate. While big firms fought competition with the government's help, cut-rate operators played on the public's gullibility with fancy sounding schemes that were really lotteries.

Politics were turning out to be as big a challenge as any to financial innovation. When the Post Office turned a deaf ear, Tappan and Farnham had only one more option, an appeal through their congressman. Their effort worked and the Syndicate had its mailing privileges restored. Post Office officials lifted the ban temporarily until there was a formal hearing, but the company could write no new business in the meantime. It was up to Investors Syndicate to prove its worth to a group of skeptical government officials before it could be fully tested in the marketplace. Though relieved by the reprieve from what surely would have been a death sentence, Tappan was hardly placated. "This seems very much like hanging a man and inquiring afterwards as to his guilt," he wrote, but he understood that legally he had no recourse other than to comply with the demands.[77]

In March, Tappan decided Farnham should go to Washington. He was not optimistic. "There is no use interviewing the second attorney general of the Post Office Department, John L. Thomas, the man who shut down on us," he wrote. A holdover from President Cleveland's Democratic administration, Thomas was not likely to be sympathetic to a Republican like Tappan. "Charges have openly been made that this man was bribed by the insurance companies. We do not think that it indicates a free country, when one man can shut down and ruin another man's business without giving him a fair hearing." Perhaps, he hoped, an appeal directly to the new Republican postmaster or the attorney general, would get around the Thomas roadblock.[78]

Unfortunately, Tappan's foreboding proved all too prophetic. "Thomas . . . was still in office when our attorney was there, and we found that we could not do anything as long as he kept his position. . . . [N]o matter how strong a pull we might get, it would be referred back to him again." One slim hope had been rumors of his ouster by the new administration. In those days of fierce partisan politics, patronage jobs were one of the most powerful and well-used tools of competing parties. Positions in Washington were relatively few in number when government was only a fraction of its current size. So federal jobs were prized plums handed out to loyal supporters who got out the vote. The Post Office was in fact the single largest government agency, in terms of jobs. Its main offices were almost always filled by the supporters of the current administration. But Tappan, who disdained this sort of political patronage, was ironically caught by just the sort of reforms for honest government he supported.

Tappan believed in honesty and efficiency in government. Though a supporter of McKinley, he was not fiercely partisan. He voted on his beliefs, in this case in hard money and the gold standard. But he did not see politics as a game to be won by fair means or foul. He and moderate Republicans like him generally supported laws designed to remove the taint of corruption and patronage from the political system. One of the prime measures for purifying politics, reformers believed, was the civil service law.

Appointees with civil service status could not be removed by an incoming administration and their job given out as a reward to some crony. Only those who passed tests demonstrating competence were allowed to occupy government offices. This effort to inject more "professionalism" into politics would continue to grow in the early twentieth century, helping to end the heyday of party politics by undercutting the support mechanisms of the great party machines and their bosses. McKinley's White House predecessor, the Democrat Grover Cleveland, a decided moderate, in fact had supported civil service measures, even though they had been proposed by upper-crust Republicans to keep unwashed immigrant masses and ignorant Democrat farmers out of office. As it turned out, Thomas occupied an office Cleveland had designed as a civil service spot! Political patronage would not work for Investors Syndicate. Professionalism, the value that Tappan turned to in defending his own operations, had now caught him in a trap.

It was turning out to be a long, hard winter. Minnesota had experienced severe weather, even for Minnesota. The ground was covered with more snow "than we have had in several winters," Tappan wrote, and the expectation was of bad flooding when the melt came. In March, the Tappan household was sick with the grippe, which first afflicted his mother and then him. While he was out of commission, Winnie began keeping the Syndicate books. Her education and experience paid off for the young company, and she continued to work by John's side during these difficult early years. Meanwhile there was little to do but wait and hope for a reversal from the Post Office.

Tappan kept up his optimistic correspondence, though he could not help but note how much business the Syndicate was losing while under the cloud of suspicion. The shutdown came just as many investors in the old Guaranty company were taking up Tappan's offer to trade in their shares for his certificates. Would-be agents were also writing from distant parts of the country, interested in selling the certificates in their territory. The depression was abating and the uncertainty over currency had been resolved. "You can rest assured that we are not going to 'throw up the sponge,'" Tappan answered inquiries, "as we intend to continue the business right along, and if we cannot possibly write new business on our present plan, we shall get up some equally good plan on which we can write business."[79] The Post Office still might reconsider, and that might just be worth all the trouble. A clean bill of health from the Post Office would act something like an official imprimatur. Investors Syndicate could look stronger and better to investors than before.

Nothing transpired for several months, as summer brought the usual slowdown of orders. Tappan continued practicing law, and enjoyed the warm weather with his family. Then, in September 1897, the break finally came. Using a new form of the original plan, Tappan was able to satisfy the Post Office. Investors Syndicate would be allowed to pay out all the old business on the books, but not write any new business except under a modified contract. The new certificates matured in less time, twelve-and-a-half instead of twenty years. That sounded more serious than it really was. The attractiveness of the certificates had always depended on their maturing fast. "Of course we never expected that any contracts would run this long [twenty years], and this was a mere safeguard so that we would be absolutely safe in issuing the contracts."[80] Tappan had always claimed that his plan was capable of generating returns in as little as two or three years. Still, by putting the required time to maturity so far off in the future, he had raised eyebrows. It would be easy for an illicit operator to concoct such a scheme, and then claim financial exigency or blame uncontrollable market forces for delaying the promised payoff as long as possible. So, in the end, the government had merely made him move his money and his mouth into closer proximity.

A few years later, in fact, Tappan again shortened the term of the contract, to alleviate public fears over the long wait between making payments and seeing a return. Given how easily investment companies folded, seeing a payout sooner rather than later became a major selling point. Accordingly, Tappan redesigned the contracts so that "by paying people part of their money quicker, it will enable us to get new business easier, as the party who has received part of his money on his contract feels more encouraged, and is more inclined to invest and help us get new business."[81] Since many investors put security first, the revised contracts also provided even more liberal surrender features, and allowed heirs to withdraw all money actually paid in upon the death of the holder, if they did not choose to keep up the payments.

For all the legal turmoil, the future of the certificates would still depend less on the blessing of some regulatory authority than on the public's faith that they were what they claimed to be. Tappan himself understood that it was really the public, not postal inspectors, he had to convince. In fact, much of his time was taken up less with matters of management than with writing to potential investors, and presenting a strong public image for his firm. These things he did personally, in numerous letters and correspondence sent to individual holders of certificates, or in answer to inquiries about the Syndicate's prospectus. The letters frankly acknowledged what was at stake. "We have conducted this company from its inception honestly and fairly and for the benefit of the members," he wrote in admission that many other companies had not. "I cannot say I blame you for being suspicious," he responded to wavering investors, "as I know what your experience has been in other companies." "We are almost total strangers to you," Tappan went on, "but I give you my word that everything is being conducted in a perfectly honorable and straightforward manner and that we intend to stick right by our members, and you need not have any fears about being used in the manner you have been by the other companies."[82]

This was the crux of the business problem Tappan faced. As a government investigation would note many years later, the face amount certificate was "nothing more" than a contract between two parties, a promise to pay. Investment of this sort looked awfully shaky compared to traditional forms of investment, which involved the ownership of something real and tangible, like property. One could argue that these pieces of paper represented real property nonetheless. Corporate stock, for example, is actually a claim of ownership on the assets of a company. But in practice, holders of stock merely receive the "residual" profits from the corporations they putatively own. They also stand at the end of the line when payment is due to creditors, workers, and suppliers. Few owners of corporate stock will ever be in a position to directly control their companies, in the way they might a piece of land or their own business. In the case of Tappan's face amount certificate, clients really could not even claim this residual right of ownership. All they really had was the company's promise to return their money with interest.

Was it still possible to do business on the basis of trust and honor, especially when the fragile financial health of men and women of small means was at stake? What would make the public trust a man whom they had never seen and a company they had never visited? Tappan was broaching these questions. He solicited money from people who did not know him, were not part of his locality, and largely had no business relationship with him. If Investors Syndicate turned out to be less than promised, or worse, a sham, what recourse did they have? Common law probably gave investors some remedy, but actual cases establishing the extent of Tappan's obligations and the rights of investors had yet to be heard. For most men and women of modest means, hiring a lawyer and hauling Tappan into court, across state lines no less, were simply not options.

One way of bridging the trust gap was through character. As the ideal of the manly independent producer waned, elite Americans sought other ways of distinguishing the worthy citizen from the unworthy. Respectability once had been signaled by one's property, by ownership of land, or by possession of a manual skill. In the new economy even the well-off did not always make their living through property ownership. Professionals such as doctors and lawyers, or incipient professionals such as investment counselors, offered their services and expertise, but the public had no way of knowing what stood behind these professions of competence. In a market-based society where presentation and representation were designed to attract consumers who knew little about the producers, the potential for fraud and deceit was great. One way around these dangers was by focusing on recognizable traits and habits of individuals, which indicated their honesty, competency, and leadership. Character, in the parlance of the time, "made a man rich."[83]

This notion of character depended less on what one did, than on what one was. It was defined by observable traits, from clothing, accent, and style, to race and ethnicity. Nineteenth-century "Victorian" America placed much more emphasis on refined deportment and manners than on the honest simplicity of earlier decades. Character could be expressed in tasteful household furnishings, middle-brow cultural pursuits, and appropriate meals emphasizing European cuisine presided over by servants. Since the line between clever deception and genuine worthiness was hard to prove, it helped to have independent validation of character. Membership in organizations, churches, and social clubs was one way to vouchsafe one's character. By the end of the nineteenth century, Americans were joining fraternal lodges and business clubs such as the Rotary and Junior Chamber of Commerce in record numbers. For professionals, validation of character was also conferred by university degrees and accreditation from responsible boards that oversaw medicine, law, accountancy, and other fields. Professions that had once been open to the self-educated or that had trained members through apprenticeships closed their doors, admitting only those who could afford a university education and probably training beyond that as well.

By making eligibility into the professions dependent either on validation from a self-selected peer group or on external behavior, the cult of character gave society a more conservative cast. Character was fixed in place, or at least difficult to acquire, except by hard work and conformity to expectations. Upward mobility was still possible, however. Tappan had, after all, brushed off the habits of the frontier, finished school, and passed the tests of professional propriety. But he had certain advantages of birth, background, and culture. Not everyone could be so lucky. Tests of character could easily exclude those whose skin color, accent, or habits did not measure up to proper society. To serve the financial needs of the white middle class, it helped immensely if one were a member of that class.

Far more than the small amount of physical or monetary capital it possessed, Investors Syndicate's future was underwritten by the character of its principal. "Any financial scheme . . . ," Tappan wrote, "is dependent largely for its success upon the honesty, integrity and business ability of the people who head it." It was crucial to distinguish Investors Syndicate from other companies that "promise too much, have no stability about them, [and are] managed dishonestly." The problem was not with the idea of an investment company, with the "principle," so much as "the manner of applying it."[84]

One reason that Tappan refused to completely disassociate himself from companies such as the Guaranty and Colombian, whose failures threatened the reputation of his own firm, was his belief that one could not shirk obligations. He wrote letters to those who had bought bonds in companies that failed, offering them a chance to transfer their funds to Investors Syndicate. This was good marketing, to be sure, but it also forged a reciprocal obligation. The bonds that Tappan took might well be worthless, or worth far less than the contracts returned. Tappan himself had invested in these other companies, and admitted that in some cases problems stemmed from self-dealing on the part of top managers.[85] Honest men, however, did not use others as an excuse. Reflecting on his involvement with the Globe Mercantile Company, which had also gone bankrupt in the depression, Tappan wrote, "We put in a good deal of time and work into this thing in trying to push and secure new business, advertising, . . . etc. [I]t proved a most disastrous enterprise to us financially, as we not only lost money and have never been adequately paid for our time and work and never expect to be, but we also induced our friends to come in, which is the part we regret the most of anything. It is because we wished to do right with you and treat you as we would be treated that we made you the offer about transferring you to the Investors Syndicate."[86]

The true test of character came during moments of failure. In the ethic of the times, defeat was to be met with redoubled efforts. Failure, in the words of popular theologian Henry Ward Beecher, "turns bone to flint," and "gristle to muscle." It was an education on the road to success.[87] Failure, though, also raised serious problems in an economy that sought to link virtue and economic success. Did failure indicate want of character? If not, then was fortune a capricious goddess, smiling and frowning with arbitrary abandon on those she chose? Panics, such as the one in the 1890s, were problems because they suggested only a tenuous connection between economic failure and moral fault. Farmers and small business owners, workers and widows driven to poverty by a massive economic downturn seemed to have done nothing to deserve their fate. When hundreds of thousands of hardworking people were facing similar circumstances, could each one really have had a secret failing that brought on their condition?

As with gambling, failure raised the frightening prospect that virtue and success, hard work and achievement, were no longer connected.[88] To ward off such thoughts, Victorian Americans thoroughly investigated the question of character. They read stories by Horatio Alger, who explained how "pluck" and hard work would bring reward to the deserving. They carefully watched the habits of their neighbors, for signs of drunkenness (one of the great taboos in Tappan's mind), profligacy, and indolence, all of which signaled an eventual unhappy ending. When a businessman came to an unhappy end, they scrutinized his life for signs that, somewhere, character was at fault. He had been a spendthrift; he had been too speculative; he had not been energetic enough; he had hoarded his wealth and refused to put it to productive investment. "Objective" information from credit agencies was frequently indistinguishable from such gossip and after-the-fact moralizing. For people who believed money was more than material, more than a means to an end, such moralizing was considered quite proper. Money was too important to be merely an object of greed or self-satisfaction. "Our right or wrong use of money," declaimed a magazine article in 1886, "is the utmost test of character as well as the root of happiness or misery, throughout our whole lives."[89] Those who successfully mastered the gyrations of a money economy were also exhibiting their social and moral rectitude.

Tappan's creation of Investors Syndicate can be seen as one more institution to support the connections between morality and economy. Gold Republicans had defended the gold standard on these moral grounds. Populists had sought to link money with virtue through Free Silver and new financial schemes to help downtrodden farmers. Tappan had gone the route of a new institution, a new type of financial instrument that would allow prudent, hardworking, and ambitious men and women a means to save that was, as he continually pointed out, perfectly safe. Through a system of careful investment, one could bring the slippery and possibly capricious nature of money under control. Through this new financial product, even the small wage earner or farmer could save money against the ill winds of an economy that threatened to blow the virtuous off course. Increasingly, the old moral connections between money and virtue would be embedded in new, rational institutions for planning and managing capital and credit.

By "personalizing" his business, Tappan formed a sort of bond between borrower and lender that helped to overcome mistrust and uncertainty. So long as Investors Syndicate remained small and local, Tappan communicated his values and character directly to the public. Growth, on the other hand, required a larger system, an organization that could advertise and sell the product nationally. Like other financial service companies, Investors Syndicate had to depend on commissioned agents operating quasi-independently to find clients. These agents, who did the actual selling, were also responsible for spreading the philosophy behind the certificate. If they did not do their job, or failed to understand the larger meaning, Investors Syndicate would become just another short-lived investment scheme. Finding and managing agents was the next crucial strategic challenge the new company faced.

From the beginning, the success of Investors Syndicate was closely tied to its sales force. Like insurance companies, the Syndicate was built around independent salesmen, who were granted the right to sell the face amount certificates and received a commission on each sale. To launch a broad national sales effort, such independent agents were crucial. Though Tappan was "hoping to put some of our men on a salary," this was wishful thinking.[90] It was simply impossible for a small, start-up firm to keep employees on salary. But commissioned agents could be found around the nation. They were paid from the business they generated, keeping $7.50 of the initial $10 up-front fee each new customer handed over.

Ideally, agents were knowledgeable about local conditions, had good contacts, and could do the sort of labor-intensive selling that was impossible to carry out from afar. In a business heavily dependent on trust, other, more impersonal methods of sales were of little use. In fact, except for the numerous letters Tappan wrote personally to prospective investors, the Syndicate shunned print advertising after "circularizing" the country a few times. Word of mouth was more effective than attractive type or bold displays. One of the few advertisements that Tappan ran, in the *Mail Order Monthly,* was a single inch display that read "$2.08 FOR EVERY $1.00 INVESTED. Sounds big, but that is exactly what we are paying for our investors, and have been for the last 6 years. No wheat or mining speculation, but absolutely guaranteed." In the end, though, Tappan came to see that "it is only by personal application that business is written."[91] Agents who asked for advice on technique received replies such as this: "Do not expect to sell contracts by passing out circulars as you can never sell anything in that way. I never show a man a circular . . . until I have thoroughly talked up the plan."[92]

On the one hand, Tappan was convinced that his plan "speaks for itself." It was simple, legal, and thoroughly safe and could be explained in a "nut shell." So there was no need to trumpet it through loud displays or with fancy printing. What was needed, however, were loyal agents who would do the legwork, going house by house, family by family, and convince the public that a safe, practical, honest, and legal alternative for their savings did in fact exist. In a giddy age of speculation, lotteries, financial chicanery, and outright fraud, this was no easy task. Simple as the plan seemed to its inventor, agents found that they had a hard time convincing people to hand over their money to an operation they had never heard of.

In the early years, public skepticism led right back to Tappan himself. The wary investor's only real assurance was the integrity of the principal, John Elliott Tappan. Tappan never tired of answering queries with his own pen, putting himself and his character before the wary public. When an agent asked Tappan to help him convince a prospect, this was the reply Tappan sent the wavering client: "We want your friendship and your good will and if you will let us place you in the Investors Syndicate we will give you four contracts and both Mr. Williams and myself will personally guarantee that these contracts will be complied with by the company to the very letter, and will give you a written statement to that effect if you so desire."[93]

There were of course no ironclad guarantees about any investment. In his short career, Tappan had already seen "companies that have promised too much, have had no stability about them, and have been managed dishonestly."[94] Still, Investors Syndicate's number-one sales pitch remained Tappan himself. Testimonials from satisfied customers spoke not only to the validity and stability of the contracts, but of the honesty with which they were treated. Company literature played up this theme. As one customer rather effusively put it, Tappan was "one of the squarest and manliest men, among all the manly men of the great North Star State."[95]

By the end of 1899, John Tappan was feeling optimistic. He and Winnie continued to work side by side, the two of them riding bicycles to the office. J. W. Earl, a former insurance salesman, joined the company as manager of agents. "While business is not booming with us yet," Tappan wrote, "we are having a steady, uniform growth, which is more healthy and substantial than a temporary boom would be."[96] Tappan was right. Growth was steady, not spectacular. Investors Syndicate had written over 300 contracts, 200 of them were still in force.[97] The company had done $100,000 in business, and paid out over $11,000 in returns to its early investors. Though these figures indicated a young firm, Tappan was proud that he returned a higher percentage of the money he took in than "any financial institution, Insurance or Indemnity Corporation."[98] It was still crucial, however, to get word out that the Syndicate actually was a new, safe, and effective alternative to banks and other traditional financial institutions. Investors Syndicate was to be an enduring institution, one committed to long-term change in how Americans saved. "We expect," Tappan wrote, "to be one of the largest financial institutions of the great Northwest." It turned out he was underestimating the firm's future. Before it reached its pinnacle of success, however, Investors Syndicate had several more challenges to meet.

CHAPTER FOUR

A TURNING POINT

Business went well for Tappan in 1900. Though there were no spectacular gains, growth proceeded at about the pace it had for the previous five years. The company was still young, Tappan knew that. He understood that building a reputation and fine-tuning the product was going to take time and patience. Meanwhile, his own law practice was providing a steady income, particularly in real estate, where Tappan took a special interest. There were lots of opportunities to buy and sell land, both in the city of Minneapolis, which was growing rapidly, and in the surrounding countryside. Winnie continued to apply her bookkeeping and secretarial skills at the offices of Investors Syndicate, until the birth of their first child that spring.

Like many young enterprises, though, Investors Syndicate experienced unexpected ups and downs. Being a pioneer of consumer financial services meant swimming in untested waters and enduring painful lessons from unknown or obscure hazards. Returning from a needed vacation and hunting trip in the fall of 1901, Tappan arrived back in the office to just such an unwelcome surprise. The Post Office decided to have a second look at the face amount certificate and did not like what it saw. Despite Tappan's hope, Investors Syndicate had not cleared the last of its legal hurdles. Though no charges of fraud were leveled, inspectors were taking preemptory action. Once again they shut down the company's mailing privileges. This was a serious blow. For a second time, the whisper of scandal threatened the young enterprise. With hardly enough time to unpack, Tappan was on the road once more, heading for Washington and a showdown with federal authorities. This time he was leaving nothing to chance, or to political fortunes.

Back in Minneapolis, new director of agents J. W. Earl manned the office. Earl's job was to keep public suspicions at bay, for cancellation of mailing privileges was tantamount to an indictment. During the first week of the crisis, no news leaked out to the public. "I called at R. G. Fisher's place this afternoon," Earl wrote to Tappan, "and he called me to one side and said that he understood that the government was after us and that we were not allowed to use the mail." As Tappan and Earl feared, rumors were threatening to spread before the investigation even began. "I laughed at him," Earl continued, "and asked him where he got such wild information."[1] It was a desperate move of bluster. Earl denied the allegations point-blank and affirmed that mail was still being delivered. He offered to show him if necessary postmarks from that very day.

Technically this was no lie. The Post Office order did not cover personal correspondence, only business. And in fact, at least one contract had slipped through the blockade. Fisher backed down, saying that he had heard a rumor all investment companies were closed down. He merely assumed Investors Syndicate was included. Earl's ruse had worked, and he concluded the meeting with his customer reassured that "Investors Syndicate would be on earth when all others had been forgotten, all of which relieved his mind very much."[2]

In Washington, Tappan cooled his heels waiting for word of a meeting. Day by day, Earl's reports grew gloomier. "Up to this time so far as local gossip is concerned, we are masters of the situation." But he admitted, "We are all on tip-toes holding our breath here at the office waiting for your telegram."[3] In response to inquiries from customers as to why they had not received receipts for payments, Earl was forced to respond that the office work had piled up and the secretary was on vacation. Every day it became more difficult to fend off inquiries. R. G. Dun, the credit reporting company, sent out word that something might be amiss with Investors Syndicate. Associated Press reporters telegrammed, trying to find out if the company was under investigation again. Local reporters were sniffing out rumors of scandal, especially after it was discovered that two competing investment companies, Diamond Contract and Northwestern Land Investment, faced the same allegations. Customers, anxious in the best of times about their money, wanted reassurance that all was well. "While I appreciate the fact that you are in the thick of the fight down at that end of the line," Earl wrote to his partner, "yet I want to assure you that it is no huckleberry picnic to stand off the curious at this end."[4]

As long as Earl could keep the investigation quiet, the Syndicate would suffer no permanent damage to its reputation. Clearing the company's name, however, meant operating in the ways of Washington. To that end, Tappan engaged a lawyer who had made a reputation handling the affairs of investment companies in trouble with the Post Office. Earl believed that "the department and he [the lawyer] are in cahoots." The Washington attorney was in effect extorting business out of investment companies with the help of postal inspectors. But there seemed no way to get around the legal barrier short of making such changes as he recommended.

On November 21, 1901, the strategy paid off. Tappan wired back to his partners, "Order revoked. Mails opened. Leave tonight. Back Saturday 2 PM."[5] The investigation had turned up one part of the contract that was problematic. To attract business, Tappan had modified the method of maturity, so that coupons of the same contract matured in different months. The idea was to make the certificates more attractive by speeding up the time when the investor first saw his or her return. But such features bordered on the "multiple" system, whereby an element of chance was added to the investment. This sort of gambling was the number one concern of postal investigators.

Investors Syndicate did not escape completely unscathed. The day the mails were restored, the *Minneapolis Journal* finally got its story, reporting that the Syndicate had been under investigation, though now it was cleared. It would not be the last time a government agency investigated the plan, but Tappan and Earl felt confident that they had strengthened their position by meeting the charges and responding. Successful resolution of the problem reinforced their conviction that the face amount certificate was legitimate and legal. A general letter to all subscribers the following January emphasized this point. "You may also possibly have noticed that different investment companies . . . have been in difficulty with the postal authorities, and we desire to say that [our] contract has been submitted to the post office department and meets with its full approval."

Even so, the outcome did not settle all qualms that Tappan felt about the government's role in his business. Most frustrating was the way these sorts of charges were launched. All it took was one dissatisfied official to file an unfavorable report in Washington. "I would like to get my cold hands upon that man Morgan [a postal inspector]," wrote Earl. It was he who had made the most damaging charges. "If he ever comes to Minneapolis again . . . I think we had better arrange to play football with him." One can assume Earl did not have a friendly game in mind.[6]

Tappan himself took away a slightly different lesson from the experience. Though he had no love for arbitrary government agents or corrupt Washington lawyers, he came to believe that a rational, coordinated regulation was needed, as opposed to no regulation at all. Legitimate plans benefited from a clean legal bill of health. Competent investigations would drive out of business the shady and suspect who tried to compete by less than honest means and thereby undermined investor confidence. Over time, Tappan would become a cautious supporter of limited government regulation.

The first years of the new century had been busy ones for John Tappan in other ways as well. In March of 1900, John and Winnie saw the birth of their first child, Ruth Winifred Marie Tappan. John was absolutely ecstatic over his new daughter. She arrived at five in the morning, with John in the room. Nearly half a century later he would recall the moment of her birth with perfect clarity. "It was 15 degrees below zero, and a poor, cold robin was sitting all humped up in a tree outside the bedroom window, and you looked at me with big, wondering eyes, trying to solve the mysteries of life."[7] Tappan, the avid nature lover and youthful bird watcher, took the robin as symbol of this moment for the rest of his life, giving his eldest daughter many gifts with a robin motif.

With a new child, the Tappans began to feel that their small apartment was too cramped. Winnie stopped working to take up the full-time duties of motherhood. They all moved into a large house on Dupont Avenue, with a nursery upstairs, and a downstairs library and fireplace. It was by any standard a comfortable home for a respectable family of the middle class, though by no means was it opulent. Minneapolis was still the West, and even the middle class did not have all the comforts of modern life, not even in the early twentieth century. The Tappans had to make use of outhouses, not indoor water closets, and they took baths once a week on Saturday in a large tub set before the kitchen stove, using the homemade brown soap Winnie fashioned from lye. The move was none too soon, however, for by December of that year Winnie was pregnant again. In August 1901 she gave birth to a second daughter, Marion Elizabeth. As he had when Ruth was born, John was present at the delivery and took off two weeks from work. He looked after Ruth while his mother Adelaide helped with Winnie's recovery and with the new infant.

These were good times for the young family. Once the postal investigation crisis passed, Tappan had enough leisure time for family vacations. Summers were often spent away from the city, where the torpid air was considered unhealthy, especially for children. In the country, John was in his element, once more outside the bounds of domestic civilization. Semi-annually he escaped all feminine influence to go on hunting trips with male companions. He also loved venturing into rough rural Minnesota whenever he could. When he could not be with his family on vacation, he would remain behind in the city and join them on weekends for picnic lunches in the fields, fishing, or just enjoying fresh air and relaxing.

Tappan's personal and professional life meshed in a satisfying way during the early years of the new century. He still was not taking a salary from Investors Syndicate, but could earn a decent living through a modest law practice. Meanwhile, his company was progressing in just the way he had planned—slowly, steadily, legally, and legitimately. Its growth was fueled not by hyperbole or improbable promises, but by solid performance. Tappan himself was content to reinvest the profits, as he advised clients to do. The future was not certain, of course. But it was at least a bit clearer. Rationally, logically, Tappan could expect the Syndicate to continue its pattern of growth. The next five or six years, at least, looked like smooth sailing.

So long as Investors Syndicate remained small, it retained a strong personal touch about it. The office was open every weekday from 8:00 A.M. until 6:00 P.M., and half-days on Saturday. Tappan himself visited the office every day, in addition to his law practice, stopping his work only for a midday meal at home. Though he employed a number of attorneys as well as bookkeepers, secretaries, and stenographers, most of the day-to-day business he himself could oversee. The agency side of things was in Earl's hands, while John was responsible for handling the money, designing the contracts, and making most of the land investments. He also acted as part-time salesman, contacting friends and drawing on a widening group of local contacts for clients. These clients were important as much for how they advertised the security and success of the face amount certificates as for the cash they brought in. Like his numerous missives and circulars to the several hundred investors, his friends and acquaintances reinforced the sense that he was taking personal responsibility for the economic well-being of people he knew. Investors Syndicate was not just a faceless bureaucracy.

This sort of close personal contact with clients made Tappan more of a financial advisor than a salesman. He looked for ways to help those experiencing temporary shortfalls to get back on the path of savings. When one woman who was behind on her payments sent her mother into the office with $10 toward her contract, Tappan wrote back, "We trust that you will not break down at your work as your mother said that it was beginning to tell on you, and if you can keep your health . . . you will certainly get your place speedily paid for."[8] Those who had money paid in sometimes found that they needed cash, fast. The loan provision of the contract allowed them access to it. "We are sorry to note that you are out of work and that your prospects are not bright for settlement," Tappan wrote to one hard luck case. "Trust that things will soon change for you. If you want the extra amount, let us know and we will fix you out at once."[9]

Such a forgiving attitude did not come cheaply for Investors Syndicate. The company itself was adversely affected by the same downturns in the business cycle that hurt its clients and subscribers. There was no disguising these facts of business life. Investors Syndicate had to depend as much on the forthrightness of its subscribers as they depended on honesty from the firm. "We are very hard pressed for money at the present time on account of having heavy obligations," Tappan wrote with candor to the firm's clients.[10] He was expecting in return those who owed money to pay up as soon as possible. "You owe us a balance of $30.34 including interest," went a letter to another. "We have carried this loan for you for about seven years and you are getting a good salary and we think that you should straighten up the matter."[11]

Financial advice necessarily touched on matters of personal lifestyle and conduct. Saving was not merely a matter of gain; it inculcated certain habits of mind. And it required a certain sort of character. If "manly" men paid off their debts and fulfilled their obligations, then successful men (or women) had industrious life habits. That meant, among other things, sobriety, both in the sense of seriousness of purpose and in the more common sense of not being a drunk.

At the beginning of America's industrial age, in the years before the Civil War, temperance had suddenly bloomed as a reform cause, reversing decades of increasing alcohol consumption. Middle-class Protestants began to advertise their moral fiber and fitness for success through external signs of self-control. Temperance never really died out after the Civil War. The long sought goal of banning alcoholic drink was finally realized with the passage of the Prohibition Amendment in 1919. Though teetotaling was hardly universal among urbanites of Tappan's class, many followed strict Victorian proscriptions concerning bodily indulgences. John Elliott Tappan was one of these.

Tappan himself was a lifelong abstainer, who had to be tricked at times into taking brandy prescribed by his doctor for "medicinal purposes." He frugally bottled his own root beer for summer enjoyment, even if at times he had to consume the soft drink all at once as the home-capped bottles began to explode open in the summer heat. Not a particularly religious man, John tolerated equally well the Catholic priests of his wife's faith and the preachers of his own family's church. But like generations of antisaloon reformers before him, he believed that drinking wasted corporeal as well as capital resources. Saving was hard business for those who did not have much to begin with, and drink was only a snare and temptation from the true path to financial freedom. Worse than even the expense was the danger that it would lead one down the road to dissipation, resulting in lethargy, self-indulgence, and loss of work or business.

These dangers Tappan had witnessed firsthand, out West in the mining and logging camps. When a friend was in danger of succumbing to such temptations, Tappan wrote him a long letter imploring him to stop before it was too late. "I do not wish to interfere with your business, but, as I have told you before, there can be but one outcome of this matter and that will be bankruptcy for you."[12] Nothing could be worse. It meant, Tappan went on, "loss of everything you have on earth, and the loss of an opportunity of a lifetime, as you will never again have such an opportunity as you have had and as you now have." Saving for the future was a lifetime commitment, something that Tappan had stressed from the beginning of his project. Plan ahead, start now, save up small increments, keep on the path of savings, and you will come out ahead in the long run.

Tappan issued a steady stream of correspondence to those who were having second thoughts or were failing to keep up payments. The letters were larded with the tenets of self-help, laying heavy stress on consistency, constancy, and sacrifice for a future reward. "Did you ever notice that when you are good and thirsty a drink seems a good deal better?" he wrote to one, obviously not referring to alcoholic indulgence. "It is the same way with your maturities. They will bring so much more when they do come and by waiting they will be all the more appreciated."[13] Though the twentieth century is usually seen as the era when Americans abandoned their inhibitions about spending and stopped saving, they received no help from John Tappan if they did. His own children would tease him for being a "real Yankee" with the dollar. But John continued to follow the traditional wisdom that "the saving of money usually means the saving of a man."[14]

It is of course extremely hard to say why people save money, except perhaps that they save to have money and with luck to have more of it by investing. Beyond the generalities of "saving for a rainy day," or protection against disaster, however, the meaning of saving as a cultural act can be extremely obscure and individual. Still, it seems clear that certain changes had taken place in American society that were also altering how and why people saved. Retirement, as noted, was becoming an important part of the saving equation. Decades earlier, insurance companies had marketed savings as a way of protecting families from the death of the male breadwinner. Both retirement and insurance were caught up with the idea of saving to consume, retirement especially so—putting money aside in order to consume it later.

In the nineteenth century, by contrast, savings had been connected to production. Savings institutions were oriented to mobilizing capital for some sort of income-generating project. Even the working class saved for production more than for consumption. Laborers in cities, for example, had access to workingmen's banks and savings and loans. Social philosophers such as Jeremy Bentham, David Hume, and Thomas Malthus believed that these "frugality" banks could alleviate poverty by assisting the "industrious and provident" poor to help themselves. Saving promoted "habits of economy, of calculation and of foresight in all classes."[15] A solid basis of savings, it was thought, would allow the poor to elevate their status, acquire land, or perhaps move from toiler to independent propitiator.[16] The banks not only made money, they taught correct habits. Many, for example, opened only a few hours per day, to discourage sudden and capricious withdrawals of money. Others gave customers extra premiums if they made regular deposits each week from their paychecks. This mixture of charity and business caught on, and by 1818, mutual savings banks spread throughout Britain and then to the United States.[17]

Savings banks were something of a precedent for Investors Syndicate. These "working men's" institutions drew the majority of their depositors from among domestic workers, unskilled laborers, skilled artisans, and lower level members of the mercantile and professional occupations. It was, as in the case of the Boston Penny Savings Bank, literally possible to open an account with a penny. Bank directors carefully investigated would-be depositors, to be sure they were from among the "industrious poor." By targeting these groups, who were generally ignored by commercial banks, the mutual savings associations grew by 1860 to become some of the nation's largest financial institutions, "financial behemoths" of cities such as New York, with names like Drydock Savings and Seaman's Bank, which advertised their origins.[18]

Social reform and professionally managed finance merged in the savings bank, in the same way that Tappan was putting them together in his own fledgling enterprise. The rich, it was assumed, had the resources and education to make their own investment decisions, presumably in land, in their own businesses, or as lenders to other members of their own class. The poor lacked the skills and wherewithal for the risky business of investment. Savings bank trustees, assisted by salaried employees, would make these decisions by collecting and diversifying the small savings of working-class depositors.

For the most part, the savings institutions seem to have fulfilled the purposes of their design—to encourage savings for production and independence. Clients made regular deposits, accumulating relatively large sums of money, kept it there for a number of years, and then withdrew it in relatively large sums. This pattern of saving and withdrawal suggests that the banks were not being used to finance everyday needs—consumption, in other words. Accumulated funds that were withdrawn in large sums were most likely being reinvested elsewhere, in land, a house, or a business. Of course, in some cases the money may have been used for some unexpected tragedy or to meet some large consumption need. But savings for consumption would more likely follow a pattern of periodic deposits and periodic withdrawals. The only depositors who seem to have fit this pattern were unmarried women and widows. Unmarried women worked most of their lives in the labor market, unlike married women. They lacked the sort of household assets of a family business, land, and children to finance their later years, and so depended more on savings to support a form of retirement.[19]

When Tappan began Investors Syndicate, Americans were saving money at a high rate. Overall personal saving was about 11 percent in the latter half of the nineteenth century. Middle-class Americans—those earning at least $1,500 per year—saved an astonishing 30 percent of their income, a stark contrast to today, when personal savings are negative.[20] Even workers, using the mutual savings banks, could put aside as much as 8 percent of a year's earnings.[21] When the opportunity arose, most people would save. By paying higher rates of interest than commercial or mutual savings banks, by offering the security of an insurance policy, but with "money while you lived," Tappan and his face amount certificate fit into a growing niche for savings opportunities aimed at the ambitious and frugal lower-middle and working classes.

Over time, though, the nature of savings would change in America. It would become more modern, with less and less money accumulated for productive purposes and more for leisure and consumption. Besides retirement, the notable change here was in the rise of consumer durable goods. In the late nineteenth century, consumer durables, the sort of purchase that requires either consumer credit or a big lump sum payment, were far less common than today. Electrical appliances such as refrigerators, ranges, and vacuum cleaners did not exist. Other big-ticket items, such as cars, were in their infancy and no more than the playthings of the rich. By 1920, however, Americans would be saving less of their income and spending more, mostly because they would be using savings to buy consumer durable items. The trend was furthered by the birth of consumer credit, which allowed ordinary men and women to finance these expenditures. When Tappan had started Investors Syndicate, consumer debt stood at about $400 million. By the mid-1920s consumer boom it would be over $4 billion.[22]

The switch to durable goods reveals the changing meaning of savings and consumption in modern capitalism. At one time, it seemed clear. Saving was distinct from consuming. It was linked directly to investment and production. It was about enhancing future income, resisting temptations for luxuries, moving from dependent toiler to independent property owner. But in the modern economy, most households no longer make their own investments directly in the productive economy.[23] Instead, high levels of personal consumption stimulate investment by businesses, who draw on savings for the capital formation necessary to production. The categorical distinction between consumption and savings has been blurred through the introduction of consumer durable goods. As goods lasting five or more years, durables might well be regarded as the equivalent of an investment. The consumer of a durable receives a stream of pleasure from the purchase over the life of the product, just as an investor receives a stream of income from an asset. Distinctions between consuming for pleasure and saving for future income no longer hold steady in a world filled with durable goods. Even savings itself can be seen as a form of psychic pleasure or satisfaction—the satisfaction of watching your money grow. If so, then what is the difference between investing to receive future pleasures from later income and consuming a durable good, with its stream of future pleasures? Defined this way, as another form of savings, consumer durable goods stood at 12.5 percent of personal savings in 1898. But by the early 1920s they had risen to 21 percent, and were nearly 36 percent by the late 1940s.[24]

This hedonistic way of thinking, common perhaps among economists today, is almost certainly not the way Tappan saw the world. Though he was far from an ascetic, enjoying worldly goods, he also reveled in the simpler, homespun pleasures of family, holidays, and outdoor life. Investment might generate income, but income for pleasure was still different from income for reinvestment and wealth building. That sort of distinction is a difficult one for people in today's world to appreciate, if they hold that, in the end, all income is finally spent somewhere to achieve pleasure.

Men such as John Tappan, who lived during this transition, had to negotiate the change in values that consumer society implied. Values of thrift, sobriety, and hard work did not simply disappear as Americans became more consumer oriented, of course. Instead, these older values reattached themselves to consumption itself. There were ways of distinguishing solid, virtuous consumption from wasteful, hedonistic consumption.[25] Some products, though expensive, had obvious utility, and were safe from the charges of luxury and indulgence. Other items, however, were more questionable, and shifted categories over time. At some point, for example, indoor toilets and washing machines became tools of household efficiency, instead of unneeded, newfangled gadgets. Men often regarded items associated with women and the home as less utilitarian than items from the male domain, treating female consumers as frivolous spendthrifts, unable to control their shopping impulses. Some members of the white middle class also accused other socioeconomic and racial groups of having spending habits that they denigrated as profligate and childlike. These consumers supposedly lacked the self-control that distinguished virtuous from degenerate consumption.

The complicated issues involved with savings and consumption can be made clearer by looking at the number one consumer durable, the leading edge of the consumer revolution, the automobile. The single greatest cause in the early-twentieth-century shift away from savings and toward consumption was automobile purchases. Tappan was an enthusiastic automobilist, an early believer that the car was a tool of progress, if also an expensive item of consumption. A strong believer in progress through technology, he bought his first car in 1910. Later, he owned a Model T, the world's first true mass production automobile. Owning a car in 1910 still put him in the vanguard. America had at that time 500,000 car owners, contrasted with the 8 million or so it would have a decade later, after Henry Ford perfected mass production of inexpensive cars.

As an early participant in an emerging middle-class lifestyle, Tappan took great pleasure in his machine, riding about town in the open-body car with a duster and goggles to keep free of dirt and sand. Before he owned the car, he had also been an enthusiastic cyclist. The bicycle industry gave birth to many of the techniques of mass production, and launched a number of the entrepreneurs who would transform the automobile industry.[26] But cars and bicycles were linked in another way as well, in their original cultural place and meaning in American society.

Both cycles and cars were taken up by men (almost solely men at first) because they provided independence and mobility. Their connection to masculinity was expressed in an emphasis on speed and danger—today's familiar and relatively harmless bicycle design was known at first as the "safety" bicycle and marketed to women, as opposed to the fast and precarious high-wheeled models men rode. Initially at least, both cars and bicycles were not consumer items for everyday use. They required the user to take an active role in repairing, maintaining, and adjusting them. High maintenance automobiles were signs of manly independence, rather than luxury and status.

When Henry Ford began producing inexpensive automobiles, he first targeted those most independent Americans—farmers and rural residents. Farmers eagerly took up the car habit as prices fell. Automobiles changed from the urban rich man's toy to a practical farm machine. Users of automobiles in fact adapted them to unintended purposes. Farmers used car engines to saw wood, grind metal, and draw water. They purchased after-market attachments for such chores as plowing fields. Rural women transferred power from the car drive shaft to churn butter or run washing machines as well.[27] Though he did not have to make his living in this literal way, with the automobile, Tappan too appreciated the car as a practical machine. Mobility allowed him to move around the city and countryside inspecting properties where Syndicate funds were placed. When Tappan bought any new tool or device, he would spend hours thoroughly understanding and mastering it, maintaining it in the same condition as when he purchased it. He had little tolerance for carelessness or shoddy workmanship, and used everything he bought to the fullest, making it last.

For members of the urban middle class like Tappan, cars had a slightly different appeal than for farmers, but they were equally a symbol of rugged masculinity. Like four-wheel drive vehicles today, they promoted the fantasy of escape from civilization, an escape perhaps, then as now, more imagined than real. Still, on the road with a car, one could go "where fancy dictates." Automobilists enjoyed self-reliance with their cars, "as a master commands a ship at sea," enthusiasts put it. Middle-class families would leave the city and pitch tents in some clearing or farmer's meadow. Tappan's first car came from the Pan Motor Company of St. Cloud, Minnesota, an early model notable for a refrigerated space in the back where one could store food or pack a lunch for a country outing. Other early automobilists left town and stayed at inexpensive motor camps and cabins that were just beginning to dot the countryside. With their cars they went back to nature and abandoned the overly civilized, highly structured life of the city. But just for a time, just until the weekend jaunt was over. From one perspective, then, the car could be an escape from the confines of the very industrial civilization that spawned it.[28]

So features that we today associate with modern automobile culture—suburban sprawl, individual isolation, the pursuit of status, heedless consumerism—may have appeared in a different light a century ago. To rural residents, cars offered freedom. With them, they could join the flow of society at their pleasure. Driving was not about isolation and alienation, but rather just the opposite. Cars were tools for productive work, rather than pleasure palaces on wheels. Henry Ford believed that widespread adoption of cars would lead urban Americans back to the country, away from crowded, noisy, dirty cities, while connecting rural Americans with the benefits of markets and technological progress.[29] Ford's image was of a nation of thriving industrial villages and up-to-date prosperous farms, a human-scale middle landscape that did not require concentrations of people or capital.

At its most utopian, automobile society was a reprise of the old Populist vision, a return to decentralization and manly independence. This reform of society by automobile technology was not conservative or backward looking. Early car enthusiasts, such as John Elliott Tappan, were generally forward thinking, enamored of the productive powers of machinery. Tappan in fact was a charter member of the local branch of the American Automobile Association, originally an automobile "user group" dedicated to disseminating information on cars, helping owners master intractable machines, and lobbying for improved roads. Improved roads were a necessary complement to the car, of course, since rutted dirt tracks brought autos quickly to a standstill, particularly during the muddy spring thaw in Minnesota. Cars and good roads, on the other hand, increased social intercourse, integrating the farm and city, allowing independent businessmen and yeomen farmers to thrive by taking the fetters off their industriousness and relieving them from dependence on railroads, a technology controlled by powerful corporations.[30]

Populists had once identified the business corporation as the most oppressive force. In the Progressive Era of the twentieth century, corporations still needed watching, but, as the automobile seemed to promise, they might be forces for progress as well. Few examples surpassed Henry Ford's booming motor car company in this regard. Ford provided for the average family an affordable, dependable machine that would help them earn their living, and to live self-reliantly and travel independently.

Cars were also caught up with one more important social change, one directly tied to Tappan's life. They helped to spread the design of suburban living. Like street railways before them, cars opened up additional land for single family homes. Tappan's main source of investment outlets for funding was this urban and suburban home-building market. Americans from the early nineteenth century had been enthusiastic homeowners, and the opportunity to purchase the roof over one's head penetrated fairly far down the socioeconomic scale. Relatively high wages and cheap land made this possible. Still, in the industrial age, many workers and even middle-class families were crowded together in dense cities, which were growing far faster than villages or small towns. Suburban living, however, was touted as an ideal compromise, more healthy and ordered than the crowded city, yet close enough to work to be practical, at least for those with good incomes and access to a streetcar line nearby. In the single family home, women could create the neat and orderly environment necessary for raising children into solid American citizens. Suburbs seemed to promise another middle landscape, between the comforting past of the country, and the dynamic but disturbing future of the city.

As the suburban fringe around cities grew, streetcars had difficulty keeping up with this vast expansion of space. Lines were often undercapitalized, and sometimes poorly run by urban political machines. In any case, they operated by collecting traffic and centralizing it at certain nodes or central points, which made the journey for outlying suburban commuters long and difficult. Cars had the advantage of offering autonomy and personal freedom, or so it seemed. The flexibility of car travel, plus the desirability of home ownership, made suburban living an almost unbeatable combination in twentieth-century America. For many Americans, cars and home ownership took on powerful symbolic meanings, connected to old virtues of freedom, independence, and individualism.[31] In their initial reception, personal automobiles, suburban family homes, and good public roads remained tied to these earlier values of production and economic independence.

Only over time did these definitions give way to more consumerist ones. Through the early twentieth century, masculine technologies started to change. Safety bicycles for dress-wearing women, cars with automatic starters rather than hand cranks, and with closed cabins to keep out dirt and dust, helped to domesticate these products. Suburbs became safe, planned enclaves, removed from earlier notions of independent property ownership. With domestication came an expanded consumer definition that widened the market but also eliminated many of the masculine associations of utility, danger, difficulty, and work. Ford's functional black cars lost out to General Motors products. The latter emphasized design, changing models and adding new comfort features on a yearly basis. Farmers who wanted Model T workhorses became less important to carmakers than middle-class suburbanites who wanted luxury appointments.

In embracing the automobile with gusto, Tappan could well have been buying into either the initial or the more modern definition of the car. Perhaps he embraced both in an unthinking way. His work for the Automobile Association, his interest in good roads, his pride and mastery of the machine, suggest the utilitarian and republican side of his relationship to the car. But it was impossible for one individual to attach to the car a stable meaning.

Tappan was also an automobile consumer. In a similar manner, the meaning of saving and investment proved slippery and elusive. With the rise of cars and other durables, people saved as much to consume as to produce.

In his own business, Tappan seems to have tried hard to keep the meaning of saving fixed in its nineteenth-century form. He encouraged individuals to save, accumulate, and gain a competency. He invested their money in something he believed was real and stable. Land was still the source of wealth for John Elliott Tappan. Land was something solid and real, the best type of investment. Money taken from investors went into mortgages backed by land, mostly improved city land. Admittedly much of this investment rode on the suburban housing boom. But as Tappan repeated in his advertisements, the funds to pay back certificate holders did not come from speculative enterprises. They came from real investments that Tappan and his fellow members of Investors Syndicate could monitor and see themselves.

At first, when the Syndicate was small, all investments went into property nearby, in and around Minneapolis, so that there was no doubt what the public's money was being lent for. Improved land was the safest investment, a point Tappan reiterated in his public pronouncements. But it is revealing that he was not content simply to follow in the footsteps of those who had gone before him. A cautious, unimaginative investor could pick well-developed land for investment. An ambitious entrepreneur would have to do more than that. In Minnesota, even in the early twentieth century, it was still possible to find investment opportunities for real frontier development, as it had been a half-century earlier during the nation's westward movement. It was still possible to make money developing virgin territory. That was what Tappan's parents had done by coming West. John decided to continue the same project, as a land developer in the remote northern reaches of Minnesota.

In April 1902, Tappan struck a business deal with Kneut Kneutson, who was developing Isle Royale in Michigan as a summer resort.[32] It was exactly the sort of wild and undeveloped country Tappan loved to get away to whenever he could take vacation time. The densely forested island teemed with wildlife, including moose, wolves, red fox, and snowshoe hares. It was the perfect place for a birding enthusiast to wander and explore. The waterways around the island made for great boating, and there were several hills that afforded panoramic views of Lake Superior. So enthusiastic was Tappan about this venture that he thought about staking his own claim to land, in a territory somewhat closer to home.

A couple of years later, in 1904, he took out a homestead claim for 160 acres of wild country about 40 miles north of Duluth. It became his rural retreat and pet project for the next two years. The land bordered the Mesabi Iron Range, which he had visited during work for the Merritts. His holdings had a fine stand of old growth timber, a virgin forest dark even during daylight hours. Though Tappan had no thought of giving up city life to return to the occupation of his father, he expressed enthusiasm about his new venture as though he were a genuine homesteader. "The soil is black, rich loam," he wrote to friends, trying to pique their interest in joining him. "Where there is a clear space bluejoint grass grows as high as a man's waist. They claim that almost anything grows up there except corn and watermelons."[33]

A decade before Tappan staked his claim in the far north, historian Frederick Jackson Turner had declared the frontier experience in American history over. There was no more wild land for virtuous pioneers to tame. Yet in the early twentieth century, Tappan was able to find in the wilds of northern Minnesota the same sort of frontier exhilaration his family had once felt in their journey westward. He was elated by his claim, working outside in the crisp fresh air with his hands, running his fingers through the heavy dark soil. He inhaled the fragrant smell of the pines and took every opportunity to steal away to Rice River, a small stream that flowed through his property. An excellent hunter whose pathfinding skills were honed during his days in California and as a surveyor in the Pacific Northwest, Tappan walked his land carrying a rifle. He met wolves, lynx, wildcat, and bear in the forest, and shot most of his own food, mainly rabbit, deer, and partridge. He drew water in buckets from the nearby river and lit the night with kerosene lamps and an open fire. But this was no mere getaway for the weary city businessman.

Like most American pioneers, Tappan was especially interested in wringing a profit from nature. His plan was to sell the old growth timber, which would fetch a high price, and then use the cleared land for farming and stock raising. He wrote in detail about the soil, the value of the timber, about the location of railroad lines for transportation and the nearest markets for crops. He explained to his friends, whom he hoped would join him, how to acquire land through the Homestead or Timber Acts. By September 1904 he was drawing up plans to get settlers set up on adjacent lands, to turn what had been largely unoccupied country into a new frontier community. Owning already one quarter section, he hoped to double his holding to 320 acres.

In October, having blazed a trail through the pine and poplar, Tappan started to build a 22 by 24 foot cabin and another house for guests, as well as a barn and a henhouse. He built his house of logs and cedar shingles, which came from the clearing of the building site. The tools he used were hardly different from those his forefathers would have wielded—a saw, an axe, an adz, a hammer, nails, and mortar.[34] That fall, Tappan cleared a total of fifteen acres with the help of friends and neighbors. He also fenced sixty more acres and built a bridge over the Rice River. Hay, potatoes and other vegetables were in the ground, and goats, sheep, chickens, and cattle were on the land.

Leaving a hired man in charge, Tappan headed back to Minneapolis in late October. He had plenty of business to keep him occupied: his growing law practice, which brought in the family income, and Investors Syndicate. But in late January 1905 his mind wandered back to his northern lands. Perhaps a stock farm would turn a profit up there. From his time in California, he knew about the hearty, thick-fleeced Angora goats, whose wool brought prime prices. They had the added advantage of being, like all goats, great eaters, and would help clear the land of brush. That winter Tappan bought twelve of them for his homestead in northern Minnesota.

In April, John decided to give his land development project more of his time. He "took to the woods" once more, now with family in tow. It was not a simple journey. The railroad had just begun to penetrate heavily timbered areas. One could travel by flatcar as far as Tower, a nearby settlement. Then it was a three-hour walk through the woods. Tappan borrowed a wagon so that they could transport kitchen equipment, furniture, and food. But subsequent journeys were made on foot. John carried Marion on his shoulders. Winnie was pregnant and due in November. Oldest daughter Ruth trudged the whole way through the forest herself. The cabin had been prepared for their arrival, including a start on a thirty-foot-deep well that would eliminate the need for long walks to the river for water. The goats were also in place, doing their duty of clearing the land by eating down the grass to stubble and devouring leaves, branches, and small saplings. Meanwhile, others were taking up John's offer and settling on land nearby. That summer the Tappans saw the beginnings of a town that eventually came to be called, naturally enough, Angora, Minnesota.

Splitting his time between his new town-building venture and his city business, Tappan went back to Minneapolis in May. But he could not leave the cabin empty for long. Claim jumpers threatened to take over any good piece of property, especially one that had been recently improved. So Winnie and the children stayed in the cabin the rest of the summer. It was a beautiful spot and the fresh air away from the city, both John and Winnie agreed, was the best thing for growing children. Still, it meant that she had to make a home in a rude cabin, with no running water and the occasional face-to-face confrontation with a curious black bear.

By August, John was back. His vacation was a pleasing mixture of relaxation and physical labor. He harvested the hay, weeded the vegetable garden, repaired the barn, and got the cabin ready for winter. Other days he took the children fishing in the river and on excursions in the woods. The plan was for Winnie and the children to remain until October, and then return to the city in time to have her baby. But John was not able to stay the whole time. In September, he was called back to testify in Washington, D.C., on Investors Syndicate's methods of doing business. It was part of the continual tussling between the company and the Post Office regarding the legality of the plan. This time at least there was no threat of adverse publicity or stopped mails. But testifying took John away from what was becoming his second home, and second love.

To help Angora grow, Tappan sought to merge his office business with his newfound avocation. It was the ultimate solution to the high transactions and monitoring costs of mortgage lending. Not only could he visit the land where the funds were going, he actually had control over much of the surrounding settlement and local conditions. Syndicate monies went to other homesteaders who wanted to buy land in the north to farm or for timber. Inquiries were met with Tappan's personal reply. "There is a good opportunity there for a blacksmith and one who can also do wagon repairing, and there is also a good opportunity for anyone with a small amount of capital to go into the grocery and feed business."[35] Later, several of his friends settled in Angora, opening a post office and putting the rough little settlement on the map. Carl Nord ran a small store, selling flour from the Pillsbury mill in Minneapolis, and stocking sugar, lard, salt pork, oats, and clothing such as overalls, shoes, and socks. Angora had a duly elected town clerk and town supervisor. "Thus," reported the rural broadsheet, *Northland Farmer,* "the progress of civilization continues on all sides of us."[36]

The frontier was gradually being civilized, which was the way men like Tappan regarded the coming of commercial enterprise and settlement. Farmers turned over the soil, lumberjacks cut down old growth timber for prime hardwood, and hunters received bounties for killing off predatory wolves. Angora soon had its first industry, a sawmill owned by the Ofstad brothers. With houses and barns going up, they provided the lumber and shingles.[37] No longer would the population have to order sawed lumber weeks in advance from as far away as Virginia, or make do with rough cut logs.

Human progress could not tame all of nature, however. Returning for Winnie and the children in October 1905, John and his family were cabin bound by a sudden, severe late autumn snowstorm. It snowed continually for several days. To feed the animals, Tappan had to dig a tunnel to the barn, and he and the children ran back and forth from the house, lighting their way with candles. While waiting the weather out, John made plans to incorporate a new concern, the Northern Livestock and Improvement Company. Letters to the State Experiment Farm in Grand Rapids had convinced him that the best use of the land was stockraising. Northern Livestock's charter was "the raising of livestock, the buying, improving and cultivation of farm lands, and business essential thereto and connected therewith."[38] With $50,000 in initial capital, the new corporation set out acquiring more land in and around Tappan's homestead claim, as well as more Angora goats. Believing his project well launched, Tappan hired a local couple to look after the farm and returned with his family to Minneapolis.

The following spring brought Tappan back to his claim, and to some disappointment. Raising stock from a distance was an expensive and complicated affair. Someone had to live on the land and tend the animals year-round, which cost money. Winnie had given birth in the fall to their third child, John Elliott Tappan, Jr., whom the family called Elliott. After two daughters, John was elated to have a son. But now the Tappan family had grown too large to simply truck out to a remote cabin several times a year and expect to get any real farmwork done. The livestock ended up costing more than it brought in, so Tappan decided to sell his goats. They went to a local man named Johnson on a farm near Ashawa. Soon Angora the town outgrew its homestead origins, and Tappan outgrew his rustic adventure.

With the sale of the trademark goats, an era ended for Tappan. Apparently no one ever tried raising Angoras in the vicinity again, though the name stuck, and to this day a painting of an Angora goat hangs on the wall of the town's post office. Tappan had been the prime force in creating something out of nothing. If it had not panned out quite the way he had hoped, the experience nonetheless was part of what he regarded as the real work of humanity. He had by his own hands turned the chaos of nature into a new community, and transformed raw land into a profitable asset.

Tappan's venture into the wilderness might seem a strange one for a man of the city with a young law practice and a struggling investment operation. It reveals his romantic side, a return more than a decade later to the adventures of his youth. But it also reveals that the flame of reform, even utopian dreaming, still burned within. By founding a new community, a new outlet for the funds of his clients, he was engaging in the sort of hopeful planning for a better future that had long accompanied America's westward movement. Angora was not meant to be an alternative or religious commune, of course, but it was meant to offer people the sort of hope for a fresh start that many middle- and working-class aspirants to success sought. In the end, though, this evocation of the frontier proved more a diversion than the main focus for Tappan. No longer, even in still rural Minnesota, would men find that frontier opportunities such as transforming land, raising crops, and tending stock would be the ways to financial success. Most of Tappan's subsequent land development plans contributed to America's pursuit of leisure, not production. He continued to purchase land along the lakes of northern Michigan and Minnesota, but with the intention to promote vacation spots and tourism, the summertime pursuits of the new salaried middle class. Most of John's own work, moreover, would be similarly unglamorous and nonphysical. He had to answer the call of the office, not the call of the wild, from now on.

Tappan made several minor changes in the business of Investors Syndicate. In 1904, for example, the Syndicate began marketing a shorter term, seven-year contract, responding to a slowdown in the economy. Unlike the normal ten-year certificate, seven-year ones had fifty coupons attached, with the first maturing in as little as four months. Subscribers could take as many coupons as they liked, paying fifty cents per month for each. All coupons would be matured in eighty-four months. There was also no "membership" fee, or up-front load, making them all in all more attractive to those with less spare income to set aside.[39] Otherwise, business continued as usual. John found agents to sell contracts in as many locales as possible. Old contracts matured, and new ones came in at a steady clip. Word-of-mouth and labor-intensive selling "on the ground" continued to be the main ways of getting business.

The general pattern with Investors Syndicate was to innovate by offering contracts that were attractive to clients lower down on the socioeconomic scale. By reducing loads, making monthly payments more flexible, and decreasing times to initial maturity, Tappan made his investment plan more attractive to the cautious or to those with only minimal savings. In 1905, Investors Syndicate introduced a still shorter term contract. This one matured even faster. All money was paid back with interest due in just five years, making it, in Tappan's opinion, "the best investment contract put on the market by any company." In addition to a shorter horizon, the contracts offered simplicity and flexibility. Investors could put in any amount beginning at $2 per month. These advantages made it for a time the firm's biggest seller.

By 1908, the contract moved toward what would become its final form. The "Ten Year Guaranteed First Mortgage Gold Certificate" required a higher monthly fee, $6.15 per $1,000 of certificates. But it paid out full value in ten years. If it cost a bit more, it offered a new feature of reassuring security. After two years of payments, it could not be lapsed for the next six years. "So that if a person is out of work or employment, he is amply protected."[40]

Three children, his business, and an avocation as town builder kept Tappan extremely busy during these years. On top of that, his main source of income remained his law practice. He had a variety of clients and conducted a general practice mainly in civil law that included divorces, real estate transactions, wills and trusts, and occasional incorporations. He also handled all the land and real estate legal work growing out of Investors Syndicate.

At home, John and Winnie experienced the joys and problems that accompanied young children. Cold Minnesota winters brought on seemingly endless rounds of childhood illness. The days before routine vaccinations and antibiotics meant late nights with crying children suffering from colds, flu, whooping cough, and croup. The winter of 1906 was particularly difficult. Marion had flare-ups of the croup several times. She would wake up in the middle of the night unable to breathe, and the eldest, Ruth, would yell out to her parents, "Marion's got the croup!" John and Winnie would leap out of bed and rush Marion downstairs, turning on the kettle and holding her head near the steam until she could breathe again.

Holidays were the real moments of joy for the family. John loved holidays and celebrations of all sorts. He liked giving surprise gifts to his children, such as boxes of candy left for them to find on Valentine's Day. National holidays brought out his patriotic side, and were a chance for him to inculcate moral lessons that he believed were his duty as a father. His favorite story for Washington's Birthday was Parson Weems' famous fable about George and the cherry tree. Tappan repeated the tag line over and over to his young children: "Yes Father, I cannot tell a lie. I chopped down your cherry tree."

Though not a particularly religious man, Tappan followed a strong moral and personal code. His primary rule was the golden rule, "treat thy neighbor as thou would be treated." But his own theology was simple and straightforward: Believe in God, who was just, and believe that heaven awaited those who were deserving. "Deserving" he generally defined as those who had led a good life. He didn't see much need for elaborate organized religions. Sometimes he took pleasure in questioning scripture or pointing out inconsistencies in the Bible. He claimed he never understood why Christ had to die, if He was all-powerful. But having promised Winnie that the children would be raised Catholic, he fulfilled his pledge, taking them to Mass every Sunday.

Over the years he and the local Catholic priest, Father Cullen, developed a close relationship. Like Tappan, Father Cullen had a teasing sense of humor. "We're going to make a Catholic out of you yet, J. E." was Cullen's favorite line. "I watched you come up the aisle. You genuflected on your left knee. You've got to learn to genuflect on your right knee, you know." Tappan had no trouble returning this sort of friendly religious fire. When he began taking his children with him on business trips, he would always find the local Catholic church. On Friday meals, he reminded them, "Now children, it's Friday, so you must order fish. But I'm not Catholic, so I don't have to. I'm going to have a steak."

Sentimentality was not the sort of emotion that stood high on the list of successful Victorian men like Tappan. He believed that life was pretty much as one saw it, and that there were few real mysteries that could not be unraveled by a cold shot of logic and reason. There were not many overt displays of physical affection in the Tappan household, and both Winnie and

John preferred to instruct and correct their children, rather than praise them to build self-esteem. "Waste not, want not," was a favorite household maxim, which John practiced on his many hunting expeditions, cooking and eating what he shot. One summer he bought some bantam chickens as pets for the children to play with up at Angora. In the fall, Tappan decided that the practical thing to do was to kill and eat the chickens, knowing that they would not last the hard winter. He wrung their necks and Winnie prepared them for dinner. But when the meal was served, everyone except John sat like statues and stared at their plates, looking at what just that morning had been their pets. Unaware of what was going on, Tappan ate voraciously until suddenly Ruth could stand it no longer. She started to cry and then all the other children started to cry, too. John looked up in surprise as Winnie herded the wailing children out of the dinning room and into the kitchen, where she made them something else to eat. John remained out in the dining room, enjoying what he would later call some of the finest chicken he ever ate.

This sort of pragmatism did not crowd out fun, however. With his family and while on vacations, Tappan loved to be entertained, to indulge his sense of humor, and to experience an almost childlike wonder at nature and the world beyond the safe, sane, and durable realm of everyday life and business. During the autumn, state fairs were popular in the countryside around Minneapolis. John usually took the children for a day that combined celebration of rural values with thrilling spectacles aimed more at entertainment than edification. They saw "Dan Patch, the fastest harness horse in the world," who attempted to "beat the world's record" at the mile. (Dan failed, missing the mark by one and one-half seconds according to the *Northland Farmer*.)[41] There were livestock auctions, acrobats and performers, rides and sideshows, and reenactments of famous disasters and fires to give the audience the vicarious thrill of danger. Much like the traveling shows and amusement parks that were becoming popular in urban locations, the fairs brought to their audience a taste of the wider world, or at least a sensationalized version of it.

It was at holidays, though, that the Tappan family had the most fun, Christmas in particular. John was closest to his children when they were young and dependent on him, and he delighted in sending them letters from Santa or leaving them anonymous gifts on their birthdays. Even on these occasions, though, John took the opportunity to teach little lessons in virtue. He mailed them letters from his office from "Santa Claus," reminding them of their lapses in behavior and promising them rewards if they stayed good.

It was in Tappan's nature to enjoy surprises, tricks, and jokes, reverting from his sober and businesslike side at these moments. Each Christmas he favored one child with a special big surprise gift. One year, he picked Ruth for the treat. She was almost eight years old, mature enough for an expensive present. John bought her a ruby ring, but he wrapped it up in the peel of an orange he had carefully removed so that it was almost whole. He put the ring box inside the peel, which he tied with a string. Then he put the orange inside an old shoebox stuffed with newspaper. That all went into a larger box, and then a still larger box, until the entire, now enormous gift was wrapped in paper and tied with a bow.

Christmas morning, Ruth tore through what seemed like endless layers of boxes and wrapping until she found the orange. When she saw her gift was nothing more than a piece of fruit, she angrily threw it across the room. John roared with laughter and said, "Wait! There's something inside of that orange." When Ruth untied the string and opened the box, she was delighted enough to forgive Santa his little joke.

Nineteen-hundred-and-six had been a special year for the Tappan family. In April, they had their fourth child, a girl they decided to call Zita. John was at home once again for the birth. Ruth and Marion were thrilled. Zita was like a little baby doll to them. They played with her and enjoyed helping their mother care for her. Of all the children, Zita looked the most like Winnie. Ruth and Marion had poker-straight hair like their father. Elliott's was curly, but blond. Zita had her mother's dark, curly locks.

The family was complete with the birth of Charles Henry Tappan, who arrived Christmas Day, 1908. He was born during what was proving to be one of the coldest winters on record. New Year's Day brought howling storms, severe even by Minnesota standards. Then, suddenly, it warmed and began to rain. Tappan described the change in climate to a friend in Seattle: "Have been having some pretty cold weather here but the last week has been like April, rain, etc. So you are not so much ahead of us in the weather after all."[42] It was on one of those dreary, unseasonable January nights that Marion came home from school feeling sick. The next day she was much worse and Winnie called the doctor. Not liking the sound of her symptoms, he rushed over, fearing the worst. His fears were confirmed as soon as he saw her. Marion was seriously ill with scarlet fever.

Scarlet fever was one of the most feared childhood killers of turn-of-the-century America. It was also an extraordinarily complex disease.

Unpredictable symptoms could leave one victim with deeply infected sores and high fever, another with a mild rash, and be all but invisible in a third. High fever, swelling of the tongue, a red rash over the whole body, coma, and death claimed between a quarter and a third of its childhood victims. Unlike many infectious diseases, it attacked poor and well-to-do alike. In 1858, Charles Darwin's young son had died of scarlet fever. Doctors would not fully comprehend its etiology or methods of transmission until the 1930s.

Though less often epidemic by the early twentieth century, scarlet fever could spread very widely from its source of origin. It passed not simply from person to person, but from animal to person. Cows harbor the same pathogens that cause the disease in people, and cow's milk proved to be an important but elusive vector for outbreaks. In 1911-1912, Chicago saw an extreme eruption of milk-borne scarlet fever that infected 10,000 and killed 200. As people moved to cities and consumed milk from commercial dairies instead of their own cows, they gave the fever a chance to spread far and wide. Less than a third of the milk consumed in the United States was pasteurized at the time. The high incidence of milk-transmitted scarlet fever would help usher in routine milk pasteurization as the link was gradually understood.

It was also extremely hard to prevent the spread of the disease to other family members once it entered the home. One bout with scarlet fever conferred immunity to the toxins that produced the characteristic bright red skin pigmentation, but not necessarily to the disease itself, which is caused by one of twenty types and sixty subtypes of group A hemolytic streptococci. A recovered patient might well contract a different strain and, though possessing no outward symptoms, still be infectious. Since children had less time to gain exposure to the various streptococci, they were more vulnerable than adults.[43]

With few effective remedies, the most that could be done was to wait and hope for a mild case. Doctor Donaldson ordered a quarantine of the Tappan household for the next six weeks. John hired a nurse to care for Marion full time, and both the nurse and Marion stayed upstairs. To warn outsiders, a sign hung on the front door—DANGER: SCARLET FEVER. So warned, people avoided the house and walked on the opposite side of the street when passing by.

While Marion was quarantined, no one, not even her mother, was allowed in the room, and the nurse was not allowed downstairs. Winnie slid plates of food up on the landing, and when they were finished, the nurse rinsed the plates in hot water and put them back out onto the landing. Winnie took them down to the kitchen to be washed in boiling water, all precautions taken so that none of the other children would come down with the deadly disease.

On February 5, 1909, Tappan wrote to his friend Sue Quimby, cautioning, "Do not come to the house because Marion has scarlet fever and the house is under quarantine. Marion has been very sick but seems to be getting along all right now although she is not out of danger. We have her shut up in the play room upstairs with a trained nurse and none of the family including Winnie have been permitted to go in the room and see her since she has been sick, as we are trying to keep the rest of the children from getting it, if possible." It was not possible. Two weeks after Marion was diagnosed, Ruth and Elliott came down with the fever, too. They were quarantined upstairs with the nurse.[44]

While his children were ill, Tappan continued to go to the office every day, at least for half the day. An unfaltering optimist, he was certain that they would recover. Soon the whole house would be back to normal. There seemed little reason to fall still further behind on work, especially during these crucial months with Investors Syndicate's new gold certificate on its way and the property at Angora to look after. By March, his faith seemed to be rewarded. Marion was getting better and the doctor was sanguine that both she and Ruth would make full recoveries. Elliott was still in some danger, but he too had had only a mild case of the deadly disease. No one else had gotten sick. Winnie was especially grateful that her infant, Charles, and two-year-old Zita had been spared an illness infamous for taking its toll on the young and weak.

The house had been tense and gloomy during the worst of the quarantine. But March was getting close to Zita's third birthday. She had not seen her older siblings for many weeks, and hardly understood the dangers they faced. To distract her from what was going on, Winnie started to tell her about the birthday party she would have, with cake, ice cream, and lots of presents. Zita was excited, and went around the house shouting, "my buffday is coming, my buffday is coming." She was an angelic child, with a sweet disposition, very loving and caring. Finally, one night when the doctor was leaving, he gave Winnie the news they had been waiting for. Marion could come downstairs the next day, and Ruth in two days. Winnie was ecstatic. She could hardly contain herself and said to Zita, "Marion will be downstairs tomorrow." Zita ran around the room, her face lit up with joy that she would get to see her older sister again.

When Marion came down the next day, Zita was so happy that she ran up to hug and kiss her sister. The following day, she did the same to Ruth. Marion still had some unhealed scabs on her face from scratching the rash during her delirium, but Winnie thought nothing of it. The doctor had said they were cured and no longer contagious.

About four days later, after dinner, Zita complained that she felt funny. Winnie called the doctor, who came over immediately. After examining the child, he confirmed John and Winnie's worst fears. Now Zita too had contracted scarlet fever. Marion may have contracted the disease from milk, which often meant a mild case. Direct person to person exchange was usually worse. Though he said nothing, Dr. Donaldson already knew that Zita was much sicker than any of her siblings had been.

Upstairs she went with the nurse. Winnie was beside herself. Just when she thought the ordeal was finished, that all of her children had escaped danger, it was starting all over again. She was too nervous to sleep, spending nights downstairs in the library, pacing the house through the early morning hours. John stayed upstairs near the sickroom. Winnie could not bear to be alone, so Marion slept with her. Winnie had never been a good sleeper and now she barely got an hour's rest each night.

Though Zita was in the same room with her brother Elliott, the two-year-old spent a good part of the first day crying hysterically for her mother. She had never before been separated from Winnie. Winnie called Doctor Donaldson and asked if she could go to her. The doctor replied, "If you go to Zita and contract scarlet fever, you will definitely give it to the baby because you are nursing him, and if he gets it he will surely die." He told her it was her decision, but if she went to Zita and contracted scarlet fever, she might lose both children. Winnie finally decided to stay downstairs to protect Charles, but she was torn to pieces every time she heard Zita. The little girl screamed, "I want my Mama, I want my Mama" for hours on end, while Winnie sat listening with the baby in her lap, tears streaming down her face. Marion remembered the scene vividly. She recalled waking up in the early morning, while it was still dark, and seeing her mother sitting at the dressing table, crying to herself over and over again, "My baby is dying, my baby is dying." Lying still in bed, Marion would watch her mother, who cried until dawn, and then, when the first shaft of light crept into the room, left to prepare breakfast for the family.

In a week or so, the doctor announced, Marion would be well enough to stay with Zita. Having survived the fever, she was now believed to be immune.

Everyone thought that Zita's loneliness for her mother would be comforted by the presence of her sister. Winnie loved the idea and it cheered everyone up looking forward to that day. But two days later, Zita suddenly got worse. Winnie grew more and more frantic, as her daughter's condition seemed to be deteriorating fast. Finally, John sent for a specialist from Chicago, who arrived the next day with Dr. Donaldson. The two men spent a very long time examining Zita, then came down the long staircase. Winnie stood at the bottom, watching them descend, awaiting the prognosis. When the doctors reached the bottom of the stairs, the specialist looked at Winnie and said, "Only God can save your child." Winnie burst into tears and fell to the floor sobbing. John tried to help her, but she was too distraught to move. She just remained on the floor, her head on the stair, crying inconsolably.

Three more days passed. Winnie could no longer wait. Taking the risk of infecting her infant son, she went upstairs to Zita. It was too late. The child had lapsed into a coma and no longer knew her mother. On March 15, Zita died. She died in the early evening, and the nurse informed John first. When he heard the news, he went to Zita's bed to look at her one last time. She lay there, her tiny form wrapped in a white blanket as though she were asleep. Her face was framed by the auburn curls that made her look so much like her mother. Her hands clenched her favorite toy. John knelt down by the bed and covered his face with his hands. Then he went downstairs to call the undertakers. They arrived that night to take Zita's body away, going up the back stairs to avoid the family. But everyone heard their heavy footsteps as they climbed to the nursery. Winnie sat in a rocking chair, saying over and over again, "They're taking my baby, they're taking my baby." In desperation, John finally said to her, "Winnie, if you don't stop, you are going to crack up." She paid no attention to him, and just kept on rocking.

1. John Elliott Tappan with sister, Carrie, in Oshkosh, WI, about 1872
(All photos from the private collection of Carol Heher Peters)

2. John Elliott Tappan—1890

3. Winifred Gallagher (left) with her sister, Anna, in Minneapolis, about 1894

4. Winnie's wedding photograph, November 1896

5. In their automobile, 1906: front seat, from left to right—Elliott, Marion, John; back seat, from left to right, Adelaide, Ruth, Winnie, Zita

6. About 1908: from left to right—Ruth, Marion, Elliott, and Zita

7. Zita with her favorite Teddy bear—1908

8. Ruth in her Easter coat, Dupont Ave., 1908

9. Marion, 1916

10. Ruth, 1916

11. Salt Lake City sight-seeing bus, about 1912: Adelaide—2nd from left, front (with glasses and hat); Winnie—4th row from left, front (in white blouse); John—back row, on left

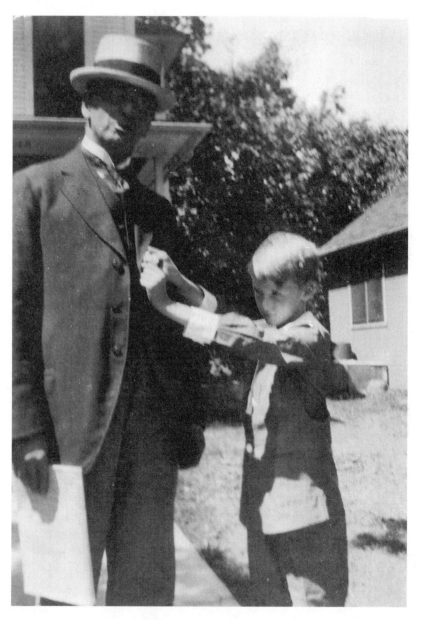

12. John with Charles, summer, 1916

13. Ruth and the Sheik of the Sakkara,
at Memphis, Egypt, 1924

14. 1924 passport photo: front—Winnie, John; back—Elliott, Charles

15. John, about 1910

16. John, about 1930

CHAPTER FIVE

ADVERSITY AND SURVIVAL

A century ago, families dealt with death in a different manner than today. To some extent, they had already begun to follow practices that would become common by the mid-twentieth century. Professionals, "undertakers," had removed much of the process of preparing bodies for interment from the hands of relatives. Outside of major cities, however, undertaking was often more part-time job than profession, a sideline of transfer, storage, and haulage companies that had wagons and carts. Memorialization of the deceased was an elaborate and well-established ritual. Each detail of the funeral was expressive, down to the meaning of the type and color of flower chosen. On the Tappan door, there was a sprig of pink roses, the traditional symbol to tell passersby that a child had died. Inside the house, Zita lay in a small white coffin. At the gravesite would be a headstone that expressed, more than could words or public display, the feelings of the family. Especially in the case of young children, monuments could be redolent with emotion. Common motifs included angels and cherubs, far different than the skulls and reminders of mortality, or stoical Bible passages, that had once appeared on graves.[1]

Men and women experienced loss and death differently, as well. After Zita's funeral, John sat down with all his children. He explained to them that their mother had taken the loss very badly and that she would not be herself for a very long time. Winnie's extreme reaction in part stemmed from her own mother's early death. As a child, she had felt deserted by her mother. So when she made the decision to stay with her infant son Charles, she believed she had repeated with her own daughter what had happened to her. She had deserted Zita when she most needed her. This sense of guilt and failure as a parent drove Winnie into severe depression.

Winnie stopped eating, and sank into a sadness that did not abate for several years. During that time, she kept the house clean, washed, ironed, and starched the clothes, and prepared three meals a day. But her movements were mechanical, as though she were working in a daze. She never smiled, never joked, and soon the rest of the children dreaded returning home from school. Occasionally Winnie would bring one of Zita's dresses out of the closet, hold it, and cry. The prolonged grief bothered John and he soon learned never to speak of Zita. Mere mention of her name would cause Winnie to burst into tears.

Though her behavior was extreme, it was not considered wholly unusual for the time. Mourning was a ritual taken seriously, and it could be practiced for years. Far from trying to forget about death and put losses behind them, parents or widows could dedicate their entire remaining lives to the memory of the departed. They built a connection between the living and dead by wearing suits of black, dressing the entire family in somber colors, sometimes even draping the house in black crepe. After the funeral, Winnie collected a few of Zita's things, such as a handkerchief she had always carried around, several pennies she had liked to play with, and her pearl necklace. She put them in a box with a card that read, "Zita Loretta Tappan, our little darling, the dearest and most beautiful flower that God ever created. Born April 27, 1906, died March 15, 1909." She kept this box on her dressing table, where her family found it thirty years later, after Winnie's death.

John's reaction was different. At his most distraught, he said to his children, "It would have been better if God had taken the baby, as he is only a few weeks old, and your mother has not gotten attached to him yet." Several months later, he wrote to a friend, revealing his state of mind. "We have had trouble since I last saw you. The children had scarlet fever, and for thirteen weeks the house was under quarantine, one child after another coming down with it, and we were obligated to keep an expert nurse all the time, and with the other expenses it made a very heavy expense, and then the worst blow of all was that we lost little Zita, and this blow we cannot get over. All of our troubles paled into insignificance as compared to a blow like that, and think how foolish we were to worry about other things which were trivial in comparison."[2]

The letter showed the sides of Tappan's personality struggling with each other as he tried to come to terms with the loss. One side is Tappan the straightforward and pragmatic man, noting even a little coldly the cost of the nursing of his children. As a progressive and optimistic personality, he was embracing a more contemporary attitude toward death. Death and grief could be best handled by encouraging words or, in extreme cases, mitigated through the intervention of professionals, increasingly secular ones—doctors, funeral directors, psychologists. Yet death was not to be so easily sanitized, not when opportunistic disease could so readily claim the lives of innocents. When the human and emotional side of Tappan dominates, he rebukes himself for worrying over trivial and mundane matters in the tragedy of the loss of his child. Ultimately, though, John was an optimist. He considered it fortunate that only one child was lost; it could have been much worse. He also understood that there were four other children who needed their parents, and they might well interpret Winnie's feelings for Zita as a wish that one of them had died instead. John did not ignore the pain the loss caused, but by his definition of masculinity, it was his job to absorb the blow, keep the household running, and get on with life.

No doubt, at some level, John was able to accept the comforting little statements that people make when someone has suffered an irreparable loss, homilies such as the one a neighbor repeated to Marion: "I don't know how your mother expected to keep Zita. She was an Angel of God, and He only loaned her to your mother for a little while. Your mother should not have expected to keep her." In this regard, John would never quite understand the long, deep sadness, the never-healed scars that Winnie would carry her whole life. He would never forget the loss, but it would not show on him.

Late that spring Winnie told John that she could no longer live in their house on Dupont Avenue. In summers past, the family had taken vacations at Lake Minnetonka, but she was reminded of Zita there, too. So that summer John found a place on Beard Avenue, on the west shore of Cedar Lake near the outskirts of Minneapolis. He decided to buy it, a new home not haunted by painful memories. It was a good change for the family. Cedar Lake was out in the country in 1909, but still close enough for John to get to work. It was a refuge for the children and it lifted Winnie's spirits. When fall came and it was time to go back to Dupont Avenue, Winnie resisted. She was not yet ready to see the room in which her child had died, or the toys and clothes still neatly stored in the closet. With the children's eager approval, John decided it best if they stayed on Cedar Lake all winter. He rented out the house on Dupont Avenue and made the necessary arrangements.

Living on the lake, it turned out, had its own problems. Although John could take a trolley from its last stop, nearest the lake, he had to cross over the water every day. He decided he no longer needed a car, but a boat. When the lake froze for the winter, he and the children could walk, but even that created new worries. Winnie would watch each morning as they set out until their bodies vanished in the distance, fearful of an accident or of one of them falling through thin ice. The local ice company cut its profits out of Cedar Lake, taking so much ice that eventually no one could cross, and they all had to walk around. To the children, it was often tempting to skate across the lake anyway, and as the spring thaw arrived, they would defy parental orders even as they heard loud cracks under their feet.

Winnie spent each day at home alone with the baby. For John, it was enough to focus on work, the core attribute of manliness. If feelings of grief stem from doubts about self-worth, then men, who gained their worth from their work, could deal with grief by working more. Activity was the accepted remedy for sorrows, troubles, and defeats. The office, moreover, was where men found conviviality, fraternity, and association. For Winnie, home had become a lonely and isolating environment, the exact opposite of the expected female realm that was supposed to be composed of a supportive network of friends and family. But few friends ventured out to the lake when winter descended. Winnie and John had always been a bit isolated from Minneapolis society. Now they were geographically isolated as well.

Still very depressed, Winnie vented nervous energy in cooking, as if taking her anger out on the stove. She made large dinners, baked breads and a pie each day. She kept soups simmering on the stove and nourished her children with the ancient home remedy "pot liquor," or the broth left over from boiling vegetables. There were treats as well. To warm up the children as they returned from the frigid walk home, she greeted them with fresh-baked cinnamon rolls.

Though her sorrow abated somewhat, she was not always capable of controlling her emotions. One cold winter morning when Elliott was late for school, he tried to beat the clock by taking his bicycle, though he had been forbidden from riding it for fear of frostbite. By the time he reached school, his nose and chin were stinging. Alarmed at the sight of him, the teacher told Ruth to take him home. With Elliott crying from the pain, they arrived and told Winnie what had happened. She was so enraged that he had disobeyed her orders that she refused to help him. It was characteristic of Winnie to be unremittingly harsh when her orders were disobeyed, but Ruth was horrified with this display of anger. Though she was supposed to return right to school, she stayed, and, remembering the treatment for frostbite, soaked his skin in cold water until he felt better. It was only a mild case and Elliott suffered no serious or permanent injury. But Winnie's reaction indicated how much pain and anger she still felt over the loss of Zita.

John was concerned enough about her state and her loneliness that he sought boarders to take up the extra bedrooms. Better, he thought, to have someone else in the house with Winnie at all times. He apparently had no luck. Winnie despised the loneliness of the winters, but could not bring herself to return to Dupont Avenue, so in April 1910, John rented the house out again. In the summer, Cedar Lake was a pleasure, especially for the children, who enjoyed swimming, walking through the woods, and picnics on the grass. In a few months, he hoped, things would improve.

That summer, John planted four trees on the property, one for each child. Winnie put in a large vegetable garden with her favorite foods: tomatoes, peppers, strawberries, raspberries, lettuce, and cucumbers. At the end of the season, she put up applesauce, pickled peppers, jams, and jellies. John and the children also began a ritual they would continue every summer. At nine each night, with the Minnesota sky still light, they all put their bathing suits on and ran down the sloping lawn for a quick dip in the lake. Then, back to the house for bed. The swim cooled everyone off enough to help them sleep soundly.

It was less lonely in the summer months. Priests came out for regular visits. John took them swimming and canoeing while Winnie prepared a large and inviting meal. Friends and family stopped by to escape the hot, humid days. Winnie was still not ready to return to their old home, however. So John prepared to spend another winter on Cedar Lake. He had plenty to do at work to keep him busy as well. Recovering from Zita's death was draining, but Investors Syndicate had its own troubles.

Nearly simultaneous with personal tragedy came a series of blows to the company. Throughout the family crisis, John had kept up his optimistic correspondence, noting that, "The Investors Syndicate is growing right along, nothing fast but has a steady growth. . . . We have at present $85,000 in assets."[3] In May of 1910, however, Tappan also expressed the first in a number of reservations about the firm's cash position. "Don't call on us for money," he wrote to Charles Featherstone, "unless you have to have it as we have never been so hard pressed for cash."[4] The sources of distress seem to have been twofold. First, as the contracts matured, the firm was not growing new business fast enough to keep sufficient cash on hand for payments. The Ten Year Gold Certificate, a new version of the face amount certificate that the company believed had great promise, proved a slow, if consistent, seller. This was a nagging, long-term problem that could only be solved by restructuring sales operations. More immediate concerns loomed on the asset side as well, however. Returns from investments were slow to come in, and Investors Syndicate was going through a change in its investment strategy.

To some degree, growth of the company entailed a movement away from the original conception. Tappan had largely placed company assets in land mortgages. Born in the agrarian controversy of the 1890s, the Syndicate had been conceived as a more democratic capital market institution that nonetheless practiced sound business policies. Any hope that it might bring capital to the farm belt, however, soon vanished. The highest profits and most secure investments were to be found in lending money to urban home builders. Lending strategy was focused on improved city real estate, an obvious choice in a growing city such as Minneapolis. The city's need for funds was so great that Tappan found, "we have never been able to obtain sufficient money to supply the demand for this kind of loan."[5] Without a single dollar spent on advertising, he was actually turning down loan applications for want of money to lend.

Urban investments had obvious advantages. America was urbanizing at its fastest rate ever. Much of this growth was not in the established East, but in new western and southern cities such as Minneapolis, Chicago, Atlanta, Houston, and Los Angeles. In the twentieth century, housing in these cities would boom, as adjacent lands were developed into desirable suburbs. New urban technologies, such as sewers, electricity, and streetcars contributed both to the urban boom and to the desire of middle-class homeowners to build modern houses accessible to all of these conveniences, or to remodel older ones for the same purpose. Nonetheless, despite this seemingly limitless demand, southern and western cities had trouble attracting capital. Like western farmers, ambitious urbanites west of the Mississippi had reason to complain that they were at a disadvantage compared to the East.[6]

The urban mortgage market, like the market for farm mortgages, had special problems that discouraged movement of funds from capital-rich areas to western locales needing funds. It was as bad, or worse, than the rural mortgage market. Capital for the expensive business of residential construction—which reached 8 percent of GNP in the late nineteenth century—had to come from the old and established markets in the Northeast. Remembering the high rate of default in the panics of 1873 and 1893, however, eastern lenders were cautious with their money. No lender wanted to be stuck with foreclosed property to sell. As with farm mortgages, it was difficult for eastern lenders to find reputable agents, or to assess the quality of information they were given. Agents of lenders had incentive to oversell properties, making their money on commissions. Urban borrowers in the West therefore ended up paying higher rates of interest, received shorter-term loans, and were permitted to borrow less money relative to their property holdings than counterparts located near the channels of capital back East. The impact was to reduce the rate of city growth, drive up housing costs, and make it more difficult to own a home.[7]

Into this breech stepped Investors Syndicate. As with the farm mortgage market, the home mortgage market fit the company's general goals of advancing capital for productive purposes to those who would have otherwise found capital hard to come by. Tappan proudly proclaimed his intention of "encouraging thrift in getting a home paid for [with] small loans on the humble home," whose monthly fee schedule was usually less than rent.[8] Before World War II, few lenders structured amortizing debt for homeowners that provided for level payments over the whole term. Most houses were constructed with short-term, renewable loans that had to be paid in full at the end in one giant balloon payment. Tappan's policy was different. He permitted relatively long-term borrowing, and installment payments to extinguish the loan. By allowing small monthly installments, Tappan was permitting "a great many" to purchase a home, "when they could never save enough to pay off a straight loan." Like his installment savings plan, the installment credit feature was, as he saw it, a great boon for the average person. For these reasons, Tappan's plan proved so popular that he had trouble keeping up with demand. By not charging any commission or up-front fees, and by giving borrowers a long time to pay back in small monthly install-ments, Investors Syndicate gained a reputation as a good place to borrow money, as well as a good place to invest money.[9]

Still, the move into the home mortgage market was a step away from the original ideas of economic independence founded in an essentially agrarian economy. Farmers were once again at a disadvantage. They did not have the sort of regular monthly income that enabled them to take advantage of the savings features of the certificates, or the payback features of the loans. Farmers obtained their income annually, when they sold their crop. Tappan's mortgages were designed to be paid off by regular remit-tances in small amounts, and his certificates were to be bought in the same fashion. Both worked best for those who received regular paychecks. Overall, farm families saved less than did nonfarm families, in part simply because they were poorer. Indeed, for much of the period between 1897 and 1920, their saving was negative. But even when farmers saved, much of their money went back into the farm, as capital equipment or to improve the land. When the farm economy improved in the 1920s, many rural families put their savings not into paper securities such as the face amount certificate, but into the "durables revolution," electrifying the home, modernizing the dairy, buying a car or piano.[10]

Urbanites, on the other hand, had many of the characteristics that fit the needs of Investors Syndicate. Urban borrowers were generally salaried workers, with steady jobs and regular incomes. Their demand for home ownership, and to improve the homes they owned, was increasing. In the western states, Tappan's stronghold, urban growth had replaced frontier farming as the mainstay of growth. Even in the farm belt, cities such as Minneapolis, Omaha, and Kansas City were maturing rapidly. These were the initial outlets for Syndicate funds. On the West Coast, Los Angeles by the early decades of the twentieth century was growing fastest of all, and it ended up absorbing the lion's share of Syndicate funds by the 1930s. About half of the monies were scattered in communities from Oregon to Florida, although New York City also took a good chunk of it as well.[11]

Urban real estate was a shift from Tappan's original plan in another way. Home ownership was not exactly the same as property for independent production. Though a capital good, a home did not by itself supply the basis for a competency. This did not stop astute urban developers and house builders from conflating the home with the masculine laborer's place of work or the farmer's homestead, drawing on the language of independence and republicanism. Leaders in the mortgage lending industry spoke of the home as a bulwark of democracy and liberty, echoing the older notion of the independent producer as champion of democracy.[12] Yet the twentieth-century American home was more a domestic space than a public one. Work and private life were increasingly being separated as cities grew and streetcars, trolleys, and finally motor cars enabled men to commute from suburban homes into the city. Cities themselves were increasingly differentiated, with the old, jumbled center, composed of shops, wharves, warehouses, and residences, giving way to a specialized downtown. Downtowns were not places to live, but to work, increasingly in giant office towers and skyscrapers. By the same token, homes were places of respite and rest from the masculine world of work. Some women went downtown to work, but generally not married middle-class women, certainly not those with children. They stayed home, now a place far from the work world.

When builders and lenders appealed to the virtues of home ownership, they were giving old language new connotations. "Property rights, especially ownership of a home makes better men and women and better citizens." These were laudable goals to be sure. But however much home ownership might appear a democratizing experience, in an age dominated by giant corporations and centralizing financial institutions it was a far cry from the independence and equality that property had once conferred. The domesticated home was, like the durable consumer good, more an item of consumption than of production. Home builders and mortgage lenders seemed to realize this, when they aimed their appeals to women, just as marketers of consumer goods were doing the same, realizing that women made the household's most important consumption decisions.[13]

Still, if Investors Syndicate was not exactly fulfilling the old agrarian and producerist dream, it was moving money into hard-to-reach western markets. For all the potential problems this entailed, the company seems to have run into few snags. Initially relying mainly on John Tappan to inspect properties around Minneapolis, it expanded its loan portfolio by drawing on the knowledge of friends and associates for more distant investments. Later, it opened branch offices in key cities, staffed by salaried employees. They provided appraisals of properties and handled foreclosures. The company did not generally use independent brokers, whose incentive might have been to encourage questionable loans.[14]

Tappan's move to Cedar Lake also gave him the opportunity to become a land developer again. He built a series of summer cabins with Syndicate funds. It was a good decision, for a few years later the city dug canals connecting Cedar and a number of other lakes, a huge dredging operation that attracted onlookers for miles around and greatly increased the value of the property.[15] He also had property in Angora that was appreciating, as well as some investments in Washington State. These mortgages were handled by friends and close contacts in each place. Former Syndicate attorney Henry Farnham had moved to Nevada, where he provided information on land investments there. In Isle Royale, long-time Angora friend Kneut Kneutson requested funds for development from the Syndicate. Tappan also had maintained strong ties to his old stomping grounds in the Pacific Northwest as well, investing in lands he knew to be valuable for their timber.[16] Other funds went into land in Montana and South Dakota, where Tappan spent many holidays fishing and hunting. He had family connections in both places as well. Winnie's sister Anna and her husband lived in South Dakota and her brother Luke in Missoula, Montana.

In all of these distant investments, Tappan had firsthand knowledge or could count on objective information from close friends. By mixing business with pleasure, and creating an extensive network of friends in the different places he visited, Tappan was able to handle mortgages in these distant locations.[17]

Problems arose when Investors Syndicate sought to expand outside of these personal and professional networks. To diversify its portfolio, the company made a substantial, $10,000 loan to the National Securities Company, a real estate loan and investment operation that made and sold mortgages on property. But the strategy backfired. In May 1910, National Securities went bankrupt, forcing Investors Syndicate to write off the loan. By placing funds with the firm, the Syndicate had gained the advantages of diversification, but at the cost of being one step removed from the actual investments. There was no easy way to supervise and monitor where the money finally ended up. When National Securities went into receivership, Tappan, as the major creditor, was forced to take over a portfolio of land he had not personally inspected. In addition, Investors Syndicate was forced to pay some of the taxes and to take up prior mortgages made before the loan was signed. All told, some $15,000 in Syndicate funds was tied up with National Securities.[18]

It proved to be a near disaster. "There has never been a time since I organized the Syndicate that we have been so hard pressed for cash as we have been and are right now," confided Tappan. "We have plenty of money out," he noted, "but it seems that when we want it in, we cannot get it."[19] He was forced to "scrape the bottom of the cash drawer," to meet a $200 obligation on a certificate. Tappan prided himself on meeting each and every company obligation on time. Yet, he confessed, "It is absolutely impossible for us to meet everything as it becomes due."[20]

This was especially irksome to a man who believed reputation all important. His frustration flashed into anger when one subscriber wrote a threatening letter and mentioned getting an attorney if he did not receive his due immediately. Tappan had been out of the office when the first request for payment had arrived, and by the time he returned, the second, threatening letter was in hand. In a detailed, personal response, he began, "We have no desire to repudiate an honest debt and are perfectly able and willing to pay our debts. But we are not on earth to be frightened, bluffed, or bull-dozed and if you wish to place it in your attorney's hands, we are perfectly willing that you should do so, in which case we would see to it that your attorney earned and got some fees."[21] "Good business sense and courtesy" meant trusting in the proven honesty and reputation of those with whom one did business. Threats were an insult, and lawyers an unnecessary expense, as far as Tappan was concerned.

The same values applied on the other end, when Tappan sought money due the Syndicate. Cash shortages made him devote substantial time to clearing the books of receivables. He wrote personally to each and every one who owed money. Those who honestly sought to pay their obligations saw his lenient side. One old friend in Chicago, who had borrowed $250 for "30 days" three years prior, still had not repaid the debt. When the man avoided a stream of notices, Tappan contacted the man's employer for assistance, before it became necessary to take legal action. The result was yet another plea for more time. Tappan then launched into a lecture on responsibility. "I hated to take the step I did," he wrote, "but you simply forced me to do it by your lack of attention to this note." After explaining the firm's legal obligations and the requirements of state laws on the company, Tappan concluded, "Now Fred, you can have the time that you ask for in your letter, that is, you can make a payment on the 15th of every month, but you must remember that you have made this same promise to me several times and you have never kept it once. . . . I shall give you fair warning that this time the promise must be kept or I am going to get the matter cleaned up and disposed of absolutely one way or another. When can we expect the first check and what amount can you afford to pay each month?"[22] Tappan could be liberal, but he still expected responsibility, and for all his dislike of legal proceedings, he was the sort of man who would pursue a debt of ten cents if it were a matter of principle.

The same month as the National Securities bankruptcy, the Syndicate received a second blow. J. W. Earl, who since 1900 had run the agency system marketing certificates, suffered a stroke. At first, it appeared a minor one, and Tappan wrote to a mutual friend, "Mr. Earl has had a stroke of paralysis and was in a very serious condition, but has rapidly recovered and we expect him to be all right within a short time."[23] Unfortunately, Tappan's optimism betrayed him. Earl was out of action for several months. It was a bad time to be without the head of the sales force. Tappan needed money, to meet obligations on maturing contacts and to lend and invest to generate income that could make up for the National Securities debacle. "We are getting some new business," he admitted, "but not a good deal." Earl's incapacity, including paralysis and inability to speak, probably hurt here.[24] In July, Earl took an extended vacation to recover in Isle Royale, Michigan. But his recovery stopped short of full. Still unable to return to full-time work, Earl finally passed away on December 28, 1910. The gap he left in the company was so large that the next two years would be the slowest in the history of Investors Syndicate.

Tappan had lost not only a crucial partner, but a man who had been with him from the earliest days, practically a founder of the firm. His passing coincided with another major personnel change. In October, Carrie Guthrie, Tappan's sister, resigned as the firm's bookkeeper, a position she had held from almost the beginning. It proved difficult to replace her. Not only were qualified bookkeepers hard to find, but the company had never fully systematized its accounting from the early, catch-as-catch-can days. Carrie had developed her own bookkeeping variations, reflecting the experimental and innovative nature of the Syndicate. It was hard to train a replacement or explain to them what she did and why she did it.

The losses came just as Investors Syndicate was hopeful that its new certificates would begin to sell. The new product helped put to rest concerns about lapsed contracts, which had always been a source of suspicion from regulators and potential customers. The new certificates contained more liberal loan and surrender features, and paid back principle plus 4 percent interest in case the contract holder died before making all payments. "They are absolutely payable at the end of the period instead of being dependent upon earnings, etc., as your present contracts are," Tappan explained to one client.[25] He wrote to each of his contract holders, explaining the new provisions and offering to exchange their existing certificates for new ones on favorable terms.

Pressed by a shortage of help, Tappan fought all winter to get things back under his control. But in November 1910, Marion came down with diphtheria and Charles contracted typhoid fever. Winnie was frantic at the arrival of another round of deadly childhood illness, not even two years after Zita's death. Given the medicine of the time, there was little to do but wait and hope. The diphtheria passed in five weeks and the typhoid fever in four. After Marion became ill, the family moved back to Dupont Avenue, believing it to be healthier than a winter on the lake. The move plunged Winnie deeper into depression, and John had his hands full trying to calm her and look after the rest of the family.

With much of Tappan's life in upheaval, 1911 started off shaky. John continued to move cautiously at Investors Syndicate, cutting costs, pressing those who owed him for money. His appeals were taking on a strained, emotional quality. To one slow-paying debtor, he wrote, "I would as soon think of cutting off my right hand as of throwing down a friend who had befriended me as I did you in this deal." While the debtor shirked his obligations, Tappan's own life was being pressed right to the margin. "You know how I have worked in trying to keep the Syndicate going," he reminded him. "My wife and myself have economized, we have not traveled around the country but have stayed at home and saved."[26]

The connection between Tappan's personal and business finance was extremely close. He still took no salary from Investors Syndicate, but he used the company funds for investments in his own lands, and projects of friends and partners. Sometimes loans made to "personal friends" required stretching the acceptable range of assets. But such loans were made on the basis of strong ties, mutual respect, and the importance of reciprocity in local business communities. Tappan still expected that he would be repaid, because in such cases "justice and right" as well as friendship were especially strong motivations.

Though today this sort of commingling of personal and business matters might raise suspicion, it was common practice among financial institutions of the time. In the early nineteenth century, the first commercial banks emerged as local institutions for mobilizing and managing the funds of a small group of shareholders, directing them into favorable local land and business deals. Deposit banking and services to the general public came later. Savings and loans continued in a similar vein. "Owned" by their depositors, they could be seen as vehicles for collective investment, placing capital into home mortgages, especially for the depositors. Many were run by real estate investors and builders, who expected to make little profit on the loans, but benefited by encouraging buyers to purchase homes they built. Even today, local commercial banks often operate in a similar manner. Though they have trustees and directors to watch out for fraud or misappropriation, the crucial investment committee that lends funds is often composed of or closely connected to important local land and business interests, many of whom are friends of the bank executives. Such close connections provide a way of establishing trust in debtor-creditor relations and supply useful information on the best new investment opportunities around.

By drawing broadly on funds from clients in different locations, Tappan was moving toward a more public conception of finance. He acted as fiduciary agent for the subscribers whose money he solicited. Yet it made sense that he invested these funds in properties that he was most closely connected with and knowledgeable about, to avoid the high costs and managerial difficulties of dealing with land mortgages. In fact, as the sour deal with National Securities indicated, he got into more trouble when lending took place at arm's length, without his close personal supervision.

Still, use of "other people's money" remained a perpetual source of tension in the public's perception of financial services. Many remembered the great stock jobbing and land boom chicanery of the late nineteenth century and the recent insurance investigations. Promoters, presenting themselves as disinterested intermediaries, solicited funds for investment in railroads, ranches, mines, and other developmental activities. But it was all too easy for promoters to overinvest, inflate promises, and sneak their profits off the top. Nineteenth-century railroad boomers were infamous for overselling lines, whose operating profits proved nil. But by the time stockholders realized this, the promoters were gone. They had already made their money, by purchasing land that appreciated along rights of way, or running the construction company that built the road, or supplying materials such as steel to the new line.

To the extent that Tappan and his network of friends and cohorts used Syndicate capital for investments in which they were personally involved or interested, the same dangers presented themselves. State examiners provided a minimal level of inspection into operations, but usually they acted only after the fact. A bad loan decision, such as the Syndicate's venture with National Securities, might be caught once it exploded, but examiners generally did not interfere with actual decisions. On the other hand, Tappan's own close involvement meant that his reputation and his money were also at stake. Poor judgement or self-interested loan decisions could destroy his position in the community and possibly cost him money out of his own pocket. Fly-by-night operators might not care about such things. Blowing into town with a new get-rich-quick scheme, they could be satisfied with hasty profits, a nasty bankruptcy, and a surreptitious departure in the dead of night. Tappan had never intended to operate that way. He was in Minneapolis to stay and he was committed to long-term Syndicate success. Thus matters of reputation and trust mattered to him a great deal. These were the sorts of things that had to be established arduously, in deal after deal with creditors and debtors. His thousands of personal business letters to correspondents testify to his willingness to perform this work.

Disentangling himself and the company from the National Securities debacle was proving to be one of the greatest challenges to this way of doing business. Receivers of the bankrupt company had started a suit against the stockholders, which included John and Winnie. John had apparently taken a personal stake in the firm that had borrowed Syndicate money. The receivers were demanding more money to get the company out of debt and up and running again. As was often the case when a corporation failed, stockholders not only received the smallest portion of the remaining assets, they were dunned for more payments to get the firm back on its feet so it could pay its secured debts. If this seemed like adding insult to injured stockholders, the alternatives were even worse. Sometimes courts simply wiped out the existing common stock, to permit the restructured corporation to float a new issue. These were the good reasons why the average person was wary of common stocks.

Tappan sought a negotiated settlement on behalf of himself and the other shareholders. The receiver told him it would cost $8,500 to stop the suit from going to trial and relieve everyone of their liability. That would be enough to pay about 20 percent of the outstanding debt.[27] The negotiations apparently failed and, in the spring of 1912, Tappan was notified that he owed nearly $7,000, due by July 1. It is unclear if the suit ever proceeded to trial, or if a settlement was made at a lower figure. Either way, $7,000 was a lot of money for Tappan. He once again wrote everyone who owed him money.

The work of scraping up funds and promoting a new product had been urgent enough, with Earl's death and Carrie's resignation. But the spring also saw a final major loss of personnel. Carrie and her husband Harry moved to Portland, Oregon, pursuing what John called "land fever." Harry had been involved with John in investments in property in Ashland, Wisconsin. In addition, Harry had served the company as director of the Monthly Installment Loan Company, a spin-off of the Syndicate that provided consumer credit by structuring loans to be repaid in small monthly amounts.[28] But he was too far away now to keep up those duties. John accepted the situation with good humor, though the separation was both a personal and professional loss to him. Chiding Harry over who produced better strawberries, Oregon or Minnesota, he wrote, "I enclose herein a resignation for you as a director of the Monthly Installment Loan Company, as you are disqualified for the reason that you are now an Oregonian and we cannot stand for having any berry-pickers on our Board of Directors. They are too low."[29]

John had kept his sense of humor, but his spirits must have been down. Most of his time was being spent asking friends for money or dunning late-paying borrowers. He had lost his right arm in Earl, and with him the crucial marketing function for increasing sales of new certificates. Close family and vital contributors to the Syndicate had moved far away. At home, the bleak mood had only abated slightly. After Marion recovered from diphtheria, the family moved back to Cedar Lake for the rest of the winter of 1912. Winnie had gone through a bad time when she first set foot in the house her child had died in. Afterward, she decided she could never again live there, a place still haunted by her memory of Zita. At Cedar Lake, Winnie now had a close friend and confidant. Mrs. Duffy, who had lost a son of her own, was the only person Winnie could ever talk with about Zita. But living on the lake kept John somewhat removed from the center of things in Minneapolis. It was still a long, cold journey across or around the lake, and then a long trolley ride to downtown. At his plea, the ice company agreed to keep a path open all winter, to allow residents the shortcut across the ice. John Tappan was now reaching middle age, forty-two years old, committed to a project he had started as a young man that still was on shaky ground.

Perhaps the crises were starting to affect his feelings about his own future. He remained a cheerful optimist, and he worked the long hours necessary to solve problems. But his own livelihood was also at stake. A few years earlier he had written Henry Farnham, the company's former attorney now living in Nevada, asking if he would consider returning to Minneapolis and become his law partner. For all the potential John saw in Investors Syndicate, it was the mundane tasks of lawyering that were paying the bills. "I have more law business now than I can attend to," he wrote, "although I am not making as much out of it as I should."[30] Despite an iron-willed dedication to the Syndicate, John was not above the temptations of an easier road or of a more promising, shorter avenue to prosperity. He had, as he admitted, "a pretty large family on my hands," a family that needed him more than ever. Perhaps it was time to admit that law was where his best hope for success actually lay.

Farnham declined the invitation, but that year Tappan and Willis Silverthorne went into practice together. John had a fair amount of legal work to handle just from Investors Syndicate's real estate and property investments. With the company short of cash, however, he may not have been seeing much in the way of payments for his services. Tappan most likely took minimal fees and "reinvested" what he earned in the company. But with a partner, he could move further afield in a general practice. In addition, he continued to conduct the business of the Monthly Installment Loan Company. All of this was handled from the same offices with Investors Syndicate.

There were other new ventures as well. Fifteen days after Zita's death, John had completed the incorporation of the Equitable Storage Company with several of his friends and associates from Investors Syndicate. Since 1910, he had been a participant in the Excelsior Baking Company with Silverthorne. The move into foods continued with a project close to Tappan's heart, the Tropical Fruit and Nectar Company. Tappan ate a healthy diet and loved fruits and berries. He hoped that this new company's product, a concoction of oranges, lemons, pineapples, and figs, would succeed as a temperance drink and medicinal product. The company failed shortly after incorporation, but the idea is revealing. A number of regional entrepreneurs in the South and Midwest were promoting new, medicinal drinks as alternatives to whisky and as curative therapies for nervous conditions and disorders of the bowels and intestines.

Some that were launched around the same time as Tappan's fruit beverage actually succeeded, most famously Coca-Cola. Like Tappan, their supporters saw both profits and social improvement in the venture.

Tappan had stretched himself thin, there is no doubt about it. On one side, he was pressed by sluggish growth, bad debts, and cash shortages to work long hours at the Syndicate. On the other, he was tempted by opportunity in greener fields to settle down and make enough money for his family, while furthering the healing process at home. Characteristically, he responded not by pulling back or focusing, but by devoting energy in both directions, the long-term needs of the Syndicate and the immediate opportunities for profits. By the very nature of local business in a growing city, a variety of investment opportunities were bound to come Tappan's way. His involvement in real estate and lending put him in touch with many people who had good ideas about where to build houses, where to invest capital, and which plots of land to buy just before they skyrocketed in value. Knowledge of such opportunities was actually vital to the Syndicate, since they provided its major source of funds—earnings on loans. But Tappan's diversification of interests also reflected something about himself.

He could be quite single-minded about things, but he also had a flexible character, as revealed in his humor, enjoyment of good times, and demonstrated resiliency in the face of adversity. One expression of this flexibility, however, may have been a tendency to withdraw a bit in the face of what he perceived to be unalterable circumstances. When home life grew too oppressive for the teenage Tappan, he simply moved out on short notice to find his own way in the West. The moves into baking, confectionery, and soft drinks, the taking on of new law business, and the personal property investments all reflected his opportunistic side, his unwillingness to be stymied by adversity. These new activities, however, also took him further away from the day-to-day needs of Investors Syndicate. He was not being entirely consistent with the advice to "stick to it" that he frequently gave his own subscribers. If the company was ever going to succeed as Tappan hoped, he had to add new personnel. Most important, with Earl gone, someone had to handle the marketing of certificates and management of field agents. For the first time since he founded Investors Syndicate, Tappan had to wonder if the project had reached the end of the road.

CHAPTER SIX

THE AGENCY SYSTEM

Tappan had been through a lot. His family life had changed tragically, and would never quite be the same again. He had moved houses and given up some of his favorite recreations. There was little spare time now for the usual hunting and fishing excursions into the woods with male companions that had once been part of his life. He had to save every penny and was still struggling with a spouse threatening to fall into depression. His business had experienced two years of slow growth and the loss of major personnel. Men and women who had been with him from the start were now gone. For nearly twenty years he had been trying to make Investors Syndicate into something big, yet it remained small, limited, and still under the clouds of suspicion that followed all investment plans. At middle age, he was making a living as a lawyer, but law was not his true vocation, the Syndicate was. The only way it would succeed was if the public came to realize what he already knew—that here was a safe, effective way to save money. The question was, How could he get that message out?

By nature, Tappan was not a salesman. True, he had sold the first contracts and did much of the early legwork to spread word about the company. His approach, however, was a simple, direct, rational one. He explained, he did not persuade. He used logic, not emotional appeals. He disdained the hard sell, the come-on, and the oily tactics commonly associated with suspect operators and get-rich-quick schemes. Sometimes, his flat, straight ahead approach even seemed a bit insensitive to customers who wanted endless reassurance. Tappan had no problem explaining how the certificates worked, encouraging people to save for the long term, and giving his personal guarantee that the operation was totally "square." But he expected honesty, logic, and trust to be enough. Those who could not understand explanations in "clear cut English language," or who still failed to catch on no matter how "plain" he put things, exasperated Tappan. He let customers know when he thought he had been "plain enough" in his letters of explanation.[1]

These simple, direct appeals were a world away from the slick salesmanship and financial pettifoggery so troubling to middle-class men and women, but so common, too. In a classic book by Mark Twain, one of Tappan's favorite authors, the pretensions of the salesman got a merciless skewering. Twain's *The Gilded Age* portrayed America as a money-grubbing parody of all that was genuine and honest. The book captured the insincerity of the late nineteenth century. Beneath the golden veneer of good times, the nation's moral infrastructure was rotting. Pursuing the almighty dollar, cardboard suitcase tycoons traded the real for the fake, the sober for the speculative, and the virtuous for the deceitful. Scam artists persuaded men and women to sink fortunes into worthless paper securities, dreaming of mansions of glory and castles in the sky. Few better representations of fast buck chicanery exist in all of American literature than the book's main character, Colonel Mulberry Sellers. A man of protean values, the Colonel moved through the country with one eye out for the main chance and the other searching for gullible investors to support his grand schemes. Yet compared to the real characters of the times, the windbag Sellers was only a slight exaggeration.

Early Wall Street, after all, was populated with the likes of Daniel Drew, Bet-a-Million Gates, and Jay Gould. Drew was the reputed inventor of the practice of stock watering, or issuing shares to the public far in excess of the real worth of an enterprise. Gates, who made and lost several fortunes, got his name from a million-dollar wager on a race of water droplets running down a train window. His whimsical bet took place at a time when the average working man earned perhaps $600 per year. And Jay Gould was probably the fieriest operator that the American financial world has ever seen. Before anyone else, Gould correctly surmised that prices in a modern securities market depended less on some "underlying" value than on the supply and demand for stocks and shares issued by companies. Demand in turn reflected what people thought a company was worth, a highly subjective matter. Thus stock prices could be manipulated simply by changing impressions. Gould masterfully acquired railroads, telegraph companies, and other properties by driving down their value, often by planting rumors in the media about the financial health of his target or by manipulating the legal system to acquire control. When all else failed, he resorted to political corruption, in one memorable case delivering bags of money to the New York statehouse door. It was not the high point of American political virtue.

In light of the memories of Gilded Age excess, Tappan had worked assiduously to establish a bond of trust with clients and public officials. A successful sales strategy, though, was a different matter. It depended on independent agents, whose understanding of and commitment to Investors Syndicate could not be assumed. Company values too had to be built into the sales force step by step.

Thus far, Tappan had avoided anything that smacked of deception. To agents who wrote for advice, he often replied simply, "About the only instructions we can give you are to read over our prospectus carefully and thoroughly so that you can explain the plan fully to any person, and be able to answer any questions concerning it." "Make no false statements," Tappan admonished. "They result only in temporary gain, if any at all, and your future will be full of trouble."[2] The idea was not business at any cost, but solid long-term performance. "Think well of yourself and your business, and say nothing about other companies in the same line unless your customer mentions them first."[3] Tappan believed that once customers understood, clearly and rationally, how an investment company worked, "you will have over one-half of the battle won."[4]

Certainly, clarity and directness were virtues. But they alone were not going to attract a wide public following to Investors Syndicate. A financial product, which resonated with all sorts of feelings connecting money to home, life, security, and the future, had too much emotional baggage for that. Good salesmen had to take an interest in the welfare of clients, had to appeal to people's feelings (and fears) connected to money. Selling savings, insurance agents had first discovered, was also about "inducing habits of economy, sobriety and forethought."[5] This was the lesson and pattern that Tappan followed as well.

As Tappan himself admitted, "it is only by personal application that business is written." In this advice, he was again following the hard-earned experience of the insurance agents who preceded him. Life insurance had received its big marketing boost in the 1840s, when mutual companies began canvassing for subscriptions door-to-door, a strategy that produced tremendous growth in life insurance for the first time.[6] The lessons of marketing a new financial product were clear by the time Tappan began. Selling was hard work, requiring agents on the ground who could do the job, painstakingly day-in and day-out at the local level. Though the home company could provide information, circulars, booklets, and the like, most of the actual effort had to be made by agents themselves. They had to personally solicit clients, explain the product, and adapt to local circumstances.

Investors Syndicate agents were generally prominent men of their communities. To find customers, they relied on strong personal contacts built through membership in associations, organizations, and lodges. This too followed the experience of insurance companies, which in the 1870s and 1880s began working through fraternal lodges and local organizations. Successful agents avoided the "office habit," and got right out in the field. "Keep a list of names and addresses of those you talk to," Investors Syndicate advised its agents. "See them frequently, and when calling upon them mention the date that you were there before. The fact that you remembered the date impresses them that you either have a good memory or a good system, and if they have told you to call on a certain date, and you do so promptly at that time, you impress them more."[7] Marketing in small towns and semirural communities, Investors Syndicate tried to emphasize personal contacts as much as possible.

With a new financial product, building up a client base almost required a sort of "multi-level" marketing. At one time, in fact, Tappan had considered dispensing with agents altogether, and instead offering "each contract holder a good commission for selling contracts with us."[8] Subscribers would tell their friends and vouch for the integrity of the investment. These new clients in turn would tell their friends, and so forth. Without any investment in sales personnel, the company would grow geometrically, each subscriber yielding at least one additional subscriber. And, unlike life insurance, Tappan wryly noted, repeat business was possible. In the end, though, such self-generated sales provided only a small percentage of new business. Professional agents were needed. Tappan stuck with one part of his original plan, though. He continued to embrace the notion of mutuality between the firm and its customers. One special form of the contract, for example, entitled holders to an extra dividend if they furnished the company with the names of ten prospects. Agents as well used family, local acquaintances, and friends for contacts. New sales agents were advised to get the names of ten friends of each contract holder, and if possible have the existing client make the first contact.[9] Such small initial steps in turn created a positive spiral, encouraging others to come on as agents and join in the business of selling.

Tappan had little time to devote to the tricky business of salesmanship, vital though that work was. It had never been his job to find good agents, or organize and motivate the sales forces. Those had been Earl's responsibilities. To anything that threatened the reputation of the company, including false or misleading sales claims by agents, Tappan often gave his personal attention. Most of his time, however, went to corresponding with customers, sending out new certificates, collecting dues, dealing with legal challenges, and finding profitable uses for company funds. His spare time was taken up with earning a living by practicing law and looking after his family. Perhaps he had underestimated the value of full-time, aggressive salesmanship. Tappan really needed a new partner.

It could have been the answer to a prayer. In 1913, help arrived, in the person of John Salmon Hibbert. An Englishman who had spent many years as a successful insurance salesman, Hibbert knocked on Investors Syndicate's door one day and inquired about a position. Years later, Tappan recalled the meeting. "Our General Sales Manager had died, and soon after J. S. Hibbert approached me and told me he wanted to take over the General Sales Agency." He arrived with recommendations in hand, but Tappan remained, as he put it, "skeptical" until he saw a letter from the Midland Life Insurance Company. The letter stated that Hibbert had been their best life insurance agent for seven years.[10]

In no position to judge beforehand if Hibbert matched his impressive endorsements, Tappan hired him on a conditional basis. One thing that may have appealed to Tappan was Hibbert's reputation. Not only had he a proven track record as a salesman, but he had not gotten into trouble with deceptive practices nor moved rapidly from one company to another. He seemed to have the combination of sales experience, personality, and solid honesty that fit well with Tappan and his vision of Investors Syndicate. At Hibbert's suggestion, they signed a contract setting aggressive sales quotas. If these were not met on time, Hibbert could be fired. He was to sell $500,000 in certificates the first year, while organizing the sales department, hiring agents, and writing sales literatures. The quota went up to $750,000 the second year, and $1 million the third. These were incredibly ambitious goals for a firm coming off several seasons of poor performance. Only a few years earlier, Investors Syndicate had claimed a modest $85,000 in assets. Now Tappan was asking for a turnaround that would, if successful, multiply the size of the company several fold. But Tappan had long believed in the certificates' wide appeal, if the word could be spread. Hibbert was a man of enormous self-confidence. Having mastered insurance sales, he believed that the same methods and techniques would work for any financial product.

As it turned out, Hibbert and Tappan had underestimated their potential. In a remarkable development that neither man could have fully anticipated, the Syndicate suddenly bloomed and revealed its full potential. The lofty sales quotas actually proved too modest, for Hibbert not only met, but exceeded them. In 1913, Hibbert's first year, the Syndicate wrote over a half-million dollars of new business. The company tripled that figure the next year, and in 1916 it added the astounding figure of $4 million of new business. Company assets grew apace, nearly quadrupling from the $85,000 mark to over $300,000 by 1917. In little more than three years, Investors Syndicate had become one of the largest and most successful investment companies in Minnesota. For a company teetering on the verge of bankruptcy just shortly before, this was nothing short of amazing. How and why it happened at that moment can perhaps never be fully explained.

J. S. Hibbert made an enormous difference, of that there is no doubt. One factor slowing growth during the early years was simply a lack of knowledge of how to set up a geographically extensive agency. Jay Cooke had developed the most successful selling agency for financial products during the Civil War, marketing millions in Union government bonds. But nationwide agencies for private securities did not catch on, and Cooke's efforts went down in flames in the Panic of 1873. Most bond traders preferred to deal with relatively large investors, reducing the cost of marketing. Retail level marketing was done individually, by local brokers, banks, and investment companies.

Insurance companies, of course, had done much better, using extensive networks of agents to sell their products to nearly all classes and groups in the nation. Tappan had already used insurance as something of a template for sales at Investors Syndicate. Investors Syndicate's first general sales agent before Earl had been J. W. Knapp, an old life insurance man. So it is not surprising that Hibbert's background was in insurance, life insurance in particular. Dealing with touchy issues of money and death, insurance companies relied on a dedicated sales force, whose motivation to close the sale came from commissions, the main and in some cases sole means of payment. When customers wanted to see a face before handing over hard-earned cash, locally knowledgeable agents working in geographically limited territory proved a durable sales system.

Agents with strong local reputations, contacts, and knowledge were also ideal in rural markets where customers were located far from central information and distribution points. A storefront office was effective in big cities where there were lots of clients, but in small towns and villages, sales personnel had to travel. Salaried employees might work in cities, where they could be closely supervised and where sales per employee were high. Agents on commission worked best in less populated regions, where motivation and effort had to be rewarded. Sales of other products in rural America, such as sewing machines and agricultural implements, grew quite rapidly through these decentralized distribution systems. Commissioned agents could do the sort of labor-intensive work of selling that was impossible from afar. At the same time, they reduced the company's own investment and liability, by remaining independent, nonemployees responsible for their own expenses.[11]

One thing that Hibbert provided to Investors Syndicate was greater systemization of the agency network. Tappan had relied on individual agents in different locations to sell certificates. Much of the early sales work was done in smaller towns and cities of the West and Middle West, places where a few successful sales quickly spread word from person to person that the certificates were a good buy. In other cases, customers approached the company directly. On their own, or by word of mouth, individuals often heard about the certificates, made inquiries, and, if convinced by Tappan's explanation, sent in their checks. Under Hibbert, this same geographically focused strategy continued, but on a much wider scale. The Syndicate expanded its base of operations first in the middle states of the nation, where word of mouth, proven examples, and close contacts between agents and customers counted most. But Hibbert also added a degree of central control to the agency structure. Marketing through agents required a careful balance between independence and central control. Agents had to have the freedom to develop business as they saw fit, yet their actions had to be controlled and coordinated so that individual actions did not interfere with overall strategy or impair the company's reputation through false or misleading claims. By 1913, in fact, insurance companies had begun to develop stronger central offices for sales and marketing. Techniques of selling were being taught in classes offered by bodies such as the National Association of Life Insurance Underwriters. Publishers printed handbooks for would-be sales agents. Still, the key to success remained the field force itself. This was true even in the larger insurance companies, which had adopted formal, central sales offices.[12]

To these ends, Hibbert opened new offices in the western and midwestern states, where the Syndicate found its best clients. Missouri, Idaho, Oregon, and Washington State were quickly added to the earlier territories of Minnesota, Kansas, and the Dakotas. In 1915, Tappan wrote to the secretaries of state for permission to do business in Iowa, Oklahoma, Mississippi, Alabama, Kentucky, North Carolina, South Carolina, West Virginia, and Tennessee as well. The new sales offices kept Hibbert in touch with agents in these territories. But he also gave agents a healthy degree of autonomy.

This decentralized structure seems to have been an important reason for the rapid growth of Investors Syndicate. Since Tappan had always treated the Syndicate more as a labor of love than a source of power, prestige, or income, he had kept the organization extremely loose and personal. Indeed, the simple realities of managing a small, start-up operation virtually required a minimum of bureaucracy and an extremely lean management. Tappan and a secretary handled most of the day to day operations. He acted as both treasurer and, in many cases, chief counsel. Investments were often funneled through friends and close contacts. Tappan merged his personal and business life at many points, using vacations as opportunities to scout around for new land, and directing company funds into his own land projects. Labor intensive work, such as customer relations, was handled simply by working longer hours. Most complaints went right to Tappan, who insisted on making himself the man personally responsible for the care and feeding of the Syndicate's loyal investors.

The new agency system maintained this tradition. It placed responsibility for sales as much as possible with those doing the work. It reinforced Tappan's original insight that "personal application" wrote business. Hibbert's contract required only that he meet certain quotas, but otherwise left him free to run matters as he saw best. Agents also had quotas, and they made money strictly on commission. Agents, not the company, paid the cost of finding clients, such as railroad tickets, hotel bills, and other on-the-road expenses. Their compensation came in the form of a fairly generous sales commission taken out of the initial payments on the certificates. They only got paid if and when they closed a sale. Hibbert himself was under the same motivation. His career at Investors Syndicate was directly tied to overall sales performance. Selecting experienced agents who could meet their sales goals, and removing those who could not, were the primary tools at his disposal.

What Tappan had long believed about Investors Syndicate was now coming true. As he exclaimed to one friend, in some amazement, "We recently sold $98,000 worth of bonds in one week. We have fourteen men working constantly in the state of Kansas alone, and the prospects of business are that it will grow to a colossal size within the next few years."[13] Growth was so phenomenal that old methods of doing business quickly became obsolete. Much of the routine work Tappan himself had once handled or did with a secretary, was farmed out to new clerical staff. In the fall of 1914, the company made arrangements with banks throughout the West to collect payments. Though banks charged a fee for each transaction, it was well worth the expense in a period of rapid growth. As an offshoot of its business, the Syndicate also added a fire and tornado insurance agency, to supply policies to mortgagees who were required to carry insurance on the property that secured their loan. By 1921, the company would hold over $3 million in insurance policies. New functions and rapid growth required one other change. Investors Syndicate had outgrown its old offices. Tappan renegotiated his lease and took over three floors of the Lincoln Building in downtown Minneapolis.

Nothing overcomes doubts like success, and by meeting and exceeding his targets, Hibbert gained Tappan's complete confidence. In February 1914, Hibbert was elected vice president and general manager of Investors Syndicate. When the original three-year contract expired, Tappan and Hibbert renegotiated their arrangement. Under the new contract, the agency system became Hibbert's sole responsibility. It was organized as a separate company, styled J. S. Hibbert. Agents were hired, fired, directed, and paid commissions by Hibbert directly. This arrangement was fairly common. Tappan's chief competitor, Fidelity Investment Association, the other major face amount certificate company, organized its sales force in the same manner.[14] By keeping the agency system separate from the rest of operations, companies reduced administrative costs and simplified operations.

One factor working in favor of sales was the attractive way in which commissions were paid. Tappan had structured the contract so that he could, if necessary, use the entire first year's payment for costs and expenses. Agents were paid by an up-front fee, or what today would be called a load. These fees meant that the agents saw their money first. It was a strategy that other new investment companies would follow as well. No load funds would not emerge until 1928, and they only started to become popular in the 1960s. Even today, they are far from universal, with many financial products marketed through networks of dealers, brokers, and agents, all of whom receive fees.

Tappan had experimented in 1904 with no load, low-cost contracts, but they had never caught on. Apparently low costs were not the key to making a new commercial product popular, at least not initially. High commissions had advantages when it came to selling something new, despite the increase in cost to the client. Insurance companies, for example, found that agent commissions rose substantially from about 5 percent of first year premiums to 80 percent and in some cases 100 percent between the 1840s and 1890s, when insurance took off. Despite criticisms of these marketing expenses, competition between insurance firms made it impossible to cut commissions. Competitive strategy depended far more on a well-paid, motivated sales force than on low marketing costs.[15] This seems to have been Tappan's experience as well.

Selling the product, Tappan knew from experience, was a labor intensive matter, especially among people of modest means living in small towns and rural counties. They remained skeptical, and only trustworthy agents who spent the time overcoming natural reluctance and fears would be able to close sales. Most of these customers invested a relatively small amount of money, although the number of hours an agent needed to complete each small sale might be no less than that needed for a much bigger sale to a wealthier client. This work had to be rewarded and encouraged with relatively high sales commissions. Healthy commissions induced extra efforts from the sales force. If these costs seemed a high percentage of value, they declined the longer the customer kept up his contract payments. Thus, the up-front load encouraged the sort of long-term commitment by investors that lay at the core of Tappan's strategy.[16] It also added to the Syndicate's financial health. Faster growth meant a higher percentage of customers making the early payments, which Tappan recorded as income on Syndicate books. Some of this income was due to sales agents as commissions; the rest was available to pay for office, marketing, and promotion expenses. This cash flow gave the Syndicate a strong bottom line, and the faster it grew, the stronger it looked.

Still, beyond the cost of selling, Investors Syndicate kept its operating costs low. Total staff was small, and by contracting for functions such as sales and collections, Investors Syndicate had little incentive to overcharge investors for these essential services. From early experience, Tappan also knew that heavy advertising did not pay, so he kept these expenses to a minimum as well. Clients' money went directly into the investments. The mortgage loans themselves were attractive to borrowers because they contained no hidden fees, commissions, or other costs.[17] Tappan found that there were plenty of high quality borrowers who were willing to pay 7 percent or more for loans, and most of these properties he could inspect himself. A low default rate meant minimal transactions costs on the investment side of operations. The result was an expense ratio of about $3.60 for each $1,000 certificate. That was far better than comparable financial services. Insurance firms' expense ratio averaged over $11 for each $1,000 in insurance.[18] Even later, when expansion came fast and furious to Investors Syndicate, total sales costs to total contract values were low relative to other products.[19]

Sales were making Investors Syndicate a success, but salesmanship in financial products also opened doors to the dangers of fraud, misrepresentation, and high pressure tactics. The devolution of responsibility away from headquarters, and away from John Tappan in particular, could lead to lack of oversight in how the Syndicate and its products were represented. Agents and companies had divergent interests. Agents, of course, made money by sales, and so might be tempted to cut corners and mislead clients into signing a contract. Honestly run companies had to worry about agents whose quest for commissions led them to make indefensible representations and endanger the company's long-term reputation.

Tappan's own experiences with bond companies were hardly reassuring. Salesmen in the field did not always know what was going on in the home office, even as they worked to overcome customer skepticism by vouching for the integrity of the firm they represented. Even honest agents could be tempted by the short-term pressures of the job to abandon the truth when it came time to close the sale, since they made no money until the contract was signed. Tappan himself acknowledged these pressures, understanding the necessity to get a prospect to sign sooner rather than later. He advised his agents to close with a man on the first meeting. The longer the client waited, the less likely he would be to hand over his money. But that eminently practical advice also invited high pressure tactics and dishonest representations designed to snare the unthinking before they had a chance to mull things over. Growth required a strong commitment to honesty if these dangers were to be avoided.

The customers that Tappan sought were not sophisticated investors ready to parry aggressive sales thrusts. Marketing efforts remained concentrated on Middle America—the midwestern states and the middle to lower-middle class of the population. A later study would show that the typical Syndicate customer was a schoolteacher. Other occupations heavily represented were housewives, clerks, salesmen, and managers. Many were women, with nurses and stenographers also prominent among the clients.[20] The typical sales target, an image taken from later advertising, was "Miss Jones," a hardworking schoolteacher. The gender characteristics are important here, particularly the suggestion of an unmarried female. Typically, unmarried women saved money in "modern" ways even back in the nineteenth century. Where families with children headed by men often saved to invest in home ownership, small business ventures, or for education, unmarried women saved for the day they no longer worked. Miss Jones was a variation on the classic "widows and orphans," who represented broad public stock ownership. Both images suggested a degree of vulnerability. Though Miss Jones was a tough and skeptical customer, demanding much work from the good salesperson, she also needed his expert guidance on matters financial.

There was potential for conflict between Hibbert and Tappan on the tricky matter of how to represent the company's products to such customers. They had differing interests. Hibbert's job was to meet quotas, and his main interest was in finding good sellers and expanding the customer base. For Tappan, on the other hand, Investors Syndicate had always been a long-term project. He needed and wanted growth, but he had invested a substantial amount of time in establishing the company's reputation for honesty, probity, and competence. Before Hibbert, Tappan had also paid agents on commission. Still, it was imperative not to allow the pressures for sales to destroy the foundation of trust that underlay Investors Syndicate.

Life insurance had in fact almost come to ruin on these rocky shoals. The commissioned agents who were so crucial to success came under fire for using tactics much like those deployed today by dishonest car salesmen. The innovative tontine plan, which had much in common with Tappan's plan, was heavily criticized and driven out of the market in part because of the techniques used by commissioned agents.[21] In the worst cases, agents misrepresented the complex financial and legal obligations that made up a life insurance contract. Customers might begin payments, but then default, unable to keep up premiums. Since agents were often paid up front, it mattered less to them than to the company whether or not the customer kept paying. As with insurance, it was tempting for agents to oversell. An unscrupulous agent could exploit such customers by getting them to sign on for more than they could manage. In other cases, salesmen used financial double-talk to convince unwary buyers they were getting more for their money than was true.

Self-regulation of high pressure tactics had a mixed record in finance. Their reputations sullied, the largest insurance companies tried to pull back, put agents on salary, or at least write codes of ethics and professional standards of conduct to discourage misrepresentation. Alone, however, individual companies could not always overcome self-interest. Unscrupulous operators, for example, might turn a blind eye toward unethical sales practices, officially reprimanding agents, but also raising sales quotas in response to business growth. This sent a mixed message of "do not lie," but also "do whatever is necessary to make your quota." Eventually, high pressure sales tactics caught up with insurance companies, as calls for investigation and regulation mounted. The complexities of modern finance pried even conservative Republicans away from their infatuation with an unmolested free market. Especially in a matter so closely related to family financial well-being as money, the old doctrine of "let the buyer beware" no longer seemed enough.

Perhaps learning from the insurance company experience, Investors Syndicate sought to avoid the same problems. Tappan understood that commissions motivated aggressive sales activity, but in 1895 he also wrote, "We are hoping to put some of our men on salary; providing they can guarantee to turn in so much business."[22] Throughout the twentieth century, investment companies flirted with this idea. Salaried agents eliminated the incentive to "churn accounts" or to make sales just for the purpose of getting more commission, regardless of the needs or interests of the investor. Merrill Lynch went to salaries for its stockbrokers for this reason in the 1950s. The experiment only lasted a decade or so, before the incentives of the commission system became too great and Merrill Lynch went back to the old ways.[23]

Tappan's resort to the salary idea may have been as much to attract good sales agents as to stem sales agents' abuses. Convincing a well-established, successful agent of the virtues of a new plan was never easy. At a time when investment companies were a rarity, strong salesmen might well be skeptical about hawking products of companies that might soon be out of business. Opportunities beckoned in established industries such as insurance. There, successful agents also had the opportunity to move up a level and become regional agents, earning a percentage of the sales of subagents working under them. Others operated general agencies, selling a variety of financial products. They were less interested in the long-term success of a firm like Investors Syndicate than in simply finding hot financial properties to market. Making agents salaried employees had the advantage of tying their long-term interests to company success. So Tappan did not immediately abandon his idea. In 1901, he again opined, "I believe the only way for us to get this company going in good shape is to put some good people on a salary."[24] He never did, as it was a proposition that would have cost the company precious operating capital. By 1905, he had become a firm believer in the motivating force of working on commission. Hibbert's success confirmed that belief.

Still, Hibbert and Tappan both agreed that, important as sales were, agents had to follow strict rules of propriety and conduct. An important part of the company's success, Tappan maintained, stemmed from its "good reputation" for meeting obligations and conforming to the often fickle requirements of state law.[25] Agents had to uphold these standards of conduct if business was to keep growing. They were to be gracious, polite, and tactful, and never use illegal, immoral, or unprofessional tactics. It was policy not to "knock" another company doing similar business or to make derogatory statements about competitors. There was no point, Tappan wrote, in running down other firms. Not only did it provoke retaliation, but it tarnished the reputation of the whole industry, to everyone's detriment. On the other hand, as Investors Syndicate grew, successful agents working for other firms naturally inquired about opportunities. Here Tappan drew the line on gentlemanly cooperation. "I do not agree with you in regard to hiring agents who are or who ever have worked for any other company," he replied to a firm that had accused him of stealing agents. As long as no "deceit or misrepresentation is done to get [an agent]," Tappan believed, individuals should be free to choose where they wanted to work.[26]

Generally, the Syndicate paid commissions at what it regarded as "market rate," or approximately the same percentage as other companies in the area who used agents.

Still, overly zealous agents became a problem for Investors Syndicate, as they had long been for insurance companies. The majority of defaults on face amount certificates came in the first two years, possibly because clients had overestimated their ability to keep up payments. It was not always easy to control behavior in the field. Answering one complaint, Tappan noted, "agents very often do things which they are unauthorized to do, and which neither you nor I would sanction . . . [and] they do this secretly without our knowledge."[27] Agents sometimes touted the company and its products by making vague but reassuring statements such as, "the state of Minnesota backed the contracts," a deception that played on the fact that Minnesota did oversee the company through its banking department.

Particularly dangerous were agents who tried to close sales by giving customers a "written guarantee," or who made the certificates sound like savings accounts. Such guarantees were impossible to enforce, since Syndicate returns depended on market conditions. They were also illegal, just the sort of thing suspicious regulators stood ready to pounce on. Claims that the customer was guaranteed to get money out whenever it was wanted were trickier. The certificates did, after some initial payments, have cash surrender features, though, if exercised early in the life of the contract, the return was less than the amount put in. More specifically, the contracts were not savings accounts, because the funds were invested in long-term mortgages. To do that, Tappan had to have some guarantee on the length of time the investor would make payments. For those reasons, the certificates tried to balance the security of getting one's money out when needed, with incentives to customers to keep their money invested.

False claims about safety and security were the oldest tricks in the book for scam artists. They remained popular methods of deceit, however, because the agent who made such claims usually suffered no direct or immediate consequences. Any guarantees they gave were not legally binding, since they were not principals of the company. Yet it was tempting to write out such guarantees, knowing that the company's track record was so strong it was all but certain the customer would get what was promised anyway, and would never be the wiser to the legal legerdemain.[28] Such conditions meant that agents had incentive to play fast and loose with the law.

Given the dangers of misrepresentation, Tappan often found himself forced into the role of judge or mediator between his own agents and his customers. He reacted by trying to be as impartial as possible. Customers came first, but good salesmen were crucial to growth, so he could not always take the customers' side if his sales force were being unfairly maligned. When a customer wrote an intemperate letter about one agent, Tappan backed up the agent, replying, "If you had made the same statements regarding me that you have regarding him, I would certainly want you to prove them." It was in his nature to place fairness and right over some narrow definition of interest or blind loyalty. To another customer he replied, "It seems to the writer, who is also an attorney of over 20 years experience in active practice, that you should have immediately repudiated the contract and returned it when you found that it was misrepresented so that we could have taken the matter up immediately with the agent."[29] The charges against the agent were "a great surprise," since the man had never been reprimanded before. But Tappan concluded, "we will not permit any salesman to misrepresent our contracts in any way," and asked for specifics so that appropriate action could be taken.

Tappan could be extremely even-handed in these tricky matters, but he had little tolerance for individuals not "on the square," and he let them know it. One ex-company agent named Makepeace had aroused suspicion by his handling of two customers. Both customers eventually complained and one went to the state Banking Department, aggravating Tappan, who was protective of his firm's good name. Though he was miffed that the customers had waited over a year before writing—at which point Makepeace had left the company—he still investigated the complaint. Once he discovered what his former agent had done, he tracked him down in Topeka, Kansas. "Now Mr. Makepeace," Tappan wrote to him, "we want to hear from you immediately as to these cases for they must be taken care of." Employee or not, there was still a bond of trust between Makepeace and the company, and Tappan was not going to let it lapse, no matter how much time had passed. "You received a commission for making these sales," he reminded him, "and you got the business under misrepresentation. The money must be refunded to these parties if they want it."[30] Nothing was more disheartening than losing a customer's trust through an agent who cut corners. Success, Tappan argued, hinged on getting customers who were "satisfied boosters of the Syndicate," instead of dissatisfied "'knockers.'"[31]

Still, Tappan was not a man to be intimidated by customers who failed to read their contracts, nor would he be cowed by unjust threats. When one correspondent from Oklahoma called the Syndicate a "gang of swindling crooks," he shot back a defense of his firm's integrity. "We would suggest that you had better watch what kinds of letters you send through the United States Mail," he replied, warning the man about libel laws. A contract was a contract, even if a customer was too thick to understand it. "We stand ready to live up to it, to the very letter, and we expect you to be man enough to live up to your part of it, and because you are not man enough to live up to your part of it, is no reason why you should turn around and accuse a corporation which has been doing an honest, straightforward, legitimate business for the last twenty-four years, of being swindlers and crooks."[32] No matter how big the business got, Tappan still believed that virtuous, manly behavior on the company's part and on the part of its customers was the basis for a successful relationship. Investors Syndicate offered an opportunity, but it was still up to each individual to take responsibility for sticking to things and paying in their money. The old ideas of virtue and manliness, now recoded as persistence and consistency, still served in the emerging world of modern finance.

Advertising, which had always been used sparingly, reinforced this message. Tappan continued to rely on simple and informative promotions that avoided anything that seemed slick, glossy, or showy. He personally penned long essays based on questions he had been asked over the years. This had been typical of nineteenth-century advertising, in which company owners more than advertising professionals set promotional policy. Often, the owner portrayed himself and his values in the appeals, ignoring the modern dictum that the message should speak to the consumer and his or her concerns.[33] One Syndicate pamphlet, entitled "Twenty Questions Answered," gave detailed and rather technical explanations of how the plan worked, why the contracts increased in value, and provided comparisons between Investors Syndicate and insurance companies. It had information on just about anything any customer might ask. Another booklet, "From Far and Near," likewise explained the structure and organization of the firm and its investments. These materials had as their underlying message the power of savings, of slow but steady accumulation. They appealed to reason, assuming that, like Tappan, the public was savings oriented and committed to self-improvement through accumulation.

Tappan's approach to advertising was extremely conservative, even quaint, in a world where people were coming to define themselves by images and media messages. In the early twentieth century, more aggressive forms of advertising were making their appearance. Magazine and newspaper copy became cleaner, and employed color wherever possible. Pictures replaced words. Subtle, non-verbal messages substituted for long-winded factual explanations. Appeals based on the character, achievements, or virtues of the firm and its owner gave way to fawning solicitude for the needs and interests of the consumer. Companies issued tokens and logos and other means of emotionally connecting customers to the products, beginning with H. J. Heinz and its metal "pickle pins." As new psychological theories of motivation underscored the irrational as well as the rational in decision making, advertisers justified their craft as a form of consumer education. Progress in society, they rather paternalistically argued, came by using advertisements to construct more sophisticated, educated consumers who would buy superior products.

Only briefly did Tappan succumb to the temptations of image advertising, but in a typically simple and low-key way. In the winter of 1915, he ordered metal savings banks with the words "Investors Syndicate" emblazoned on the side. Each bank came with a key, so it could be used as a piggy bank to save money for monthly payments. The items proved extremely popular with salesmen, who gave them away with each contract. But the message remained the same one Investors Syndicate had been promoting in the nineteenth century. It was not the advertising fantasy of personal fulfillment or individual freedom that was creeping into other product promotions. Rather, it was the most traditional of messages—slow and steady savings.

Not everything remained unchanged at Investors Syndicate. Some new traditions were being established as well. Growth required access to larger amounts of capital, and that meant a public issue of stock. In 1908, the state of Minnesota had forced Investors Syndicate to issue stock, to increase the firm's capitalization.[34] Most of that issue was taken by the principals of the company, including Tappan, though for the first time, outsiders owned shares. With the firm now writing as much as $50,000 in new business a week, it needed a larger base of capital for operations, which ranged from New York to San Francisco, and many points between. So in 1916, Investors Syndicate doubled its capital to $100,000. New stock, both common and preferred, was offered first to existing contract holders. Rather than putting the shares of what was still a small, relatively unknown firm in a new industry onto the market "promiscuously," as Tappan put it, it seemed wiser to sell to those who knew the company and had had good experiences with it. To long-time contract holders, the offering was a chance to "come in with us on the same basis as the rest who got in on the ground floor." Subscribers could surrender their contracts and take, instead of cash, a greater amount in stock. New stock was also used to acquire another company in St. Louis, the Central States Trust Company. Central States offered to the public a similar contract, though one that only paid simple 5 percent interest. Tappan bought the client list of the company, and offered to exchange their bonds for certificates from Investors Syndicate.

For most of its history, Investors Syndicate had not really had to think about competition. It was so far out in front of others that there really was none. Being in the advanced guard of financial change was a mixed blessing. The company was often forced to make a market on its own, or to settle thorny issues without precedent to rely on. Investors Syndicate operated in the interstices between existing financial services available to the public. It was different than a bank, a savings and loan, or an insurance company, though it borrowed ideas and approaches from all of them. Eventually, however, success brought imitation, and the more that word got out about the Syndicate and its longevity, the more tempted other entrepreneurs were to try the same thing. In 1911, Fidelity Investment Association of West Virginia began operations, selling its own face amount certificates. A year later, it had grown to more than two-thirds Investors Syndicate's size.[35] By the most sincere form of flattery, the imitator confirmed the worth of what Tappan had been trying to do, though it never matched him in this market. Still, it was one of the few earlier imitators to have a long and healthy life. Others, such as the Central States Trust Company or Bankers Realty Trust Company of Nebraska, disappeared into obscurity, their clients taken over by Investors Syndicate.

One important difference between Investors Syndicate and its would-be competitors lay, Tappan maintained, with the great security he had written into the contracts. Several competing companies, Tappan noted, sold contracts "with practically the same terms and conditions as ours." But the differences were instructive. Investors Syndicate created a true trust fund to pay off contract holders, by holding and keeping intact first mortgages in the amount of $110 for each $100 of liability. Other companies simply promised to have on hand funds to meet their obligations. They offered nothing like this guarantee that there was a source of money available for all matured contracts. Tappan placed great emphasis on this direct connection between customers' money and investments made with that money, a point he explained again and again in the literature. Reinforced by a twenty-three-plus year track record of paying as promised, it proved an extremely valuable strategic asset in a market for consumer financial services that was still in formation and that varied widely throughout the nation.

Customers did not have to rely solely on past performance, however. As Tappan saw it, a common commitment to the long run linked the interests of Investors Syndicate with its clients, eliminating the problem of principal-agent conflict. Contrary to fly-by-night ventures, the Syndicate had the same financial interests as its certificate holders. Both, Tappan maintained, benefited the longer their money was invested with the company. Investors Syndicate benefited, because the source of its income was long-term amortizing mortgages. It wanted investors who kept their money at work in these investments. It did not seek speculators who defaulted on payments, took cash surrenders, or quit as soon as their contracts matured. "We do not wish a certificate holder to surrender his contract before maturity. We want him to carry it through as agreed for the full ten year period, and receive his money back and 6 percent interest compounded annually," Tappan wrote.[36] Those who left their money in for the full ten years gained the best returns because long-term mortgages earned top dollar. The steadier the behavior of certificate holders, the lower the firm's transactions costs, the less need it had to keep idle balances on hand to pay claims, and the more of its assets it could have working in the form of loans. This was an extraordinary approach to take in an age when investment and insurance firms expected to make high profits by the inability of clients to maintain payments for the full term. In some insurance companies, half the policyholders eventually lapsed. Other investment firms, selling products similar to Investors Syndicate, reached rates of lapsation as high as 60 percent. Lapsed policies, however, were an unsought source of profit at Investors Syndicate.

Customer service is a term easily abused today. To Tappan, it meant more than glossy brochures or endless client contacts that were really thinly disguised sales calls. He truly believed that his customers were participants with him in the venture. The contract each investor signed contained a clause that read as follows: "the obligations of the Syndicate hereunder and of the owner to make payments as herein stipulated are mutual. Each payment shall be deemed a covenant by the owner to make the remaining payments herein provided for." In other words, both parties to the contract, the investor and Investors Syndicate, were mutually obligated to make the payments promised. Tappan fully expected the client to "live up to [the] agreement."[37] If the client kept paying his monthly dues, the firm would pay back the money and interest promised. Perhaps the second half of this obligation was not surprising—no one would invest without some assurance they were going to get their money back. The first part of the obligation, however—the notion that with each payment the investor takes on an obligation to continue—was more unusual.

The sense of mutuality, of the reciprocal obligations connecting company to client, had been present from the start. It can be glimpsed in the hope that customers themselves would be the face amount certificate's chief sales force. As Tappan saw it, in giving him their money, clients were not simply "loaning" it to him. Many companies structured their contracts in this way, borrowing the public's money and paying it back with interest. In theory, the common law doctrine of "buyer beware" applied in such cases. It was the investors' responsibility to decide beforehand if they were confident about the proposed use of their funds. If the investment went bad, there was little recourse. But to attract a broad swath of the public, Tappan needed to offer greater assurance. It was simply impossible for most of his investors to take a direct, active role in managing company operations, or to go through the bother and expense of hiring a lawyer to recover money in case of bankruptcy.

What Tappan sought was a new type of relationship with his investors. They relied on him for his expertise, but they remained well informed as to where their money went. They sent in their funds, but those funds were tied directly to a particular investment system, rather than being used at the discretion of the company and its principles. In this way, investors had a measure of control over what happened to their funds without having to possess the full level of expertise necessary to actually make the investment themselves. They knew, with legal assurances, where the money went. Tappan insisted that customers be kept fully informed, in fact expected them to master a level of detail about "their" company. They had responsibility, too, which was why he could be surprisingly harsh with complaints that reflected ignorance or failure to understand how the investment worked.

Today, full disclosure is at the heart of securities laws and regulations. Investment companies are required to send investors prospectuses about operations and keep them informed of policy changes. In resorting to an investment company, clients do not actively manage their funds. But they are somewhat more responsible for their own money than, say, in a traditional company pension plan or with social security. They can choose from a wide variety of funds and managers, with different assets and different investment strategies. Tappan's Investors Syndicate was striving to establish just this sort of modern investment relationship with clients years before it became common or mandated by law. He wanted clients who were educated, loyal, informed, and committed to the long haul.

The cement that held together all the elements that made up Investors Syndicate, that bonded clients and firm, that anchored the strategy, had always been John Tappan. From the beginning, he had been the firm's moral center. With expansion and acquisition, however, this role began to change. Tappan was rubbing elbows with a new assortment of fellow executive officers. He had never been president, but always secretary/treasurer, the position from which he felt he could best look after his customers' money. Others served as the nominal head of the company, occupying the president's office. Burns McClain, who had served since 1902, was replaced by A. W. King in 1915. King had come by way of a $10,000 investment in Syndicate stock, made when he closed up a competing company and joined forces with Hibbert and Tappan. Hibbert served as vice president and agency manager. E. E. Crabb was also a vice president and, with Tappan, a treasurer.

By December 1914, Tappan owned less stock in Investors Syndicate than did others. Some of the new investors who had come in with the public offering of stock were simply wealthier than Tappan. Laboring twenty-plus years to build the business, he had not amassed a large amount of savings, ironic for a man who admonished others to save. Other new stockholders came with acquired firms, giving up ownership in exchange for Investors Syndicate stock. In one sense, percentage ownership did not really matter, since the growth of the firm would increase the value of Tappan's holdings whether he was a minority or majority owner. Still, Tappan personally believed that his historic involvement with the company, his role as founder and point of contact with the public, was crucial. As the firm issued new stock, he still reminded customers that he was "manager of the company," and that customers who knew him, knew from personal experience "how I conduct the Company . . . that it will be conducted honestly, and that it is practically my lifework."[38] Maybe for this reason, Tappan decided to borrow money and purchase a larger ownership stake. He was by 1915 again the single largest stockholder, though he did not hold a majority 51 percent interest. The company had grown too large for him to be its owner.

For three years Tappan had struggled to keep Investors Syndicate afloat during its darkest days. For three more years, he had the pleasure of running with success. Business grew so fast that he could barely keep up with the combination of new customers, new investments, and new laws and regulations that arose as the company crossed into more states. The only reward that he allowed himself was a modest salary. For several years, he had drawn $50 per month or less for his work at the Syndicate. In 1915, he increased his draw to $75, though with the expectation that most of the money he made would come from dividends on stock.[39]

Investors Syndicate was growing in another way as well—in public image. The rest of the world was starting to take notice of the company. Tappan had long seen one of his major functions as defending the company's reputation against public criticism. When newspapers, magazines, or zealous state attorneys attacked the company as some sort of money-grubbing scam, Tappan often shot back long letters in reply. Customers who wrote in angrily that they had been cheated sometimes got similar treatment, with Tappan reminding them about libel laws when he felt he or his firm had been unfairly maligned or attacked out of ignorance. It was the sort of response of a man who indeed took his business extremely personally. Of course, there was little he could do to control the flow of information about the company if reporters or investigators were really determined to do a hatchet job on the Syndicate. But he tried nonetheless, answering inquires from periodicals such as *Review of Reviews, Metropolitan Magazine,* and the *Chicago Examiner.* More of the articles were favorable now, and several recommended the Syndicate's certificates to its readers.

As word got out, there was also renewed attention from another source—the government. Once the early postal investigations had passed, the company had been largely free from clouds of legal suspicion. But as more of the public began participating in financial markets in the early twentieth century, some state governments decided that they should have a closer look at where this money went and how it was being used. There would be no federal regulation of financial markets until the creation of the Securities and Exchange Commission in the 1930s, but a series of state "Blue Sky" laws appeared on the books to regulate financial practices. The laws took their name from the popular term for inflated promises—literally anything, including the blue sky—that fast-talking investment promoters used to seduce the unsophisticated public.

The first law was passed in Kansas in 1911, and soon several more of the western states in which Investors Syndicate did business had similar legislation. Eventually every state in the union but Nevada would follow. To prevent fraud, Blue Sky laws required companies to register any securities they traded publicly, and to obtain licenses for personnel involved in securities sales. Blue Sky laws were less radical or moralistic than those proposed decades earlier by Populists. The laws largely accepted the existence of securities and stock markets, and focused on informing the public in order to prevent fraud, abuse, or manipulation of insider information. Still, they recognized a public and social responsibility in the market. By preventing well-placed Wall Street brokers and financiers from fleecing residents of rural America, such regulation was designed to prevent the flow of capital out of western states and into the hands of New York bankers. Properly safeguarded by public authorities, securities trading would give investors in places such as Kansas or Minnesota a fair chance to profit from their investments.[40]

As a man who believed in disclosure and a fair market, Tappan was not worried about the new laws. "We have complied with all the requirements of the Blue Sky Law so called, and intend to live up to it in 'letter and spirit,'" he wrote. Agents were expected to do the same and comply with the licensing provisions. Tappan had long sought to increase customer assurance about the security of their investments, so, if anything, the new law was a benefit. He also understood that good customer service did not mean caveat emptor, or devil take the hindmost, leaving the credulous at the mercy of the unscrupulous. It meant treating the public's money with trust and impeccable fiduciary responsibility. The only thing that bothered him was the sometimes unpredictable nature of state regulation.

Since 1906, Investors Syndicate had been under the supervision of the Minnesota public examiner, and then later the superintendent of banks.

These authorities checked contracts and printed matter, and issued permits allowing financial companies to do business. Investors Syndicate was the first firm in Minnesota to have a permit issued when the law was passed.[41] Tappan had also voluntarily deposited with the state first mortgages as a sort of guarantee or backup on the contracts. He was heartened when the state proposed a law that would require such deposits from all financial companies. "Nothing would please us better," he wrote to subscribers, "than to have such a law passed so that we could comply therewith."[42]

Even so, relations with government did not always proceed as smoothly as Tappan would have liked. The Minnesota Banking Department naturally tended to understand banks better than it did new types of investment companies, since these were the institutions officials dealt with the most.[43] Nor were state regulators particularly professional. "The main trouble," Tappan lamented, "is that the officers change when different administrations go in and every new man will have some new or different idea from his predecessor, and it is hard to suit everyone."[44] Investors Syndicate lost its license for a period in the state of Missouri, a result, Tappan believed, of a commissioner who was "either crooked or else does not know anything."[45] Times like these made Tappan suspect that an "under-current" was at work, probably petty jealousy from local banks or building and loans who saw Investors Syndicate as a competitor.[46] A trip to Jefferson City finally straightened matters out in Missouri. But similar problems popped up in South Dakota, Nebraska, and Oklahoma. In Iowa, the law proved so restrictive that Tappan thought about simply closing up shop there and concentrating on more open markets. "I think that is nothing but a hold-up game on their part," he wrote to one of his agents in Iowa, "and you can tell them that I said so."[47]

Sometimes the company got a friendly reception from state officials, often too friendly. In a few cases, examiners promised to smooth the way into the state, but wanted in turn to go right out the revolving door and become an agent of Investors Syndicate. Tappan wanted his customers to feel "perfectly safe and satisfied as we are doing business right," but it would be a lot easier to comply if regulation was handled in a less political manner.[48]

In this attitude toward government, Tappan once again showed himself a modern Progressive. He had never embraced the radical restructuring of the economy proposed by Populists at the turn of the century. But he had long believed in the need for reform in the public's interest. That notion lay behind his founding of Investors Syndicate, and his strong commitment to a long-term, thoroughly honest approach to investment. The most important public benefit anyone could provide, Tappan believed, was to do their job efficiently, effectively, honestly, and professionally. These same values he hoped to find in government. When officials acted rationally and with the public interest at heart, everyone benefited by having an economy that was safer, stronger, and more dependable. But politics as usual, the give and take of elections, the heated rhetoric of campaigns, strong partisan attitudes—these in Tappan's mind were delusions, focusing attention in the wrong direction. Partisan politics of this sort worked against consistency and rational management. Though, so did a kind of blind faith in markets or the unabashed pursuit of self-interest.

Tappan's goal was to position himself and his firm between the naked self-interest of the greedy speculator, who only cared for the public's money, and the retrograde hostility to modern finance that agrarian radicals seemed to embrace. There was between these two poles a course for businessmen to take, where they could put to use their high levels of skill, professionalism, and personal integrity. Tappan hoped for the same from government officials. The state could be a partner in support of his project, rather than an antagonist. He objected to laws and regulations that some states had passed as so restrictive that they stifled legitimate business. But he held up Illinois' statute as a model of securities regulation and recommended it to politicians in other states in which the company did business. The Illinois law was neither slipshod nor overly broad. It supervised and controlled companies as it should, while giving "grafters and stock jobbing concerns" a "hard time." Chicago, as Tappan knew from his own early experiences, had once been a "regular hot bed of fake stock promoting schemes."[49] The new law was clearing that up. Only about 10 percent of the companies that applied in Illinois, Tappan noted approvingly, made it through.[50] Of course, Investors Syndicate was one of them.

The three years between 1914 and 1917 proved to be the turning point in the history of Investors Syndicate. The suddenness of success is almost impossible to account for. Certainly Hibbert's arrival and aggressive marketing through the creation of a nationwide agency system is the immediate explanation. Yet there was nothing mysterious about agencies, which had been used in many businesses, including other financial services. Plenty of good, experienced insurance agents existed in the country, though few of them thought about moving laterally into a new, untested type of financial product. There was also nothing mysterious about the product that Investors Syndicate sold. Other companies also sold financial products to the public. But many that had started around the same time as Investors Syndicate had already folded. Getting the right combination of factors lined up at the right time was apparently far more difficult than it seemed.

As it turned out, the key to success in the business of selling the public new financial products came down to little more than consistency, security, and high quality customer service. Innovation was fine, but people wanted to know where their money was going, and to know it was being invested in something that was safe, honest, and proven. Tappan's years of hard work in the face of slow or no growth, his consistent performance on a small scale, and his careful, security-first organization all mattered. So did an unimpeachable track record and a willingness to meet every legal criticism by adjusting operations until they conformed to the law, rather than evading the law. Over time, the sort of people—average, working, hard-saving people—whose money Tappan sought responded to these achievements. In the end, the simple but timeless business advice of trying "each month to put our business on a better and better basis and to keep it on such a basis that it will be absolutely beyond criticism" seems to have triumphed. Investors Syndicate now had assets of nearly $1 million.[51] But there was no time to rest on past achievements. It was 1917, and the guns of August were echoing now on both sides of the Atlantic. The United States had entered the First World War.

CHAPTER SEVEN

WAR AND BETRAYAL

At age forty-eight, John Elliott Tappan was too old to serve in the First World War. But he remained extremely fit. Nothing about him was diminutive. Six feet tall, he was ramrod straight, muscular and athletic, with a loud, hearty laugh. His once slender frame had filled out since the days of tramping through the West with no money in his pocket. The one indulgence John could not control was his sweet tooth, particularly his affection for chocolate. Not even the diabetes diagnosed a few years later would curb that. His deep blue eyes were still his most striking feature, though now they were more often hidden behind spectacles. The occupational hazard of close work in the office had taken its toll. Otherwise, he was as vigorous and active as he had been when he started Investors Syndicate. In bed at nine, he rose with the dawn. He continued to read widely with diverse interests and definite opinions about matters of the day, which he expressed quite freely. Affecting a formal style of dress and stance, he wore a suit every day. Not a man for small talk, he could appear somewhat imposing to those who did not know him well, an image reinforced by rare but explosive displays of anger. But he also had a droll sense of humor, which sometimes fooled people who were unsure when he was being serious and when he was teasing.

Living on Cedar Lake with his large family, Tappan remained an avid outdoorsman, taking his children hiking and teaching them how to swim in the cool lake waters. He was a powerful swimmer, and more than once was called upon to pull drowning vacationers out of the water. One summer evening, while relaxing after dinner with a lemonade, Tappan was surprised by a frantic man bursting through the door of the house. "Hurry John," he yelled, "Two men are drowning!" Tappan rushed to his car, followed by his children Elliott and Marion. Two railroad workers had decided to cool off in the lake after eating their dinner. Either they did not know how to swim or had ventured out too far. Without stopping to remove his clothes, John dove in, dragging one man out while a second rescuer found the other. They tried to resuscitate them on the beach, but to no avail. The drowned men were as white as a fish's belly.

Work and family curbed some of John's recreational activities. Only occasionally could he venture up to Angora or Isle Royale for the hunting season or even for a simple vacation. The days when he could expect to spend a winter in the northern Minnesota wilderness as a part-time stockman were now gone. His leisure time was taken up instead by a somewhat tamer pursuit, golf. Just before World War I, the golf craze hit the American middle class. Men began the endless quest for time away from the office to chase a small white ball around a manicured green. With knickers, sweater, and cap, Tappan drove off Saturday afternoons for rounds with other Minneapolis businessmen. It was a far cry from the sort of direct contact with nature that had always been important to John's life—a pale suburban substitute for the woods and the meadow.

He did not, however settle completely for modern recreation. One season he took up a somewhat older hobby, beekeeping. When a local beekeeper came out to the house to remove a large hive from one of his trees, John questioned the man about his work. With his help, John coaxed a group of bees into a white wooden hive, and soon had all the necessary equipment: protective suit, netted face mask, and heavy gloves. Ever practical, he learned how to remove the honey, which he served to his family for breakfast. When the bees swarmed, Winnie called him at his office, and he rushed home, put on his gear, and tried to persuade them into another hive.

Between 1917 and 1919, though, Tappan got little peace out of these domestic pursuits. The war was having a major impact on the investment business. In May 1917, the United States government sponsored its first

Liberty Loan drive to raise money for American troops in Europe and to support the Allied powers. Two-thirds of the U.S. war effort was financed by drawing down the public's savings into government bonds. Taxes paid for the other third. In five bond drives from May 1917 through May 1919, the Treasury raised some $21.4 billion, about $270 billion in today's money. Just as important was the way the money was raised. To soak up excess spending power and keep inflation under control, Treasury Secretary William Gibbs McAdoo marketed the bonds as widely as possible. By encouraging all Americans, not just the wealthy, to buy Liberty Bonds, he hoped to give the entire nation a stake in the war.

It worked extremely well. Backed by a massive advertising campaign, volunteer salesmen and women and a network of brokers and dealers collected all the money desired, and more. Several of the loans were actually oversubscribed. The spirit was infectious, as banners, posters, and flags blaring "Buy More Bonds" appeared in every town and city. References to German atrocities in Belgium stirred deep emotions. Hollywood stars such as Douglas Fairbanks and Mary Pickford spoke before enormous crowds. Patriotic marchers in cities carried effigies of the German Kaiser and Chancellor Hindenberg. From the Treasury, through the Federal Reserve Banks, to commercial banks, brokers, investment houses, and commissioned sales agents, the bonds made their way through the American economy, supported by a specialized marketing organization—the War Loan Organization—run by volunteers from the nation's large investment banks. It was a nationwide, cross-class sales effort that far exceeded anything any private intermediary had attempted since the days of Jay Cooke and the Civil War bonds.

People were soon spending every spare cent on bonds to show their patriotism and to support the war. This sudden flooding of the bond market could not help but leave Investors Syndicate with a smaller market. Yet in the long run, it was also a positive experience in financial services. The war bond sales helped to accustom people to buying and holding paper securities. National savings bulged dramatically in 1917-1918, and just as importantly switched temporarily from durable goods and tangible assets to paper securities.[1] Unbeknownst to the Treasury, it was actually laying the foundation for a massive increase in public participation in the stock and bond markets during the 1920s.

Tappan was instinctively patriotic, and he supported the war by purchasing a good number of Liberty Bonds himself. But he had some immediate problems to handle as a result. Nineteen-eighteen was an extremely difficult year. Many of the Syndicate agents were drafted, which depleted the sales force. Contract holders were also drafted, and many feared that they would not be able to keep up their monthly premium while in the service. To each of these investors, Tappan wrote a reassuring letter. All would be carried on company books for two years from their last payment without lapsing. Making just one payment in that time, just one, would extend the contract another two years. Those who could not even make one payment would still not be cut adrift. "This company will not take advantage of the man in service," Tappan repeated in his letters. Those who defaulted were entitled to a partial payment. But his hope was that the liberal default features would leave soldiers "amply protected." This was a far more generous attitude than financial companies usually took in times of war. Insurance companies had required extra premiums of policymakers who signed up for duty during the previous American military conflict, the Spanish American War.[2] Perhaps Tappan was more generous because he optimistically believed that "undoubtedly the war will be finished long before the two years have elapsed, at least it should be if the United States goes at it the way it should."[3]

Going at the war "the way it should" meant full support from all Americans. Besides buying Liberty Bonds, the Tappan family also volunteered its time and effort, as did many citizens. Winnie, Ruth, and Marion worked for the Red Cross. Ruth knitted socks for American boys in France, and she and Marion rolled bandages all through the cold winter of 1918. Sometimes, however, the call of patriotism placed Tappan in a bind. Several contract holders wrote asking if they could have their money back in order to use it to buy Liberty Bonds. "While we are heartily in sympathy with people purchasing Liberty Bonds," Tappan replied, a contract was still a contract. It could not be violated even for a worthwhile patriotic sentiment. There was, however, another option. "You have a right to let your payments with us get behind for a period of two years before your contract would lapse or you would forfeit what you have paid in. By letting your payments run behind a little," Tappan concluded, "you will be enabled to get your Liberty Bond," without sacrificing the investment.[4]

One reason Tappan wanted to maintain the rules of the contract, even during war, was that he understood that some of the soldiers who went to France would not be returning. The families of some of his clients would be filing for death claims, under contract provisions that entitled them to their money back and a payment of 4 percent interest. Financially, the war was going to put a strain on Investors Syndicate. "The company will be hit pretty hard under the death option clauses in our contracts," Tappan informed stockholders. Each death surrender lost money for the company. The death of young soldiers was going to be especially hard, for many of them had just started to make payments when they went to war.[5] To live up to the terms of the contract in these cases, Investors Syndicate could not afford to make exceptions in others.[6]

The war also meant an emotional strain. When the first casualties were announced, Tappan found himself writing letters to the families of dead American servicemen, offering condolences and then dispassionately explaining to the family their options. They could either surrender the contracts, or keep up the payments the deceased had started until the contract matured. This work lent a somber mood to the times. Although Tappan's oldest boy, Elliott, was only fourteen and too young to serve, Winnie's nephew Tom Gallagher was a student at St. Thomas Military Academy and might well land in France if the war ground on.

The mood was reflected in a Christmas gift to Ruth that year, a copy of Robert W. Service's *Rhymes of a Red Cross Man.* One poem in the collection, a memorial to Service's brother who was killed in action in August 1916, spoke directly to the family's apprehension about Tom and other young men they knew. Entitled "Young Fellow, My Lad," the poem is largely filled with noble, pro-war sentiments about duty, honor, and sacrifice as a young man goes off to war. But in several wrenching stanzas, the father waits for the letter from his son that will never arrive.

At home, the war brought an unprecedented increase in government involvement in the economy. To direct the nation onto a wartime footing, Washington created new organizations for overseeing production and distribution in accord with military priorities. These were coordinated by the War Industries Board, a massive agency responsible for assuring adequate output of guns, munitions, uniforms, food for soldiers, and fuel for ships and planes, while keeping the economy healthy. In good Progressive Era fashion, the government did not simply take over the economy. With the brief exceptions of railroads and telecommunications, which were nationalized for the duration, industry remained in private hands. Most of the administrating was done cooperatively, between government officials and "dollar-a-year men," executives released from their firms to serve in Washington, for the nominal salary of a dollar a year during the war.

This belief in business-government cooperation was one of the hallmarks of mainstream politics of the times. It found its fullest expression during the war, but the ideas stretched back to the turn of the century, to the same intellectual milieu in which John Elliott Tappan had evolved his financial innovation. Progressives like Tappan were fundamentally nonradical, in that they believed in progress through rational decisions and slow social evolution, rather than extreme restructuring. They also believed in reform, however, and understood that purely self-interested behavior could lead to waste, fraud, and abuse, common enough problems encountered in the early, unregulated consumer financial markets.

New expert agencies, above mere politics, were a favorite Progressive Era way of balancing public interest with a private, market oriented economy. In 1913, Tappan had witnessed the birth of the Federal Reserve System. Democratic President Woodrow Wilson signed legislation creating a new central bank, which presumably made public control of money possible. It completed, through a modern administrative agency, one of the old Populist dreams. Earlier, Republican President Theodore Roosevelt had put his considerable energy behind efforts to conserve natural resources and regulate pharmaceuticals and food through the Pure Food and Drug Act.

The war allowed Progressives to show what they could do in managing affairs in an objective and presumably nonpartisan way during a time of crisis. Still, their efforts did not always proceed as smoothly as they believed they would, and even supporters of the general drift of Progressivism like Tappan could run into difficulties. One part of the new economic administration created for the war was the Capital Issues Committee. Like every other vital resource, capital was scarce and had to be rationed. The Capital Issues Committee was concerned with preventing competition in the market for Liberty Bonds that might deprive the nation of the funds it needed to fight the war. All investment companies selling $100,000 worth of securities per year had to apply to the Committee for a permit to do business. Tappan quickly complied, and for several months engaged in back and forth negotiations, in and out of Washington, to keep his firm operating.

The status of Investors Syndicate was unclear. Only a few other firms in the nation operated as it did. Several, Tappan noticed, had simply continued to do business, assuming they were exempt. Tappan had always had great respect for the law, reflecting his profession and his belief that it was better to operate with official sanction and public approval than to try to skirt the law. So he wanted a ruling as soon as possible. Unfortunately, as he predicted, the "unique" nature of the Syndicate's business left members of the Committee scratching their heads. Composed of several Federal Reserve Board members with an advisory group drawn from the commercial and investment banking worlds, the government body was made up of people who generally regarded Tappan and his company as competitors to their own businesses.[7] Certainly Investors Syndicate was not the sort of operation bankers and Wall Street financial men were familiar with. Tappan headed off to Washington once more, to present his case.

On August 20, 1918, he arrived to meet the Committee. A week later, when he boarded the train back to Minneapolis, he still did not have a clear answer. The Committee's mandate was to prevent fraud and abuse in the capital market. Liberty Bond drives were selling securities to people who had never bought them before. Many resold the bonds in secondary markets. Unscrupulous operators tried to take advantage of unsophisticated customers by getting them to exchange their conservative, government backed securities for speculative investments. In the interests of wartime finance, the Capital Issues Committee sought to stem such abuses, which would hurt future bond drives.[8] It was unclear if the Syndicate could continue writing new contracts during Liberty Loan drives. Possibly the company would have to stop making mortgage loans as well, a use of funds that competed with war bonds. In October, however, the Committee agreed to let Investors Syndicate accept Liberty Bonds at cash value for payments on Syndicate contracts. Face amount certificates were deemed sound enough to be offered to the public. Indirectly, the company would be helping to fund the war effort by making the market for Liberty Bonds more liquid.

The Committee's final ruling, a bit later, was less favorable. Investors Syndicate would only be permitted to write 1,000 contracts for the year. Apparently, the Committee still did not understand the nature or scope of Tappan's business. The Syndicate had already written more than 1,000 contracts for 1918. Worse, the ruling was proposing to limit the company to far less business than Tappan felt it could write for the following year. It would be difficult, he reminded committee members, to take $100,000 or more in Liberty Bonds, if the company could not write business on at least 6,000 new contracts.

The wisest course seemed to be to retrench and conserve resources while the uncertainty of the war loomed. On October 26, Tappan informed company stockholders that business would be slow for as long as the European conflict lasted. He noted that though he had secured a permit to continue business, the amount of new business was limited. No dividends would be issued until matters with the government were clear. Business was down to such a trickle that Tappan decided to shut down the company's offices in Chicago and St. Louis.

Then, less than two weeks after he made that decision, it was all over. On November 11, 1918, an armistice was announced. In Minneapolis and every other American city, news that the war had ended was met with wild celebration. Sirens were set off, whistles blew. People ran out into the street and men threw their hats into the air. Tappan had been writing a letter to a client worried about meeting his payments if drafted, when he heard the news. He was able to conclude his response to the man happily with, "the whistles are still blowing in celebration of the signing of the armistice by Germany. We presume now you will not have to enter the service."[9]

With the end of the war, the Capital Issues Committee ruling no longer applied. Liberty Bond drives were over and throughout the nation the hope was for a return to business as normal. Indeed, "normalcy," a new word coined by President Warren G. Harding in 1921, was what everyone desired. Although Progressivism had had a chance to show its colors during the war, people were not ready to expand government economic involvement permanently. In fact, World War I actually signaled the end of the Progressive agenda. In its place came a decade of much more strongly pro-business feelings. The private sector would once again lead, with government reduced to a smaller supporting role until the economic crisis of the Great Depression in the 1930s. For Tappan, a businessman first who believed in a positive though limited role for government, the future portended strong opportunities for his growing firm. But it was hard to see the future clearly in the immediate aftermath of the devastation wrought by global conflict.

Although optimistic that his firm was "flourishing," Tappan admitted, after the signing of the Armistice, that "business conditions are not adjusted even if the war is over."[10] Despite America's relatively brief and highly successful military experience overseas, the return over the next several months of bodies of young men killed in action was a sobering and disturbing event. The First World War was the first modern, technological war. Poison gas, armored tanks, and machine guns killed in astoundingly high numbers, and killed like nothing before ever had. Perhaps most frightening of all was the routine but deadly use of high explosive artillery shells in combat, which "blew men apart along no known anatomical lines," as Ernest Hemingway observed during his stint as an ambulance driver. High explosives did more than their share in leaving battlefields strewn with over a million unidentified or unidentifiable dead by the war's end.

Even the return home for the living was fraught with peril. In 1918, a new, deadly strain of influenza appeared. Following soldiers overseas and back again, it circled the globe in four months, killing more people than all the losses on all sides in the war. Medicine, so proud of its recent achievements in combating typhus, yellow fever, smallpox, and venereal diseases, was helpless before the virus that would in the end take twenty-one million lives worldwide. War-wearied populations in Europe suffered heavy losses, as did peoples in underdeveloped nations. But even in the United States, which still had a healthy economy and a well-fed population, 300,000 died from the flu in eight weeks. When the disease had fully run its course, over a half-million excess American deaths could be pinned on it. Nothing in human history killed as many people in such a short space of time as this plague. Its global demographic impact was exceeded only by the terrible devastation of World War II.[11]

Minneapolis had a relatively mild bout with the flu, though it was one of the few cities to be visited by the pest in both 1918-1919 and again in 1920. A little over a thousand citizens succumbed in the first round. In a city of 380,000 people, that was less than one-third of 1 percent. Port cities at the epicenter of the infection, such as New York and Boston, fared far worse, losing three times that percentage.[12] Still, witnessing just one death could weaken the knees of even the toughest person. The virus was at its worst when it joined forces with an opportunistic pneumonia infection. Victims of this deadly duo could die in a matter of hours, their lips blue from lack of oxygen, their lungs gray and heavy, filled with frothy, bloody liquid.

None of the Tappan family or employees of Investors Syndicate were among the victims, but nearly everyone knew someone who was. What was particularly insidious about this killer was that it took not just the very young and very old, but men and women in their prime. Marion's best friend, Mildred Sweeny, lost her mother to the epidemic. One long-time client and friend, Arthur Thomas, lost a young daughter. Though it had been ten years since Zita's death, both John and Winnie felt the sense of loss for their friend deeply. Winnie burst into tears when she heard the bad news. John wrote back, "we know" how a loss of a child "strains the heart strings."[13]

These conditions meant no possibility, for the near term, of business as usual at Investors Syndicate. First, there were the expected deaths of contract holders from the war to deal with. Then there were the unexpected deaths from disease. By killing off adults in the prime of life, the flu was "an actuarial nightmare." It took those whom investment firms were least prepared to lose—men and women still working and paying premiums. Indeed, this flu seemed to have an appetite for the healthy and robust. Most of the nation's insurance companies were forced to suspend or reduce their dividends because of it. Depending on similar demographics, Investors Syndicate was placed in a similar squeeze. With the highest percentage of deaths occurring in the twenty to forty age range, the influenza outbreak made many contract holders and borrowers of the Syndicate its victims.

There were also longer term consequences. Unlike more feared infectious killers, the influenza virus moved wide and shallow through the population. It killed a relatively small percentage of its victims, compared to smallpox or yellow fever, but it stayed silently around for months until nearly everyone caught it. That high rate of infection resulted in the astounding death totals. But even among the survivors there were scars. As the standard joke of the times went, influenza is a sickness you don't get over until a month after you're done with it. Survivors were often left weak, debilitated, with severe depression. Nearly every customer of Tappan's would likely have contracted the disease or attended to sick family members who had. That meant lost work, missing wages, doctor's bills, and financial hardship.

Those sick or recovering from the illness were granted the same liberal terms for payment as soldiers. In one case, a woman whose husband had died of the flu wrote, claiming that she knew her husband had kept up his payments. But Tappan could find no record of them. He simply wrote back, "We did not wait to trace this down before sending you your check, as we thought that we could do that later, and we would hurry on this much money to you so that you would have it to use."[14]

As he struggled with the devastating aftermath of the war, Tappan unexpectedly received another slap in the face. In 1920, the state of Minnesota sent word that it was suspending Investors Syndicate's permit to do business. It was certainly a shock. Tappan had expected trouble from other states, where Investors Syndicate operated as a "foreign" corporation or was new and untested. But not from his home state. For years, he had been the company officer to deal with these issues of public accountability, law, and regulation. Once again, it was his job to defend the Syndicate, its reputation, and its purpose in an age when the rules and laws of finance were unclear and inconsistent. He rose to the occasion, as never before.

In response to eleven specific allegations, Tappan penned a detailed twenty-six-page reply, a long letter even for him. He explained all facets of the company and its operations. He noted that in Minnesota and several other states, he had voluntarily deposited deeds of trust, which showed that the company in fact used subscribers' payments to make investments as promised. Such safeguards would not be required generally of investment companies until the 1930s.[15] Tappan also pointed out that he had done business for fourteen years before there was *any* supervision of investment companies in Minnesota. When the law was passed, he noted proudly, the public examiner "came into our office and found everything ably, honestly and faithfully conducted. We were complimented upon the economical and able manner in which the business had been conducted." Since then, every examiner had given Investors Syndicate a clean bill of health.

After noting his company's long history of legal compliance, Tappan then did a surprising thing. He placed the lawyer in check and finished not with legal reasoning, assertions of rights, or even by returning to his firm's envious track record. Instead, he closed by referring back to the very origins of Investors Syndicate, to John Elliott Tappan and his own personal integrity. This had always been Tappan's strongest case, his deep commitment to the success of the enterprise and his abiding belief that the Syndicate served the public interest by allowing people to save and to securely invest their earnings. His words were revealing.

"I started the Syndicate without a dollar," he wrote, "all I had was a good character, good reputation, honesty and lots of energy." The first certificates he had sold to his closest friends, and now many of them were not only customers but stockholders as well. Tappan believed that the reason people bought the certificates was, in part at least, based on "my having charge of the business," and their belief in him as "honest and faithful to my trust." His motto from the start had been, "meet every obligation promptly when it fell due," and "deal with our certificate holders in an absolutely honest and honorable manner." He would "almost as soon lose life itself as have anything happen to the Syndicate or its certificate holders." He put the company "above almost everything in life," having watched it "grow and develop as a child might grow up."[16]

Perhaps in an age that had seen its fair share of financial chicanery and quick-buck artistry, the state securities watchdogs were taken aback by the depth and sincerity of the appeal. Here clearly was no ordinary financier. After reading Tappan's letter, the commission reversed its suspension. Once again, the vagaries of state law and politics had threatened to trip up Investors Syndicate. But once again, Tappan placed his personal integrity on the line, and came out victorious.

Problems with state regulation did not turn Tappan into a rabid free market ideologue. Far from it. He was happy to see the dishonest regulated out of existence. Government certainly had an obligation, Tappan believed, to prevent any company from "putting out a contract or certificate that it cannot carry out."[17] His appeals to various state bodies, like the one to Minnesota, were usually couched not in terms of his "rights" to free enterprise, but to the public good his firm brought. What Tappan relished most were expressions like those written to him by one Syndicate client: "I consider your company a public benefactor in furnishing such an easy system of saving money, and paying such a liberal rate of interest with the best of security." It was a perfect statement of the principles of private action taken with public interest in mind that Tappan sought.[18]

The threatened revocation from Minnesota and the constant negotiating with other state authorities convinced Tappan of one thing. There definitely needed to be a single national law on these matters. The war experience reinforced his sense that national uniformity and efficiency were the best cures for inconsistency and variability in state law. For all his frustration with the Capital Issues Committee, Tappan came away pleased that its investigations found the Syndicate's business plan and methods of operation sound and legitimate. The committee, he believed, was composed of some of the "best known and ablest bankers and financiers in the United States," which meant largely bankers from New York. The power and prestige such men wielded had been one of the sore points of Populists and other supporters of economic decentralization. To Tappan, however, they appeared more like the best and the brightest. Under wise tutelage, the nation could have a sound financial system, but also room for experimentation and local initiative, as demonstrated by Investors Syndicate.

With Minnesota placated, it seemed at last that the worst was over. Investors Syndicate could get back to what it had been before the war—a business on the fast track. But there was one final hurdle to clear before a return to normalcy. With the war over, the overheated economy suddenly took a plunge. Europe faced dismal economic conditions in the aftermath. It had been battered by death, disease, and destruction, and barely had money to feed itself, let alone to buy American-made goods. Excess capacity at American manufacturing plants forced massive shutdowns and layoffs. The global economy went into a sudden, sharp depression, the final act of the global war.

Fortunately, the depression only lasted a short while. Born in the nineteenth century's most severe economic crisis, Investors Syndicate had little trouble weathering this squall. Farm belt states like Minnesota, and the West, where Tappan did most of his business, were not hurt as badly as the nation's urban manufacturing centers. By 1921 in any case, the economy had cleared. As wartime sacrifices faded into memory, America started on what proved to be a decade-long boom. Improvements in production and productivity drove down prices. Consumer goods rose in quality and availability all through the 1920s. Soon 60 percent of American families had cars. A whole new array of technologies became available to the average household. Families purchased labor-saving devices such as vacuum cleaners, washing machines, and refrigerators. Radios, a new product at the start of World War I, reached 40 percent of households by decade's end. New homes wired for electricity were being built and occupied in record numbers by a growing middle class. More Americans had telephones, indoor plumbing, electricity for heat, light, power, and of course automobiles, than any other peoples on the face of the earth.

The boom of the 1920s was also reflected in financial markets. As Tappan had predicted, for all the disruption, the war experience was good for the investment business. "When the war is over," he had written in 1918, "the Syndicate should be more than prosperous as people then will be educated, not only in savings, but in bonds. . . . They [the public] will fully understand what a bond means and we will do more business than ever before."[19] The desire for investments in paper securities did indeed increase as Tappan had predicted. But he, like most other prognosticators, missed the real significance of this financial revolution. The greatest beneficiary of the public's new sophistication was not the bond market, but the stock market.

The great 1920s bull market in stocks was quite a reversal of financial traditions. Until 1900, common stocks were notable for both their risk and unimpressive returns. The small, illiquid market for industrial securities was generally outperformed by bonds, and did no better than commercial paper. The New York Stock Exchange was oriented toward the big spenders, and even charged high commissions for those who wanted only to dip their toes into the market. Brokerage houses were common in most towns and cities across the nation, but they offered a minimum of services, little help or advice, and no discounts on sales. Odd lot sales—less than a hundred shares—cost the investor much more than larger purchases. Cheaper, over-the-counter issues not registered on the major exchanges were even more speculative, and newspapers entertained the American public with stories of fortunes won then lost in so-called penny stocks.

Stockbrokers themselves had a shady reputation, and customers had no way of knowing for sure who was honest, who was a thief, and who was a self-interested salesman more focused on generating commissions with "hot" stock tips. Exposés with titles like "Frenzied Finance" and "Other People's Money" told of rings and pools run by stock jobbers. Speculators enticed the public with tall tales of fortunes to be made in the market, then used those funds for runs on selected stocks.[20] In a speculative frenzy fed by the purchases of deluded investors, share prices ran up to impossible heights. The smart traders quickly got their money out at the high point, just before stocks came crashing down and wiped out the small-fry who had come late to the party.

Under these conditions, it was impossible for the average person to invest in stocks a few dollars at a time, as they could with bonds, insurance policies, and Tappan's face amount certificates. It was this situation, in fact, that gave Tappan his opportunity to market a structured debt instrument at a time when variable investments performed poorly. Low transactions costs and the hard-earned trust of the investor allowed him to compete successfully with other financial instruments, even those like corporate securities that had tempting, if uncertain, rewards.

After World War I, though, public appreciation for the stock market began to increase. In the 1920s, large numbers of Americans began for the first time to put money into common stocks as they began their historic rise as the best long-term investment measured by real rates of returns.[21] A number of economic factors were responsible for the change. Under a Republican administration, interest rates fell, lowering bond returns and increasing those of stocks. Though Wall Street was still disdainful of the small investor, returns of blue chip corporations were solid, steady, and proven. Big corporations had traded their stocks publicly for decades, but they had not emphasized widespread public ownership. Growth and consolidation during several merger movements, the first after the 1890s depression and the last starting with the 1920 downturn, increased corporate capital needs. Then, too, Progressive Era hostility to self-absorbed, but economically vital, big firms gave rise to a new generation of professional corporate managers by the 1920s. To cement their place in the good graces of the public, companies began to emphasize widespread stock ownership, giving erstwhile critics a stake in their firms. America's largest corporation, AT&T, led the way, becoming famous for its mythical "widows and orphans" shareholders.

Perhaps as many as one third of American households owned common stocks by 1929.[22] These investors were often sophisticated urbanites, who had less fear of paper securities than had their rural parents or grandparents. Loosened from their parents' conservative views of money, the bolder, freer-wheeling generation of the roaring twenties was willing to take a chance on the promise of high returns in new, booming glamour industries such as airlines. Growth in size of the stock market in turn encouraged further investment, by making stocks more liquid. Soon, indexes of stock market performance were running up to unprecedented levels. Annual volume on Wall Street rose from around 170 million shares at the turn of the century to over a billion shares at the end of the 1920s.[23] Before the great crash of 1929, which reversed much of this new trend in the public's investment patterns, the market reached an all-time high.

The move toward the stock market was also encouraged by a new type of financial intermediary, the investment trust, a precursor of modern mutual funds. A few mutual type funds had made their appearance before 1920, growing out of private trust operations. They were popular in England in the late nineteenth century. Not so in America, however. As late as 1924, the United States had seen a grand total of only eighteen such funds, including several already out of business. In America, pooled investments in the stock market were generally restricted to private trust activities for the wealthy. Investment trusts, however, were public funds. Anyone could join. They collected savings from a variety of participants and placed that money into a diverse array of investments.[24]

Beginning in 1925, investment trusts skyrocketed in popularity in the United States. By 1928, 200 were in existence.[25] Their range and diversity was impressive, even by today's standards. Some specialized in common stocks, or the stocks of certain industries; others emphasized fixed investments; and still others sought to maintain a balanced portfolio. One was run by a union, the Amalgamated Clothing Workers. Whatever the investment strategy, investment trusts followed the same basic principles of intermediation and diversification that Tappan had followed when he started Investors Syndicate. Many of them began small, established a track record, attracted investors, and then grew with the rising stock market of the 1920s.

In many ways, the investment companies were the next logical step in the growth of financial services. Banks, whose lineage stretched back centuries, pooled savings for investment in a diversity of projects. Insurance companies invested the public's money in return for protection against unexpected death or loss. Private trust funds handled portfolios of wealthy individuals. All of these institutions provided expertise in managing money and a degree of diversification individuals alone could not achieve. Tappan had built on these precedents, extending the opportunities for diversified investment and providing expertise and assistance to groups largely excluded from financial services.

Investment companies opened up new classes of securities for the middle-class investor by providing access to the stock market. But they had their limits. The first ones were "closed-end" funds. That is, they sold their own stock (and bonds and preferred stocks as well) to the public, and then used these monies to make other investments, presumably generating a return to pay back investors. Once a person purchased shares in the investment company, he or she could only get out by selling those shares in secondary markets, as they would any other asset. Closed-end funds generally were not listed on the major stock exchanges, so liquidity depended on the less secure over-the-counter market. This lack of liquidity would have made closed-end funds unattractive to those with modest amounts to invest.

Nor did the investment trusts always do a good job of maximizing their clients' returns. Sometimes, the share price of the closed-end fund was actually higher than the underlying value of the investments the fund was making. Such a misalignment of values meant the average investor would have been better off ignoring the mutual fund and putting money in the stocks himself. Modern, open-end mutual funds, by contrast, avoid these problems of value and liquidity. They issue shares continually as investors come to their door. They also buy back shares when the investor wants out. With open-end mutual funds, values fluctuate only with the underlying value of the fund's portfolio of investments. The first open-end funds appeared in 1924, facilitating the small investors' movement into the market. Overall, though, the closed-end model dominated, managing some $2.6 billion of the public's assets by 1929, compared to only $134 million in open-end funds.[26]

Even with these new intermediaries, the stock market boom of the 1920s was a wild ride for those who had never experienced the ups and downs of variable investments. In some ways, the market took on aspects of a speculative mania. People bought stocks on margin, or on credit, purchasing more than they could afford in the hope that their stocks would rise in value.[27] Rather than provide objective information, the financial press fed these speculative dreams.[28] Few rules, except internal ones followed by stock exchanges themselves, assured or controlled the amount or quality of information offered in support of a particular stock. Like most forms of self-regulation, this one was as leaky as a sieve.

To attract new investors, investment trusts hawked their wares as did any other business with goods to sell. Dealers and brokers advertised for new clients, and fed the mania for hot stocks using hard-sell tactics. As one observer noted, stocks were sold with the same techniques used to sell soap.[29] Like other cagey advertisers, investment companies appealed less to reason, and more to emotions and desires. Just as manufacturers encouraged consumption with national chain distribution and brand name goods, so brokers used stock tickers, telephone sales, and offices throughout the nation to encourage the consumption of financial services. Direct mail solicitations, media advertising campaigns, displays, pamphlets, and magazines all sought to entice new buyers. Like their counterparts in consumer goods, financial houses used advertising to create little human interest dramas in print and on the airwaves, or sponsored radio entertainment programs punctuated with "sound advice" on financial matters.

All successful financial service firms, of course, must attract customers. Investors Syndicate was no different on this score. But the stock market boom and the rise of the investment trusts was a further step toward a new definition of investment. In a speculative boom, there is little pretence that some underlying real values are what matter. What mattered in the 1920s stock market was simply that stock prices were going up, and everyone thought they would continue to go up. It was a big change in how people conceived of their investments. The public's participation in the stock market was becoming indistinguishable from its participation in any other consumer market. By the 1920s, people were buying financial assets that played on fantasy in a manner no different than the fantasy surrounding cars, clothes, or toiletries. Perhaps most revealing, they used the same device, consumer credit, to purchase stocks on margin as they did refrigerators on the installment plan.

This conflation of savings, which had once invoked words such as accumulation, self-denial, and stewardship of resources, with consumerism, would have sounded strange when John Elliott Tappan was growing up. One reason Americans had historically refrained from stocks and investment trusts, despite British precedent, may have had to do with cultural values about savings and investment. In the nineteenth century, American savings did not go into investment trusts, but rather continued to go into real assets—land, houses, businesses.[30] Savings went into entrepreneurial assets, which owners could actively manage, such as small businesses. These patterns of investment reflected the nation's strong belief in the virtues of independent ownership and producerism. Small business ownership did not cease with the growth of stocks and investment trusts, of course. It remains a strong tradition in America even today. But it no longer held the central stage it once did in the nineteenth century. Passive investment strategies became more important to American households in the 1920s.

In many ways, Tappan remained a traditionalist on this score. His original conception of Investors Syndicate was more producerist than consumerist. He relied on a dedicated network of agents, direct appeals to clients, and a minimum of advertising or hard sell, pie-in-the-sky promises. He sold paper securities, of course—passive investments. But he envisioned active, educated, rational clients, not dependent, easily led consumers. Even through the stock market boom, Investors Syndicate continued to invest in land, the true source of wealth for those who believed that fundamental or real values guided the economy. Investors Syndicate sold its face amount certificates and stayed out of the stock market.[31]

The new interest in the stock market was not a threat to Investors Syndicate, however. Anything that increased public faith and interest in securities, Tappan regarded as a positive. Investors Syndicate was also a large operation relative to the upstart investment companies. Although these firms would grow rapidly, in 1924 the entire investment trust industry consisted of less than twenty firms managing about $15 million in capital.[32] Investors Syndicate had over $13 million in assets. It was more than ten times as large as it had been at the outbreak of World War I. As the bull market reached its apogee in the 1920s, many of the same people who had bought face amount certificates could now purchase common stocks and other financial assets. This did not slow Investors Syndicate, though, for the general growth of public investing meant more money for all financial services companies.

Confident that the stock market boom was not a threat to his own business, Tappan continued to expand operations in the 1920s. In 1921, his nephew Tom Gallagher joined the law practice, which handled the abstract, title, and mortgage contract work for Investors Syndicate. Tappan continued to ride around the state in his car, inspecting properties for mortgages, now with Tom at his side. The law office took up the fourth and fifth floors of the eight-story Lincoln Building. The Syndicate occupied the second and third floors. Around them were offices for doctors and lawyers, including one for the aviator Charles Lindbergh's father. Tappan sat behind a huge, roll-top desk, with a secretary and stenographer. The company receptionist operated a four line, twelve phone switchboard and handled routine clerical work. The office was open, as it always had been, from eight to six Monday through Friday, and a half-day on Saturdays.

For the next few years, things hummed along smoothly. This was the way Tappan liked it. His personality had not changed through all the adversity.

He had long ago "trained himself not to worry," and advised his friends and children to do the same. Perhaps it was partly as a reaction to the extreme pressures that fell on his shoulders after Zita's death, when both his business and family seemed to be spinning out of control. "I could lose everything I had," he once claimed, "yet I could go to bed and get a good night's sleep." His practice had long been to make difficult decisions with a clear head after a night's rest. The survival mechanism had served him well.

Changes had come to the Tappan household during the years surrounding the war, though. In October 1914, John's mother Adelaide died at age eighty. She was found slumped over the ironing board where she had apparently collapsed from a heart attack. John was away at the time, on a rare hunting respite from work, and rushed home. He buried his mother in Lakewood Cemetery. In 1915, his brother-in-law, Charles Guthrie, also passed away unexpectedly at age fifty-seven. He and John had been as close as brothers. Tappan's own children were growing up. Ruth had entered the University of Minnesota as a freshman in 1918. Always interested in science, she decided to major in chemistry, and started her college education as one of only five women in the chemistry department. Raised almost exclusively by his mother, John was a firm believer in the abilities of women. He encouraged Ruth in her plans to become a doctor, and thought that women should prepare for careers that would enable them to be self-sufficient, should they need to be. Like her father, Ruth had a cerebral side and took her studies seriously, preferring to spend time reading rather than chatting or pursuing a social life on campus. During weekends, John picked his daughter up from school, and spent Friday nights discussing issues like the war and politics with her.

Winnie had improved psychologically, but she was easily fatigued and complained of being tired all the time. For some time, her doctor had been advising rest and a more salubrious climate, away from the harsh, depressing Minnesota winters. Winnie had always loved California and its warm sunshine ever since a trip she took years before to visit relatives. After some checking, Ruth decided to transfer for a year to the University of California at Berkeley. Marion would join her there as a freshman, and they and Winnie would live in an apartment near campus, while the youngest child, Charles, could enroll in a California grammar school. John and Elliott would stay behind.

It proved to be an excellent decision. Though John was lonely that winter, the McCutchan family moved in at Cedar Lake to keep house for him. Winnie and the girls enjoyed California immensely. Then, in the summer, John and

Elliott came out for a visit and vacation. They spent five weeks traveling back to Minnesota, touring the American and Canadian Rockies, Glacier and Yellowstone National Parks, and relaxing in hunting lodges in the rugged Montana wilderness. Days were spent boating on lakes and hiking the mountains. Visiting the West and spending time in nature, as close to its raw state as possible, was the sort of recreation John had always preferred. He had missed it sorely in the past decade, when work, family, war, and other crises had absorbed too much of his time to allow him to get away.

Occasionally, he had been able to take some or all of his family with him on excursions to Syndicate field offices in different states during the years of rapid geographical expansion. On one trip South, Tappan and his family cruised on an old-fashioned paddleboat down the Mississippi, stopping off at Joplin and Hannibal, Missouri, and visiting Mark Twain's birthplace. Twain was a Tappan favorite, and John had read nearly everything he wrote. Only Ruth seemed a bit bored by the whole thing. She spent much of her time in the ship's library, going through it quickly. When John asked why she did not take in the beautiful scenery, she replied that there was nothing out there but a bunch of craggy rocks.

Ruth had more sophisticated tastes and wider aspirations than her father. She had graduated from the University of Minnesota in 1922, and worked for a time at Investors Syndicate, redoing the firm's files. But she soon had her own career, putting her degree in chemistry to good use by working as assistant city chemist and bacteriologist, a position of unusual responsibility for a woman. As it was Prohibition, one of her tasks was checking blood samples for the presence of alcohol, and testifying in court against those who violated the new law against drinking. That was certainly a career that made her teetotalling father happy.

Still, John decided that perhaps he needed to do something more to advance the social life of his daughters. Many years of living on Cedar Lake had left both Ruth and Marion isolated and a bit shy socially. It was hard during their teenage years to have close friends, given the family's location. If trips to classic American sights or the rugged outdoors did not satisfy their desire for adventure and experience, maybe a trip overseas would.

The war was long past by 1924. The combatants had recovered from the devastation, disease, and economic depressions that roiled the world in the conflict's aftermath. America was now far and away the biggest, most productive economy in the world and a creditor nation, taking over much of Britain's old role as center of world finance. The dollar was strong in Europe. Things were going smoothly at Investors Syndicate, which was celebrating its thirtieth year of business. Few investment companies could claim a tenth that longevity. Contracts were practically flying in from customers, who had money they wanted to invest and greater confidence in financial markets. A. W. King and John Hibbert had now been connected with the firm for almost a decade. It seemed a perfect time for Tappan to take what he had never had—a real, full-scale grand tour trip to Britain, the Continent, and beyond.

⬱

John had always loved to travel. Most of his adventures had been in familiar territory, in the country, out West, to the mountains where he renewed his contacts with nature. Evenings at home he often spent as an armchair traveler to more exotic locales, reading his subscription to *National Geographic*. The European tour would give him a chance to plan a grand adventure like a full-scale military campaign. He proposed, after extensive research, a five-month trip to Europe, North Africa, and the Middle East. All the family would go.

John reveled in each and every detail, pouring over guidebooks and maps, making notations on a pad of paper. In November 1924, Winnie began closing up the house, putting away linens into trunks, storing blankets in mothballs, turning bed mattresses, taking down window curtains, and beating rugs. Then, it took another two weeks to pack, as the family chose clothes carefully for travels through several seasons and climates. They prepared for horse riding, golf, tennis, and hiking, as well as the formal dances that would be held shipboard as they crossed the ocean on the Cunard line steamer, the *Baltic*.

Ruth kept a detailed diary of the entire journey. They visited Gibraltar, Algiers, and Greece. They saw the Parthenon in Athens and thousand-year-old mosques in Muslim countries. In some places, signs of the war were still fresh. As the ship went through the Dardanelles and stopped at Gallipoli, Ruth watched a woman scatter a bouquet of flowers in memory of the soldiers who had died there. At Constantinople, they steamed up the Bosphorus and into the Black Sea, then down to Palestine, where they stopped at Jerusalem, the Dead Sea, and Jericho. Eating oranges and playing bridge seated beside hills of red, orange, and white flowers, they watched Bedouins "in their biblical costumes" pass by, and saw an old shepherd carry a lamb under one arm, "looking for all the world like Abraham or Isaac," Ruth wrote. In Cairo, the next stop, they watched snake charmers and all kinds of musicians while sitting at the terrace of the Hotel Continental. For two weeks in Cairo, the family took camel rides and visited ancient ruins, shopped at bazaars, and attended formal teas at the hotel, in a bustling city filled with British officers and German aviators who had stayed on after the war.

The cruise ended in Italy. There, John hired a car to take them through the country to Florence, Venice, Milan, then on to Lucerne, and finally to Paris. On the way through France, Ruth described in detail the devastation left by the war in the battlefields. "As we advanced on Verdun, the desolation, even after five years, was terrible. Town after town with buildings and churches practically pulverized, broken stumps of trees, huge shell holes in the fields, zigzag lines of trenches, dug-outs, barbed wire entanglements, and even gas masks and helmets strewn about."

Everyone was excited by the time the family reached Paris, which was reckoned as the highlight of the trip. But there, Tappan received a telegram from A. W. King, imploring him to come home immediately. Several states were again threatening to oust Investors Syndicate, and he felt that only Tappan could remedy the situation. John wired back that he would leave for Minneapolis at once. The disappointment was palpable, as the family had been expecting two weeks in Paris. Winnie also wanted to end the trip with a visit to her relatives in Ireland, whom she had not seen since she left for America in 1886.

To compensate for the disappointment, John offered to take everyone to London first. As a special treat, he agreed to allow Ruth, Marion, and the other children to fly over by airplane, then an exciting new way to travel. It was a brave offer, for while John loved technology, he still thought airplanes too dangerous. In 1924, passenger service across the Channel was brand new, and it would still be three more years before Charles Lindbergh's historic solo flight over the Atlantic. John, a powerful swimmer, had little fear of boats, so he and Winnie planned to cross by ferry. But when the time came to buy the plane tickets, Winnie announced, "I'm going to fly, too. If all my children are going to be killed in an airplane crash, I want to be with them. I don't want to be left alone." Her decision left John with little choice, for he and Winnie were traveling on the same passport and had to make the journey together. "Cross as two sticks" at having to get into a plane that looked more like a box kite than a modern airliner, John debated with the clerk on whether the greater likelihood of a crash would come from a nosedive or a tailspin. He steadied his nerves by indulging in a rare drink, a bottle of wine with lunch at Le Bourget airport. Though the three-hour crossing went off without a hitch, John never took another plane ride. "I know what they're like," he responded to suggestions, "they're not safe."

In London, John and Winnie separated. She did not want to miss her chance to revisit her home country, and continued on to Ireland with the girls. John and the boys boarded the ship *Olympic* bound for New York. They sailed for a week and took a three-day train journey from New York to Minneapolis. When they arrived, John went immediately to his office. Whatever had caused the crisis cleared up quickly after his return. Apparently, he could not expect to take extended trips from the office, despite the company's success. Organization, still highly informal, more like a partnership than a bureaucracy, depended on Tappan's daily presence. He was only disappointed that, in cutting his trip short, he was unable to see where Winnie had grown up. As he suspected, it was to be his only chance, for he never returned to Europe.

Winnie, Ruth, and Marion spent two weeks in Ireland and arrived home three weeks after John. One unexpected benefit of the journey came to Ruth. She received a letter from a young man she had met aboard the *Baltic*. His name was Dr. Joseph Dowling, an ophthalmologist from Rhode Island. Though she had grown extremely fond of him, she thought nothing would ever come of it, as they lived so far apart. In his letter, however, he told her that he was coming to Minnesota for a conference at the Mayo Clinic. He promised to stop in Minneapolis and call on her. For a week he visited, and by the time he left, he and Ruth were engaged to be married. The wedding was held the following June. After a honeymoon in Europe, Ruth went to live in Providence, back East where the Tappans had come from two generations before. The house seemed quieter with the eldest daughter gone. John had the first indication that he was starting a new phase of his life. He was in his mid fifties now, and his children were growing up fast. In a few years, Marion would marry Dr. Vincent Ryan, a dermatologist from Rhode Island. She too would move back East to live.

Tappan still had his work to keep him busy. By the mid 1920s, the Syndicate had 75,000 contract holders and thousands of agents operating all over the country. The future could not have been any brighter, until the day in the fall of 1925 that John Hibbert and A. W. King walked into the office and announced that they were thinking of selling their shares in Investors Syndicate.

The news was a shock. Tappan probably reacted to it in the same collected manner he took in most things, though his lively temper may have been threatening to flare up. He did not like surprises, especially if they hinted at secrecy and backroom deals. With everyone, he was open and straightforward, and expected the same in return. But the more he investigated the situation, the less he liked it. Hibbert's proposal was to sell out to an entrepreneur from Oregon named John Ridgeway. Tappan thought the suggested price too low, but agreed to consider it if they all believed it was in the best interests of the shareholders. He was annoyed, however, as he realized that Hibbert must have been discussing this deal behind his back for some time.

Tappan and Hibbert were very different sorts of men. Hibbert, the consummate salesman, clearly enjoyed his newfound wealth in a way Tappan found somewhat ostentatious. He had bought a large house, hired a staff of servants, including a butler and maid from England. He rode around town in a chauffeured limousine. His driver wore a uniform to match the color of the car he was driving that day, one a pale champagne, the other a dark burgundy. Every year, Hibbert made a trip back to England to visit relatives, with an entourage of servants in tow to look after his wife and children. Still, Tappan had always trusted him. But sometime during a vacation in Canada in the summer of 1925, Hibbert had spoken to an old friend, Charles Farrington, who ran a bond and mortgage company in Portland. When Investors Syndicate was growing fast, Farrington, along with Ridgeway and another friend of Hibbert's, E. E. Crabb, had invested in the company's stock. For a time, these men held executive appointments, a result of their investment. But sometime around 1915 or 1916, they had all left the company. During their time there, however, they had had access to Syndicate books, and knew how the business worked, and how fast it was growing.

Hibbert had apparently rekindled their interest in Investors Syndicate after meeting with Farrington in Canada. He suggested that Farrington, Ridgeway, and Crabb take another look at how well Investors Syndicate was doing. They did so, secretly. While Tappan was away, Crabb arrived in Minneapolis, announcing that he was "an examiner from Oregon."[33] The ruse worked, and the staff allowed Crabb to examine the company books. He came away impressed enough to recommend to his partners that they make an offer to purchase Investors Syndicate.

Tappan had no knowledge at the time of what was happening. With the offer on the table, however, he decided it wisest to investigate all options. A company in California had also expressed interest in making a bid for Investors Syndicate. Though still opposed to selling, Tappan left to hear what they had to say, if only to satisfy his partners and himself on the worth of their firm. Before he left, he was reassured by King that no decisions about selling would be made until he returned. King also made a verbal commitment not to sell his stock in Investors Syndicate unless Tappan sold his shares as well. Together, the two men had a controlling interest, so no buyer would want to close a deal with Hibbert unless at least one of the other two partners agreed.

Confident that he was free to negotiate as he saw fit, Tappan spent a week in California. He listened to the offer, and though maintaining that Investors Syndicate was still not for sale, he was impressed by the price quoted. It was far better than the offer Hibbert had brought him. Elated that now others were starting to recognize the value of the business, Tappan returned to Minneapolis with the news. When he walked into the office the next day, Hibbert immediately informed him that he and King had sold their shares to Ridgeway. Tappan was stunned. It had never occurred to him that his partners would be disloyal, especially not King, who had given his word. King and Tappan had known each other for fifteen years, and Tappan considered him a close friend. King surely knew how deep John's commitment to Investors Syndicate ran, how he regarded the company as an extension of his life.

There was only one conclusion that Tappan could draw. They had deliberately waited until he was out of town so that they could take action behind his back. Perhaps in King's case it was cowardice, the inability to face up to the man he was about to betray. For Hibbert, the benefit was quickly obvious. In selling his stock, he profited from the run up in Investors Syndicate's value, but he retained control of the agency, which was an independent organization. Hibbert thus cashed in on the value of his shares, while still retaining his position as vice president and general agent.

As it turned out, Hibbert had been too clever for his own good. The new owners soon determined that a totally independent sales agency was not desirable. So two years later, Hibbert's contract was bought out and the sales agency incorporated into Investors Syndicate as a wholly owned subsidiary. Ridgeway took over as general sales manager, and Hibbert's association with the company ended. Officially, the reason for the move was to allow greater direction over field staff from headquarters. Perhaps the new owners also understood the dangers of relying on a man who had already betrayed one partner.

A second reason for the sellout may have had to do with Tappan's basically conservative financial strategy. He had founded the Syndicate with a single-minded vision, and kept it going through many years of hardship. He was dedicated to the notion of building a perfectly safe method of investing for the common man, putting people's money into land. By the 1920s, however, stocks were offering even more attractive rewards, yet Investors Syndicate had not taken the plunge. Tappan had expressed no overt hostility to the stock market, but a year after the sale, policy changed at Investors Syndicate. In 1927, almost 6 percent of the Syndicate's assets were in stocks and bonds. By the mid 1930s, the percentage had risen to 40 percent. Securities offered both greater returns and greater liquidity for the fast growing business. However, even long after Tappan's exit, the company continued to invest in real estate, to a far greater degree than its chief competitor in the face amount certificate market. It also placed most of its funds in the most stable and conservative securities—bonds, notes, and preferred stock.[34]

Tappan could have continued with Investors Syndicate, as a part owner. He still had more shares than anyone else. But he did not have a majority. He never thought his own partners would engineer his downfall, and so was caught unprepared by the takeover. Over the years, he had borrowed money, much as he disliked being in debt, to maintain his ownership percentage. But with the growth of the company, Hibbert and King together owned more shares than he did. Once they sold them, Tappan became only a minority stockholder in the firm that he had founded, with a new management in charge that had its own ideas of how to run things. After considering his options for several days, he reluctantly decided to sell, too, at the price that Hibbert and King had negotiated. The offer from California was better, but Tappan considered it only honorable to follow the decision of the majority, even if that decision was based on deceit and betrayal. Once the sale was complete, Tappan never spoke to either Hibbert or King again.

The Tappan era at Investors Syndicate came to a close. Despite the deceit, the transition raised little public notice and caused no problems for the health of the firm. Only later did John Elliott Tappan express the depth of the pain he experienced. When he ended his association with Investors Syndicate, he said, it was as though he had lost a child. Those were the strongest possible words from a man who knew just how such a loss felt.

CHAPTER EIGHT

INTO THE SUNSET

Nine years after the sale of Investors Syndicate, when he was no longer connected with the company, John Hibbert met Marion Tappan in a club in Minneapolis. He went over to her and inquired about her family's health. Then he said, "Please give your father a message for me. Tell him that selling my shares of the Syndicate was the biggest mistake I ever made, and he is the most honest man I've ever known."

The loss of Investors Syndicate was wrenching to the man who had devoted more than half his life turning an idea into a growing, living, breathing thing. It did not, however, destroy him. John Elliott Tappan had too much self-reliance for that. He was a Victorian man—everything balanced. This loss, hard as it was, in the end was taken in stride. Tappan still had plenty to do, and several business ventures to keep him busy. Over the next thirty years, he continued to practice law. He continued to live as he always had, comfortably but not opulently. His children grew up and moved away, but his eldest son, Elliott, became his partner of sorts. The two of them ran a baking company Tappan had started during the slow years of the 1910s. The business was a modest success, until it folded in the Depression of the 1930s.

Through the 1920s, Tappan retained the same interest in politics and important matters of public life that had turned him into a financial innovator in the 1890s depression. He and Winnie both took a boldly nonconformist stance in the 1928 election, backing the liberal, urban, Democratic candidate, Al Smith, a New York Catholic, in Republican, rural, Protestant Minnesota. John continued to support what he regarded as progressive causes, in the Theodore Roosevelt model. By the 1930s, though, his brand of moderate liberalism was again under siege by more radical forces.

The Great Depression provoked heated debate over the direction of American capitalism, just as the 1890s depression had. John, who had supported workingmen's unions in the early twentieth century as giving wage earners a fair shake, now became ardently anti-union, as workers organized successfully in large numbers during the 1930s. It did not help that his bakery business shut down in part because of strikes by truck drivers. But more important, the beliefs in self-reliance and self-help that characterized John Tappan's notions of reform were pushed aside by the Depression and the New Deal, which created the modern welfare state. Old producerist values of independence, on which Tappan had founded his response to the problems of the modern economy, lost currency. They were no longer relevant with the growth of big government and strong unions alongside big business. Tappan, the moderate to liberal Republican and occasional Democrat, became the strident anti–New Dealer and Franklin Roosevelt foe. It was more an indication of how much the world had changed than of Tappan's change of heart.

In 1938, personal losses also began to take their toll on Tappan's world. In April, Winnie died, after a long illness, at age seventy. Into her sixties, she had remained trim and kept active outdoors, especially with gardening. Only her gray hair and glasses made her look close to her real age. But one winter she slipped on ice and broke her hip. Though she recovered enough to get around with a cane, she was never herself afterward. Losing her pep and enthusiasm, she deteriorated physically until she had to go into the hospital, where she eventually died of a stroke. With Winnie gone, John continued to reside in Minneapolis, living in the house on Cedar Lake. He kept active and vigorous, rising early and exercising each morning, though he began to develop a physique that suggested solidity more than muscular leanness. In the summers, Marion and Ruth came back for visits with the grandchildren. Tappan still had his hobbies, such as golf. He spent time outdoors, hunting and fishing in the north Minnesota woods. But he was no longer as physically or mentally independent. Finally, when he was eighty-five years old and could no longer care for himself, he boarded a train and went back East, to be near his daughters. He took the same journey but in the opposite direction that his father had made a century earlier. On January 16, 1957, John Elliott Tappan died in Warwick, Rhode Island.

～

Why had Tappan let Investors Syndicate get away? It certainly was not for lack of love of the business or pride in what he had started. John never lost his affection for the firm he had seen "grow and develop as a child might grow up."[1] Ridgeway gave him permission to stop by whenever he wished, and he often did. He would arrive unannounced, stand in the doorway, watch, and listen. He only remained long enough to be certain that the company was still well, much as an estranged parent might secretly read a letter his child had written to someone else.

The fate of John Elliott Tappan and the company he founded tells us something about the nature of entrepreneurship in American finance. There is no doubt that Tappan was an innovator. He was one of the first to see the possibilities of bringing the benefits of diversified, pooled investments to the average person, the little guy who watched the manipulations of the corporate economy and its new stock market as though they were taking place on another planet. Tappan worked, determinedly, at making this vision a reality, in the face of what must have seemed insurmountable odds.

We know, in retrospect, that financial markets did grow and improve. The interest rate differentials and monopoly control of money that so disturbed Populists abated. New financial intermediaries more responsive to the average saver appeared on the scene. How did all this take place? The rules of rational investment are clear and straightforward—pool funds, avoid risk through diversification, and maximize rates of return. Financial institutions and rules, however, do not just sprout overnight like so many mushrooms after a summer storm. Nor do abstract definitions of risk and reward control human behavior. Saving and investment defined in a textbook are simple. Lived in real life, they mean thousands of uncertain choices and possible paths for the individual, with only one life in which to choose them. For centuries, people have been told to put a bit of money aside and accumulate wealth. Sage advice to be sure, but turning it into a behavioral reality required the sort of products and services offered by Investors Syndicate and other financial pioneers. Nothing in life happens automatically, nothing transpires without human volition.

Take too macroscopic a view of the economy and you can easily miss the crucial work performed by men like John Elliott Tappan. Making saving into a behavioral reality required innovators who had a broad understanding of the culture of saving and the meaning of money in their times. It meant probing the psychology of the average investor, knowing the constraints they faced, the day-to-day realities that shaped their lives, so that a product appropriate to these conditions could be designed. It also meant going beyond the individual level to the political ramifications of changing financial institutions. The issues surrounding controversial new definitions of risk, speculation, trust, fraud, and gambling were social ones, collective definitions of appropriate behavior for investors and fiduciaries. Even the law offered little guidance in these crucial matters, and indeed, legal doctrine itself had to be made and shaped in light of the actions of men such as Tappan.

Tappan practiced a special sort of entrepreneurship. It was hard enough to promote a new financial institution, but to do so in relatively remote Minneapolis, in the face of the tremendous dislocations of the late nineteenth century, took a dedicated, even somewhat eccentric mind.

Innovations from outside the centers of wealth and power have been an important, but overlooked, part of the American economy, making it more competitive and more responsive to non-elite groups than that of other modern capitalist nations. Many of America's greatest innovators have had traits similar to Tappan's. Two of Tappan's near contemporaries, Thomas Edison and Henry Ford, had remarkably similar backgrounds. If they achieved fame in their own fields on a greater scale than Tappan, nonetheless the pattern was very much the same. All three were men who grew up in a rural society where values of self-reliance and individual initiative mattered. All were native born, white Anglo-Saxons. All were Protestants with a belief that achievement was a desirable, even necessary part of salvation. None, however, was particularly religious, and so their energies went into worldly matters of technology, production, and innovation. Above all, they were practical men who believed the purpose of life was to build something lasting. Tappan did not see himself as a mere money-maker, the sort of financier that

Americans from the Populist farmers to Henry Ford himself scorned as parasites on real producers. Tappan saw himself as a builder and maker of things, in this case a product that brought security to the middle class and encouraged frugality and savings.

What is also similar, and surprising, about these successful white men from the Midwest was that, to a degree, they were all outsiders. They grew up on the rural margin of an America becoming more urban, more industrial, and more bureaucratic. All three projected the image of self-made men who had journeyed their way from country to city. Their stories could be read symbolically as resolutions of the split between rural and urban America, between a modern industrial, machine age, and the bucolic, pastoral past of frontier myth. Even though they were helping to make the age of the machine, technology, and big business, they still identified with rural citizens, farmers, and others who felt besieged by faceless economic change. They were uneasy with the polished eastern bankers, industrialists, and lawyers who seemed to be the agents of so much of this change. Henry Ford, for example, was notorious for his dislike of bankers, his distrust of gold, and his search for a currency that would be tied to "real" production that came from soil, air, nature, and human work. Interestingly enough, Ford also sought to harmonize the interests of workers with the middle class by paying his factory employees decent wages and an annual bonus, which they were encouraged to save and invest, perhaps in just the sort of safe, modest financial product that Investors Syndicate offered. Tappan, of course, had far less trouble with the financial world, but even he believed that the way money was being used had turned against the public good, and needed to be changed.

None were outsiders in the usual sense. They were part of the majority, not members of minority groups. The nineteenth-century America they were born into was still largely nonimmigrant and, in the northern states, white. But all three had the sort of inflexible commitment to the genius of their own schemes that let them fly in the face of conventional wisdom and surmount opposition by shear acts of will and determination. Only a financial man who also stood at margins of the financial world could have understood what Populists, farmers, and small-town critics of money and banking were saying, without dismissing it as backward nonsense.

A commitment to reforming capitalism from within can be seen in the career of each man as well. Ford, most famously of course, would be connected with a positive image of capitalism. His humming, efficient factories turned out cars, a symbol of individual freedom for the common man. His car itself was an emblem of rugged, efficient dependability, stripped down, simple in design. His workers were paid the astoundingly high rate of $5 per day, a rate that socialist economies of the time never equaled. Edison likewise was the wizard of light, harnessing private enterprise to technological innovation in everyday life for the average family, via electricity, incandescent lamps, phonographs, and motion pictures. Tappan saw himself as bringing financial opportunity and the chance to accumulate wealth to a similar group of small-town, rural, and urban working-class Americans. He was building the foundations of a "people's capitalism," or at least a popularized financial world that would emerge in fuller form after World War II.

All three tended to be highly independent thinkers, often repudiating conventions despite what could be regarded as a highly conventional upbringing and background. They delighted in rejecting dogma. Edison emphasized the freethinking agnosticism of his father's household and his own engagement with the radical democratic theorist Thomas Paine. Tappan, though less committed to religious rebellion, had little interest in theology and only tolerated organized religion for his family's sake. Like Ford and Edison, he held few a priori assumptions and was a practical man. But like his cohort, he was a practical man with an imagination, believing there were simple solutions that any reasonable person could find to complex social problems, like the currency question.

All three, then, were oddly positioned at a moment of change, and shared personality traits that reflected this transitional moment. They reveled in nature, Ford and Edison taking camping trips together and wintering in remote South Florida side by side; Tappan in hunting, fishing, and home-steading in the north woods. They embraced the virtues of the simple life. They were producers, not parasites. They touted efficiency, not monopoly. They despised waste, but also dependency. They advocated temperance and moderation.[2] The world these men knew was being replaced by a far different, modern one, in part through their own hands. Yet they went forward by looking backward. They looked back to rural virtues, frugality, and simplicity in a world that was leaving such values behind. Ironically, to be successful innovators they needed this strong grounding in traditional values.

Such personalities as these give rise to a particular type of entrepreneurship. One way of making money in business is to be flexible and opportunistic. Such entrepreneurs seize every chance for earning a higher return on their capital. They generally see themselves clearly reflected in the world in which they live, and therefore lack the necessary distance to produce a striking new insight or perspective. This sort of "normal" entrepreneurial behavior can be quite profitable, though it is rarely innovative. In moving assets around to their highest return, such entrepreneurs merely take advantage of opportunities crafted by other forces.

A second sort of entrepreneurship is more creative. It often anticipates change rather than following convention. Henry Ford built his first car the year Tappan founded Investors Syndicate. It took nearly two more decades, however, before Ford revolutionized automobile production. Creative entrepreneurs have to withstand tremendous skepticism, and, as Tappan would have said, "keep everlastingly at it to get ahead."[3] After all, what they are doing is disruptive, or better, visionary. They seek to move toward a new world that does not yet exist. Ford failed with his car several times, ignoring the doubts of financiers and keeping at it to perfect his system of production. Edison had his failures, too. His giant Portland Cement Company went bankrupt and his prefabricated concrete houses never sold. Tappan waited patiently for decades before he made a dime out of Investors Syndicate. Visionaries of any sort must have great internal resources to draw on. They must remain confident in their systems, despite pressures from peers to follow the market and conform to conventional business wisdom.

The source of these internal strengths, at least for Tappan, Edison, and Ford, was their notions of character, masculinity, and self-reliance. They believed that change for the good came from individual acts, more than from organized institutions or planned revolutions. They believed that men, especially men, had an obligation to take responsibility for their own fate, and to not be dependent on others. They assumed, incorrectly perhaps, that their work would increase the capacity for self-reliance among others. Ford's automobile was to be just that: a self-sufficient means of mobility. It was aimed at the rural market originally, at farmers who could convert it into a work truck or use the engine to power farm machinery. Tappan's financial innovation was similar— a tool for the average person to achieve self-sufficiency through savings that would otherwise be impossible. It mobilized resources for home construction and other capital needs of the average person.

Their strong internal focus sometimes put these men out of step with changes taking place around them, even changes they were helping to foment. Henry Ford, the innovator who lent his name to a whole new worldwide system of manufacturing called Fordism, was still traditional enough to be adverse to consumerism. The car Ford popularized stood foremost among modern consumer items. Yet Ford initially refused to sell his cars on credit, even after his competitor, General Motors, had begun the now universal practice of financing automobile purchases. Interestingly enough, Ford's response to General Motors' credit was to start a sort of "car savings club," where would-be buyers put a little money aside each month, invested for them by the company, until they accumulated the purchase price of a new automobile. The scheme was not popular in the credit-crazy twenties, however, and soon ended.[4]

Even changes taking place in the business world sometimes elude creative entrepreneurs. Neither Ford, Edison, nor Tappan had much sympathy with or understanding of corporate growth. All three also ran into problems with the shift from individual leadership to bureaucratic management. Yet the traditional values they clung to were also the source of their strength, enabling them to face adversity and ignore criticism. Only because they were so inflexible, unyielding, even stubborn in their ideas, could they innovate. Their refusal to yield often meant that other, more flexible and commonplace entrepreneurs ended up taking over and adapting their innovations as they achieved broad popularity. Yet their entrepreneurial commitment, though seemingly irrational, promoted change.

Tappan shared finally one more thing with the class of creative entrepreneurs who came out of Middle America at the end of the nineteenth century. Like Ford and Edison, Tappan was less driven by money or the simple desire for material comfort and success than by a commitment to his ideas. He had learned from early experience working for the Merritt brothers and with shady financiers such as George MacDonald that the pursuit of the almighty dollar led to dishonest self-dealing. He never desired the big house, conspicuous consumption, the trappings of great wealth. Neither he nor Winnie made material things the center of their lives, preferring quality to quantity. Not that Tappan was a saint or unworldly ascetic. He defined success in large part by material achievement, like everyone else. But creative entrepreneurs rarely find money for its own sake very attractive. Instead, they want to change how the world works. Tappan blended individual achievement and initiative with a sense of justice and fairness and the desire to meet what he perceived as a social need. He wanted to remake the financial world, not, as other reformers suggested, through politics, but by operating outside of the mainstream, in his own, highly individualistic way. Through individual initiative, he believed, social reform was possible, and everyone could be made better off. In the end, this sort of motivation, like Ford's desire to bring the automobile in reach of the average person with ruthlessly efficient new methods of production, or Edison's celebration of his own technological wizardry, was the lasting, deepest one.

The stories of such men do not always have happy endings. Henry Ford's once admirable determination made him, by the 1930s, an irascible, prejudiced, paranoid dictator, who did his company far more harm than good. Thomas Edison's failures came from ill-conceived attempts to apply his good ideas in inappropriate settings. Tappan, of course, lost control of the very enterprise he had founded. Creative innovators are often at their best when fighting against skepticism and adversity. They lose their edge at the moment of success. They tend to be people with one big idea. John Elliott Tappan had one idea, a good one. He never stopped thinking about financial services, or about the firm he founded and the changes taking place in the industry. But he never again had a business insight of the same originality or depth as the one that boldly led him to found Investors Syndicate in the depression of the 1890s.

In a sense, it may have been fortunate for Investors Syndicate and for the financial services industry that Tappan left the scene when he did. True, he never shared quite the level of single-mindedness that drove the likes of Ford and Edison. Though he had absolute faith in his ideas, Tappan lacked the sort of monomania that would compel him to control everything, the way Ford did his company, or Edison his invention laboratory in New Jersey. Both Ford and Edison had great difficulty sharing credit and power with subordinates, which helped to make them more famous as public figures than Tappan, but less admirable human beings. Perhaps their egos allowed them to pursue their ideas further, too. Tappan, for all his insight, never dominated financial services. His success was never as great as these other men, nor his failures so spectacular. His was a more modest ambition—to show that his system could work, and to serve the customers who had faith in him.

Tappan led not by grasping at fame and power, but by example. His hero was George Washington, the patriot who declined to make himself king, but whose modesty, quiet leadership, and example shaped the presidency for all time. This modesty of ego may partly explain why, in the end, Tappan was forced out. He had never structured the company to make himself the supreme power, even though he believed that he personally was the one most responsible for the company's integrity and the fulfillment of its promises to the public. A more self-centered person might have used this as justification to make himself the man in charge—the notion that with responsibility comes power. Tappan, however, seems to have lacked some of the drive that make men seize and hold power. He did not shy away from conflict or from telling people how he felt. He did, however, prefer to be right rather than victorious. He was often "too proud to fight," the phrase another Progressive Era leader, Woodrow Wilson, once used. "Association is assimilation," Tappan once said in explaining why he did not practice criminal law. It was better to remain true to one's values and ethics than to compromise with the dishonest or unscrupulous for the sake of success. Tappan's past history suggests that he would, when betrayed by those he trusted, withdraw, tend his own garden, or light out for new territory. A belief that such new territory, new opportunities, were available and an option, shows that Tappan remained in the end a man of the nineteenth-century frontier West.

Tappan's ouster from Investors Syndicate came at a symbolic moment. In 1894, all the financial action was on Wall Street, with the great battles for control and profit taking place among powerful, wealthy corporate titans. Rural and small-town America saw such battles as immoral, and probably detrimental to the interests of plain people such as themselves. That gap, between the financial world of Middle America and the world of high finance in the East, was what gave Tappan his motivation and his opportunity. By 1924, however, the gap had narrowed considerably, and the values and visions that motivated Tappan to innovate no longer seemed so pressing.

Tappan's notion of financial democracy was based on traditions of cooperation and mutual benefit within the framework of the private market. He sought the best of both worlds. Organization would provide the security, expertise, and diversification that individuals needed, but the firm would remain close to its clients, responsive to their needs and situations, even if Tappan had to write five letters or more a day himself for twenty years. It would be an organization based on values of independence, frugality, and long-term needs, not mere money grubbing and "get all you can while you can." Finally, it would be an organization composed of many, with agents and investors across the nation. But it would also be embodied in the virtues, values, and character of one man, who would take responsibility.

By the time Tappan left Investors Syndicate, many of these older ideas about independence, self-employment, and the dignity of labor were being challenged by a new consumer-oriented mentality. People increasingly saved not to buy land or a business; they saved for retirement, which is to say, they saved to consume when they could no longer work. They bought consumer durable goods such as cars. Tappan, who roamed the West, built his own town in northern Minnesota, practiced law as an independent professional, and started and ran his own firm, lived the life of the independent producer. His clients, many of them lifetime members of the working class or white-collar cogs in corporate machines, did not. One group of independent producers—farmers—it turned out, were the least likely clients for Tappan's contracts. Unlike middle-class salaried men and women, they lacked the steady monthly income to make payments.

Tappan himself preached a message of frugality and savings, but the financial world around him had other ideas. Investment trusts run by professional managers marketed their securities to the public, just as any product was marketed. They took a profit from the investor for this service. In a like manner, the relationship between the saver and the investment company also changed. Tappan envisioned a mutuality between himself and his investors, based on a shared set of values about savings and long-term investment, rather than in speculation or the search for quick profits. Though he played the classic role of intermediary, providing to clients both an opportunity and his own expertise, he believed that investors had to be kept fully informed, and that they had a mutual responsibility to him when they signed contracts to pay in their money over ten years. The experts who ran investment companies, however, became increasingly remote from the public. "Investors" became more consumers of financial services than the mutual participants that Tappan envisioned. Tappan personally stood for the integrity of his firm, at a time when solid financial information and trustworthy advice was hard to come by. After the 1930s, however, even these problems abated. Government played more of that role, as guarantor and regulator of financial practices, making the market more open and transparent to all investors.

John Elliott Tappan used traditional values of independence, mutuality, and self-reliance to establish a relationship with his clients. The irony was that he himself was also helping to move saving away from these values and toward the consumer model grounded in expertise and housed in national corporate institutions. His hope had been to invest in land, always the source of wealth for a man who had started life on a farm. But he did not invest in rural America, so much as in urban America. He helped middle-class families purchase homes, a worthy cause to be sure when the mortgage market offered high interest rates and few amortizing, long-term loans. But purchasing a home for an urban resident was already a half-step away from the older vision of a nation of independent, land-owning producers that was at the heart of the controversies of the 1890s.

Crucial to this transition was the notion of saving small amounts at regular intervals, which is where Tappan began his ideas. The face amount certificate was purchased through regular, small monthly payments. People had always saved, of course, but in the nineteenth century a whole host of new institutions arose to regularize the practice of saving. Each of these was built around the notion of disciplined saving in regular amounts to meet a financial target, the behavioral manifestation of the new culture of saving. Of course, it was important for men of Victorian values like Tappan to distinguish the hard work of real saving from mere games of chance, lotteries, or irrational speculations. That was one reason he spent so much time in his thousands of letters to clients advising, admonishing, and teaching the ways of saving. Installments of small monthly outlays certainly increased the opportunities for those of modest means to acquire assets or borrow money.

In the end, though, these same means changed the underlying values that had once connected savings with virtue and characterized consumption as a wasting of resources. The meaning of money, that most hotly debated of all terms, had changed. Installment buying and consumer credit became tools of a much different economy. Regular monthly payments of money could instill the discipline to consume as well as to save. Installment credit for consumer durables grew rapidly in the early twentieth century. So did installment loans for homes—home mortgages with level payments that paid off interest and principal together. These two markets, interestingly enough, were ones that Tappan anticipated through his installment sales of financial products and installment credit.

So, whatever the original inspiration, the success of Investors Syndicate owed as much to the new consumer-oriented economy as to the old producer-oriented one. Where people worked for regular wages, installment systems worked well. They allowed individuals to save money without relying on pure will and self-denial. Instead of putting money into land, property, and children, instead of saving through the sweat equity of making a farm, they saved by purchasing pieces of paper and incurring with them the obligation to make and maintain regular payments.

Tappan's story suggests two important modifications of traditional historical perspectives on this moment in financial history. First, for those who think that history can be divided among the winners and losers, Tappan's tale tells a richer, more ironic story. Here was a man who should be placed among the winners. He was from a respectable family; he had all of the personal, educational, and cultural advantages for success; and he lived a long, healthy, productive life. By any conventional measure, he was successful, as a lawyer, as a father, as a business entrepreneur, and as a financial innovator. Yet by the time he reached middle age, the world he knew had changed around him, and he himself was, for all intents and purposes, obsolete. He had been an agent of change, yet the changes he helped to bring about made a world far different than the one he had imagined when he set out. He had built a firm on trust, mutuality, and partnership, only to see it thrive as a bureaucratic corporation without him. He had created a new means of saving to encourage thrift and productiveness, only to see financial services plunge into a speculative orgy that would end with the great stock market crash of 1929. He had built his world on the values of labor and the "real" economy, only to see consumerism take center stage. As one historian has noted, and as Tappan's life illustrates, the changes that made the modern economy were "never a matter of smooth integration but of social, cultural and psychic strain—among the victors as well as the vanquished."[5]

Second, Tappan's tale reminds us that not *all* of the political, social, and ethical values once attached to money simply disappeared into the maw of endless consumption. With installment saving and installment credit, the practices of saving and spending may have undergone a subtle shift. But people did not turn into zombie-eyed consumers with the rise of installment paying. The discipline imposed by the need to make regular payments could be just as harsh and unremitting a master of hedonistic impulses as Victorian codes of self-denial. So too with installment savings. Older notions of property accumulation and self-denial did not just disappear with paper securities. Rather, they were transformed into modern equivalents. Savings and accumulation meant constant "stick-to-it-ivness," in Tappan's words.

This does not mean that all worked out for the best in the end. Financial innovation remains in tension with fundamental political values now as it did a century ago. Tappan thought he was "democratizing" capital by his innovation. Events showed that democratizing capitalism is no easy matter. Providing people with consumer financial services might give them better access to higher returns, but it can also make them highly dependent on those who run the services and manage the money. A constant in the critique of investment trusts, mutual funds, and professional money managers is that their position and expertise allow them the opportunity to take advantage of those they serve. Perhaps they can offer a client somewhat better returns than that person can acquire on his or her own. But managers of other people's money can also have incentive to rake off a substantial profit for themselves. From insurance companies in the nineteenth century to investment trusts in the 1920s, again and again in American history this unequal distribution of knowledge, information, and expertise has raised important questions of fairness and power in financial affairs.

Periods of great financial innovation have often been periods that, initially at least, redistributed wealth upward, to those who could seize the opportunities being created. In the 1890s, the 1920s, and the 1980s, wealth became less equally distributed as new financial markets blossomed.[6] One reaction to these periods of inequality has been reform aimed at putting the brakes on free-wheeling finance and redirecting capital into more hands. Some of these efforts have come through government, most notably in the twentieth century, with Social Security and the Securities and Exchange Commission, both created in the 1930s. But law and regulation are blunt weapons that can do as much harm as good if too restrictive. As Tappan's life shows, the tradition of financial reform in the interests of the larger population has also included private sector action by private citizens. Tappan may not have accomplished all he hoped in this regard, but the questions he confronted have never been fully answered. The solutions he proposed continue to find their way into the financial services industry. The money business, which is so much about making money, cannot survive if it is *only* about making money. At some point, the temptations of profit become too great. Without periods of reform, money takes on a life of its own, and the good of the public, the economy, even the individual investor whose money it is, gets lost in the rush to profit.

The industry seems to need characters like John Elliott Tappan from time to time. Less important even than their originality may be the force and commitment they bring to the idea of financial service as something more than money making. After Tappan, Charles Merrill "discovered" that Wall Street was not serving the needs of Main Street. The perennial conflict between the centers of financial power and the majority of the nation living outside those centers appeared to Merrill after the Great Depression of the 1930s, just as it had appeared to Tappan in the time of great monetary conflict in the 1890s. Merrill responded by creating a new type of brokerage business aimed at ordinary investors who wanted a chance to get into the stock market. Taking his cues from the supermarket, in which he was a major investor, Merrill created a new sort of brokerage firm, one with the intent of serving small investors by accepting narrow profit margins and generating a high volume of business. Like Tappan, Merrill's innovation actually came at a moment of change and uncertainty in the financial world, on the heels of the Great Depression, in a depressed stock market with low volume. Like Tappan, Merrill confronted the problems of establishing far-flung agencies, gaining the trust and confidence of the skeptical public, and assuring investors that he represented their interests, not the interests of those who ran the markets. Like Tappan, he found that to make the market safe for the ordinary investor, he had to act in a highly professional manner, refuse short-term profits in favor of long-term customer relationships, and provide investment opportunities that were safe rather than speculative, based on knowledge of market conditions, not on fluff or captivating but vague promises of high returns.

Just about every decade has produced a similar sort of financial innovator. In the 1930s and '40s, A. P. Giannini launched his attack on mainstream banking practices. He made his immigrant savings institution into a universal bank, branching out into the remote rural counties of California and eventually becoming a national institution. He used the small trickles of savings from immigrants and workers to finance big changes in home ownership, urban and suburban growth, "integrating his business interests," his biographer notes, "into the social interests of large numbers of people."[7] In the 1960s, Charles Schwab took on the cushy club of brokers who ran the New York Stock Exchange, opening a series of storefront discount brokerage operations. Using the telephone and, later, the computer, he made it easier for small-scale traders and savers to participate in the stock market on their own. It broke the back of the Wall Street club, with its high commissions that made trading stocks expensive. In the 1980s, Michael Milken rehabilitated the reputation of highly speculative bonds, to provide new start-up capital to a host of emerging firms that otherwise would have had trouble getting the finance they needed to grow. He helped to widen the capital market by making it easier for entrepreneurs to raise capital. In the 1990s, John Bogle of Vanguard worked to return mutual funds to the sort of enterprise John Elliott Tappan would have appreciated. By keeping costs low and minimizing the discretionary power of "professional" fund managers, Vanguard permitted small savers to diversify in the stock market through index funds.

Each of these entrepreneur-reformers shares something with John Elliott Tappan. Each began with a commitment to some class or group excluded from full participation in financial markets. Each was an outsider of sorts, though knowledgeable about the financial world he was seeking to change. Merrill grew up in Florida and made himself into a successful stock market player in the 1920s. Milken and Schwab were Jews who never quite fit in with the clubby world of East Coast investment banking. Like the Italian immigrant Giannini, they chose to make their mark on the West Coast, in the more open and entrepreneurial culture of California. Bogle came from the East and, like Tappan, could be termed a member of the establishment in family background. But also like Tappan, he brought an older sense of public service and personal integrity to the mutual funds business, and a disdain for the hard-sell tactics that seemed more designed to squeeze money out of unwary investors' pockets than to serve the customers' interests.

These innovators also launched their innovations in the face of powerful, if questionable, prevailing wisdom. Merrill began to serve small clients at a time when most brokers saw business as so scarce that they concentrated on the high-profit, big investors. He ignored warnings that an emphasis on client service would only attract "free riders" who would seek his advice and then place orders with other brokers. He eliminated high fees on "inactive" accounts, allowing the average investor to practice that time-honored strategy of "hold and wait," a good choice for the average investor. And he violated the almost sacred tenet of the stock market, that the broker's profit came first, in the form of high fees charged on every transaction. Every bit of common wisdom said to Merrill, "do not do what you are planning," yet he did it anyway, despite having already lost $1.5 million in the brokerage business. Milken, an intense, focused, almost single-minded man, discovered a truth about the latent value of low-grade bonds that almost everyone else missed or denied. In a like manner, John Bogle revised accepted wisdom. The usual practice in mutual funds was for fund managers to take profit by charging a substantial fee for their services. Bogle's Vanguard instead revived the old agrarian-era notion of the cooperative, whereby the investors themselves own the institution that is to serve their needs.

Perhaps most striking, these financial innovators expressed, quite sincerely, a commitment to something beyond their own profit. Even those who have generated great wealth for themselves, have generally led rather frugal personal lives and kept up a strong interest in the social consequences of their work. We might question the impact of what they did, but there is no gainsaying that they were driven by some larger vision. When Charles Merrill stated, "I can think of nothing that would build a stronger democratic capitalism, than the wider ownership of stocks,"[8] he had no reason to lie. He was already wealthy and would in fact gain little personal wealth from the success of Merrill Lynch. With his statement, though, he captured the long, and today under-appreciated, social meaning that Americans have always attached to money. In the words of John Tappan's contemporary, the popular preacher of the Social Gospel, Washington Gladden, "money is not a mere material entity. It always stands for something."

Intermediation is a simple enough idea. Solicit funds from the public, use expertise and organization to invest those funds at a higher return, and pay clients out of those returns. When done with knowledge, efficiency, and a commitment to client interests, it is a game with only winners. But the temptations of other people's money can all too easily blot out the purpose of intermediation, and can place the profits of the organization above the interest of clients. The financial services industry has, and probably will again have to relearn the lessons of its own past. Fortunately, it has many examples upon which to draw, examples that stretch all the way back to its beginnings, to the early years of John Elliott Tappan and Investors Syndicate.

Epilogue

The living embodiment of the tradition of financial service John Elliott Tappan started is his very own descendent, the child he nurtured, the firm that continued on in his absence. American Express Financial Advisors is of course a much larger, and much different, sort of creature than the small partnership Tappan ran. Yet it remains attached to this history, in ways that the men and women who now work there may not notice, but connected nonetheless. When American Express took over Investors Syndicate (by then renamed IDS), it also acquired a long and successful tradition of customer service, and a culture of commitment to the needs of ordinary savers that Tappan had first articulated.

The power of Tappan's original idea can be seen in the fate of the company since his departure. By 1929, Investors Syndicate had assets of nearly $30 million. Most of its money was still tied up in western mortgages. When the great stock market crash finally came in October of that year, many upstart investment trusts were wiped out. Investors Syndicate, on the other hand, sold $1.5 billion worth of face amount certificates during the 1930s and 1940s.[1] As banks disappeared and took with them their customers' savings accounts, Investors Syndicate paid out $100 million to its clients. They and their friends and neighbors would not forget this performance, "never a day late nor a penny short." It was the Syndicate's finest hour, exactly the sort of commitment and security that Tappan had promised when he started the firm during the depression of the 1890s. "Meet every obligation promptly when it fell due," he had pledged, and the company did, even under the most extreme conditions.

By 1936, Investors Syndicate had a sales force over 3000 strong and offices in every state of the union.[2] The agents were part of a complex divisional structure that included regional supervisors and division managers. Investors Syndicate also indulged in national advertising, its name recognition now strong enough to benefit from the national media. Still, its advertising budget remained modest by the standards of American consumerism, just over $100,000 per year. More important, its message would have been surprisingly familiar to John Tappan. Sales personnel were reminded of the importance of "personal application." They sold clients "living protection," a message, like Tappan's own "money while you live," that played off insurance, while offering a better investment return. There was more emphasis now on old-age dependence, reflecting the growing role of pensions and retirement savings in American life. But another theme, "compulsory savings," accented the long-term, "stick-to-it-ivness" notions that Tappan had emphasized. By putting away a small amount each month, one could watch one's savings grow over a lifetime. These were exactly the themes advertising executives were using to promote banks, whole life insurance, and other savings products in the 1930s and 1940s, ideas that Tappan had first employed forty years earlier.[3]

Change at Investors Syndicate had come mainly in size and in the new opportunities growth presented. Company assets had ballooned by 550 percent during the Depression years, from $28 to $153 million. This performance gave the firm a tremendous advantage as the economy recovered and people were ready to save again. Neither banks nor the stock market had a very good reputation in the immediate aftermath of the Depression, but face amount certificates did. Stocks, needless to say, were poison to the middle class after the debacle of 1929. Those who had gone to the wall by purchasing them on margin not only saw their investments wiped out, but were left with a debt they could not repay. From the high point of 1929, the Dow lost 89 percent of its value in the crash. It eventually recovered, slowly. But the nearly ten-year depression that followed the market collapse did nothing to revive the reputation of Wall Street. Trading volume dropped substantially. By 1942, fewer shares were changing hands than in 1905. Less than 10 percent of the public owned stocks.[4] The shift of funds out of the stock market reflected the hard-earned experience of the investor and the failure of the boom market of the 1920s to live up to its hype and reputation. Public opinion polls even in the 1950s showed that most people thought that stocks were a speculative investment and mistrusted brokers.[5]

The supposed protectors of the common investor, the investment trusts, came in for a drubbing on this score as well. One reason for the rise of investment trusts in the 1920s was that they provided (or claimed to provide) the sort of brand name security and reputation that individual stock dealers lacked. The crash of the market, however, revealed that the trusts were not always honest in their management or in their promotional advertising. Too many of them were sponsored by investment banks, as a way of marketing questionable new securities. Rather than providing objective information, the trusts acted as marketing tools to fatten underwriters' profits.[6] As Tappan understood, the successful firms, the ones that would survive in the long run and promote the long-run interests of their clients, backed up promises with performance, and attracted clients with integrity and a bond of trust.[7]

New government regulations were passed during the troublesome 1930s. These had the purpose of assuring the secure operation of financial markets, limiting speculative use of the public's money, eliminating fraud, and repairing fiduciary breaches. The Securities and Exchange Commission oversaw financial markets broadly, including publicly traded stocks, while the 1940 Investment Company Act took aim at the practices of mutual funds and other firms that presumed to manage the public's money for it.

One result of these laws was a revival of the investment company and a modest renewed faith in the stock market. Having weathered the Depression with its assets and reputation still intact, Investors Syndicate was prepared to jump into this now secured market. In 1939, it moved into common stocks, organizing and managing a balanced fund, Investors Mutual. Then, in 1945, it added a bond and preferred stock fund. At a time when there were only one hundred mutual funds in existence, the Minneapolis company had three of the largest. Reflecting its more diversified lines of business, Investors Syndicate abandoned its original name in 1949 and became Investors Diversified Services, or IDS.

By the time John Elliott Tappan died in 1957, IDS was truly a diversified financial management company. It had operations in Canada as well as in the United States. Agents, now full-time employees, sold the company's financial products exclusively. The products included stocks, bonds, insurance, and of course face amount certificates. Even the way business was done had changed. At the start of the 1950s, the company still entered customer accounts in hand-written ledgers, as Tappan himself once did. But with growth, it took over one hundred people in four departments to keep track of customer accounts. Before the 1950s ended, computers were replacing posting ledgers and hand-operated adding machines. Direct distance dialing, introduced in the 1960s, permitted sales agents to keep in close touch by telephone with clients in remote rural regions.

Still, for all the changes in products, technology, and organization, IDS did not abandon its successful heritage. Often chided by elite East Coast institutions for its folksy ways and unsophisticated clients, it remained the financial services company of Middle America. Unlike many other firms, IDS managed and underwrote its own mutual funds, rather than relying on outside management. The source of the company's strength remained its close contact with the public, and a network of thousands of agents spread throughout the nation. While its products were more diverse, IDS also stuck to its traditions in one more way. By 1958, Tappan's face amount certificate had subscriptions worth $500 million.

In the expanding postwar financial services industry, IDS continued to differentiate itself from other firms by its long-term commitment and through outstanding customer service. It was labor-intensive work, calling on customers in every state, many of whom lived in rural areas. More than just a sales force, IDS agents emphasized planning and steady accumulation through a balanced portfolio of assets. These were exactly the sorts of values Tappan, in his own way, had also sought to inculcate in clients. Product took second place to the larger goal of accumulating wealth for individual investors.

IDS's own investment portfolio was more diverse than in the days of exclusive holdings of first mortgages on improved property. But the company also rode the crest of the great postwar home-building boom, a boom spurred by a growing economy and new federal mortgage assistance programs for home buyers, such as the FHA. For a time, IDS was among the top originators of FHA mortgages, and the largest lender of funds for new construction. This too harkened back to Tappan's commitment to real property and home ownership by the average wage earner.

As John Elliott Tappan had predicted, commitment to the long term paid off. With total assets of $2.75 billion, IDS was the biggest investment company in the United States by the 1950s. In the 1960s, it saw its mutual funds business take off in the stock market boom of that decade. With assets of $6 billion, IDS had the largest family of mutual funds in the nation. In 1972, the company moved into a sleek new tower designed by renowned architect Philip Johnson. It occupied the largest building in Minneapolis, the city that had been its home since Tappan took his first offices in room 240 of the Lumber Exchange Building on July 10, 1894.

Today, in a new century, American Express Financial Advisors manages close to $300 billion in assets for over 2 million clients. It has 11,000 advisors. The heart of the company remains this field force, as it did in Tappan's day. The agents are still deeply rooted in their communities, often men and women who came to the work with no previous experience in financial matters. They are still close to the center of Middle America, average people who emphasize trust, not flashy or high-flying financial pyrotechnics. They sell more products now, but the goals are the same. As the CEO at the time of the American Express takeover, Harvey Golub, stated, "We hope to help individuals and small businesses achieve their goals in a prudent and ethical manner better than any other financial firm."[8] Separated by a century from the company's origins, Golub had reaffirmed principles that John Elliott Tappan would have instantly understood—an orientation toward the interests of the client first and foremost, a long-term perspective on wealth and security, and a bond of shared values that connects clients, company, and agents.

NOTE ON SOURCES

John Elliott Tappan produced a wealth of business correspondence along with financial wealth. These letters, nearly twenty thousand running from 1894 until 1919, formed the basis for most of our work. The original letterbooks are held in Minneapolis, at American Express Financial Advisors, 70100 AXP Financial Center, Minneapolis, MN, 55474. Microfilmed copies and photocopies of this correspondence are also in the personal possession of Carol Peters.

For information about family life and personality, we relied heavily on interviews with family members and others who knew him. These include Ruth Tappan Dowling, Marion Tappan Ryan, Marian Dowling Heher, Vincent J. Ryan, Jr., John Dowling, Joseph Dowling, and Florence O'Connor.

For the later period of Investors Syndicate, several government investigations provided useful material. This information also bore on Tappan's period as well, giving us insight into competing operations and financial services generally through the 1920s. Most important are United States Securities and Exchange Commission, *Investment Trust and Investment Companies*, Report, part 1 (Washington, DC, 1939), a summary of the investigation; and a subsequent volume, United States Securities and Exchange Commission, *Investment Trusts and Investment Companies: Companies Issuing Face Amount Installment Certificates* (Washington, DC, 1940).

The histories of Investors Syndicate and American Express Financial Advisors are recounted in several company publications, notably *IDS Going on 75* (Minneapolis, 1968); *Investing in the Future: A Century of IDS* (Minneapolis, 1994), and Reed Massengill, *Becoming American Express: 150 Years of Reinvention and Customer Service* (New York, 1999).

Financial history is an extensive subfield, so there are many works one could consult for further information. The most important ones we used can be found in the endnotes. But several deserve special mention. George David Smith and Richard Sylla, "Capital Markets," in *Encyclopedia of the United States in the Twentieth Century* vol. III (New York, 1996), provides a brief, informative overview of American financial history, with references to other works. Milton Friedman and Anna J. Schwartz, *A Monetary History of the United States, 1867-1960* (Princeton, NJ, 1963), remains the standard work on monetary policy. Raymond W. Goldsmith, *A Study of Saving in the United States* vol. I (New York, 1969 [1955]), is a massive statistical look at investment, savings, and financial institutions. See also his *Financial Intermediaries in the American Economy since 1900* (Princeton, NJ, 1958). Other overviews of financial history, though covering the more recent past, are Joseph Nocera, *A Piece of the Action: How the Middle Class Joined the Money Class* (New York, 1994), and Robert Sobel, *The Big Board: A History of the New York Stock Market* (New York, 1965). Jonathon Barron Baskin and Paul J. Miranti, Jr., *A History of Corporate Finance* (New York, 1997) provide a historical account of practice that shows how actual behavior of investors can vary from the predictions of theory.

On the politics of money, Gretchen Ritter, *Goldbugs and Greenbacks: The Antimonopoly Tradition and the Politics of Finance in America* (Cambridge, 1997), is a useful recent summary. But see also the older work, Walter Nugent, *Money and American Society* (New York, 1968), as well as the important work on Populism, Lawrence Goodwyn, *Democratic Promise: The Populist Moment in America* (New York, 1976). On American economic thought more generally, James Huston, *Securing the Fruits of Labor: The American Concept of Wealth Distribution, 1763-1900* (Baton Rouge, LA, 1998), is excellent.

Understanding the culture of money in which Tappan lived was a major task of this book. Three works deserve particular mention here. Ann Fabian, *Card Sharps, Dream Books & Bucket Shops: Gambling in 19th-Century America* (Ithaca, NY, 1990); Walter Benn Michaels, *The Gold Standard and the Logic of Naturalism: American Literature at the Turn of the Century* (Berkeley, CA, 1987); and Lendol Calder, *Financing the American Dream: A Cultural History of Consumer Credit* (Princeton, NJ 1999). Each in its own way places the history of money and finance into a broader framework of values, thought, and politics.

Finally, on specific financial topics most directly related to the themes of this book, the following works were most useful. For insurance, Morton Keller, *The Life Insurance Enterprise, 1885-1910: A Study in the Limits of Corporate Power* (Cambridge, MA, 1963), remains the single best work, while

J. Owen Stalson, *Marketing Life Insurance; Its History in America* (Homewood, IL, 1969 [1942]), is an insider's account filled with interesting information on forgotten corners of the financial services industry. On mortgages, Kenneth Snowden's work is invaluable. See especially, "Mortgage Lending and American Capital Market Development in the Late Nineteenth Century," *Journal of Economic History* 47:3 (September 1987), 671-91. George Alter, Claudia Goldin, and Elyce Rotella, *The Savings of Ordinary Americans: The Philadelphia Saving Fund Society in the Mid-Nineteenth Century* (Cambridge, MA, 1992) deals with a slightly earlier period, but is one of the few studies of the behavior of savers. Two recent books trace the history and development of retirement, and the subsequent changes in saving and investment practices that went with it: Dora Costa, *The Evolution of Retirement: An American Economic History, 1880-1990* (Chicago, 1998); and Steven Sass, *The Promise of Private Pensions: The First Hundred Years* (Cambridge, MA, 1997).

NOTES

PROLOGUE

1. On Giannini, see Felice Bonadio, *A. P. Giannini: Banker of America* (Berkeley, CA, 1994).
2. John Kenneth Galbraith, *Money: Whence it Came, Where it Went* (Boston, MA, 1975), 44.
3. Many books have been written on this theme, though few have considered how it affected economic activity and organization. One of the best on the subject is Wilfred McClay, *The Masterless: Self and Society in Modern America* (Chapel Hill, NC, 1994).

CHAPTER 1

1. Walter Benn Michaels, *The Gold Standard and the Logic of Naturalism: American Literature at the Turn of the Century* (Berkeley, CA, 1987), 31-32.
2. On the American version of this theory, see James Huston, *Securing the Fruits of Labor: The American Concept of Wealth Distribution, 1763-1900* (Baton Rouge, LA, 1998), 357.
3. Quoted in Bruce Palmer, *"Man Over Money": The Southern Populist Critique of American Capitalism* (Chapel Hill, NC, 1980), 16.
4. James Huston, "The American Revolutionaries, The Political Economy of Aristocracy and the American Concept of the Distribution of Wealth, 1765-1900," *American Historical Review* 98:4 (October 1993), 1079-1105.
5. In extreme free labor rhetoric, all those who worked for wages could claim to be "enslaved" to others, or "wage slaves." The ideal, in the mid nineteenth century, remained not the well-paid worker but the worker who became an independent proprietor.
6. Jackson Farewell Address, in J. Rogers Hollingsworth and Bell Wiley, eds., *American Democracy; A Documentary Record* (New York, 1963).
7. In contrast to the late nineteenth century, when farmers were calling for softer money or a larger supply of currency, if anyone violated financial orthodoxy before 1873, it was manufacturers from the West, who needed working capital and did not mind devaluing the nation's currency if it encouraged exports. Walter Nugent, *Money and American Society* (New York, 1968), 35-36.
8. Milton Friedman and Anna J. Schwartz, *A Monetary History of the United States, 1867-1960* (Princeton, NJ, 1963), 7.
9. George David Smith and Richard Sylla, "The Transformation of Financial Capitalism: An Essay on the History of American Capital Markets," *Financial Markets, Institutions & Instruments* 2:2 (1993), 1-62.

10. Jeremy Atack and Peter Passell, *A New Economic View of American History*, second edition (New York, 1994), 511-15.

11. Friedman and Schwartz, *A Monetary History*, 42, 93.

12. Friedman and Schwartz, *A Monetary History*, 513. On the role of money center banks, see C. A. E. Goodheart, *The New York Money Market and the Finance of Trade, 1900-1913* (Cambridge, MA, 1969); and John James, *Money and Capital Markets in Post Bellum America* (Princeton, NJ, 1978).

13. Friedman and Schwartz, *A Monetary History*, 114.

14. Strictly speaking, this took place not simply because of the relative value of the two metals, but because there was a fixed ratio between them, whereby a certain number of ounces of gold equaled a certain number of ounces of silver. Thus, when the marketplace value of gold fell compared to the "fixed ratio," people purchased gold cheaply on the open market. They then took it to the mint for silver, used the silver to buy still more gold, and repeated the process until all the silver was in the mint and only gold was in circulation.

15. Charles Calomiris, *Greenback Resumption and Silver Risk: The Economics and Politics of Monetary Regime Change in the United States, 1862-1900* (Cambridge, MA, 1992).

16. Friedman and Schwartz, *A Monetary History*, 99-100

17. Friedman and Schwartz, *A Monetary History*, 91.

18. Quoted in Nugent, *Money and American Society*, 153.

19. Quoted in Nugent, *Money and American Society*, 51-52.

20. *The Emigrant's Handbook and Guide to Wisconsin* (Milwaukee, 1851).

21. Clarence Danhof, *Change in Agriculture: The Northern United States, 1820-1870* (Cambridge, MA, 1969).

22. Atack and Passell, *A New Economic View*, 367.

23. Kenneth L. Sokoloff and Georgia C. Villaflor, "The Market for Manufacturing Workers during Early Industrialization: The American Northeast, 1820 to 1860," in Claudia Goldin and Hugh Rockoff, eds., *Strategic Factors in Nineteenth Century American Economic History: A Volume to Honor Robert W. Fogel* (Chicago, 1992), 36.

24. Richard J. Harney, *History of Winnebago County, Wisconsin, and Early History of the Northwest* (Oshkosh, 1880); Publius V. Lawson, *History, Winnebago County, Wisconsin: Its Cities, Towns, Resources, People* (Salem, MA, 1908).

25. Harvard University Graduate School of Business Administration, Baker Library, R. G. Dun manuscripts, Oshkosh—Winnebago Co., 373.

26. United States Bureau of the Census, U.S. Census Schedule, 1870, Oshkosh, Wisconsin, reel 1746.

27. *Weekly Northwestern,* October 10, page 3, col. 6.

28. Viviana Zelizer, *Morals and Markets: The Development of Life Insurance in the United States* (New York, 1979); Morton Keller, *The Life Insurance Enterprise, 1885-1910: A Study in the Limits of Corporate Power* (Cambridge, MA, 1963).

29. E. Anthony Rotundo, *American Manhood: Transformations in Masculinity from the Revolution to the Modern Era* (New York, 1993), 51.

30. Letters of John Elliott Tappan (originals at American Express Corporation and copies privately held), Tappan–R. J. Parkhill, May 10, 1895.

31. Robert E. Ficken and William R. Sherrard, "The Port Blakely Mill Company," *Journal of Forest History* 21:4 (October 1977), 204.

32. A vivid picture of the dangers of logging is found in Andrew Mason Prouty, *More Deadly Than War!: Pacific Coast Logging, 1827-1981* (New York, 1988).

33. Robert Wells, *Daylight in the Swamp!* (Madison, WI, 1978), 88.

34. Quoted in Robert E. Ficken, *The Forested Land: A History of Lumbering in Western Washington* (Seattle, 1987), 134.

35. As reported in *Minneapolis Journal,* October 1 and 2, 1891.

36. On the Merritts, see David A. Walker, *Iron Frontier: The Discovery and Early Development of Minnesota's Three Ranges* (Minneapolis, 1979), 76-90.

37. Quoted in Allen Nevins and Henry Steele Commager, *Short History of the United States* (New York, 1969), 300-301.

38. Thomas Misa, *A Nation of Steel: The Making of Modern America, 1865-1925* (Baltimore, 1995).

39. William T. Hogan, *Economic History of the Iron and Steel Industry of the United States* (Lexington, MA, 1971).

40. Tappan–Henry Farnham, January 13, 1911.

41. The conflict between Rockefeller and the Merritts has never been fully resolved, but a good account of the perceptions of the two sides and the motivations are found in Walker, *Iron Frontier,* 144-70.

42. Ron Chernow, *Titan: The Life of John D. Rockefeller* (New York, 1998), 382-93. Though to be fair, Rockefeller offered them the option of repurchasing the stock at $10 plus 6 percent interest a year later. He then extended the option for two of the Merritts, who eventually exercised it to considerable profit when United States Steel was created in 1901. Walker, *Iron Frontier,* 181-82.

43. Quoted in Walker, *Iron Frontier,* 155.

44. Quoted in Walker, *Iron Frontier,* 187.

45. Walker, *Iron Frontier,* 191.

46. Tappan interview, *Investors Syndicate Broadcaster* (Minneapolis, 1941).

47. Raymond W. Goldsmith, *Premodern Financial Systems: A Historical Comparative Study* (New York, 1987).

48. Kenneth Snowden, "Building and Loan Associations in the U.S., 1880-1893: The Origins of Localization in the Residential Mortgage Market," *Research in Economics* 51 (1997), 227-50.

49. George Alter, Claudia Goldin, and Elyce Rotella, *The Savings of Ordinary Americans: The Philadelphia Saving Fund Society in the Mid-Nineteenth Century* (Cambridge, MA, 1992); Raymond W. Goldsmith, *A Study of Saving in the United States* vol. I (New York, 1969 [1955]), 407.

50. Goldsmith, *Study of Saving* vol. III, 182.

51. H. Burton and D. C. Corner, *Investment and Unit Trusts in Britain and America* (London, 1968), 1-70; Hugh Bullock, *The Story of Investment Companies* (New York, 1959), 1-13. Also William Howard Steiner, *Investment Trusts: American Experience* (New York, 1975 [1929]), 17-38.

52. Quoted in Burton and Corner, *Investment and Unit Trusts,* 16.

53. *Arthur Weisberg Investment Company,* 1949 (New York, 1949), 14-15. United States Securities and Exchange Commission, *Investment Trusts and Investment Companies,* Report, part 1 (Washington, DC, 1939), 35-42.

54. Roger L. Ransom and Richard Sutch, "Tontine Insurance and the Armstrong Investigation: A Case of Stifled Innovation, 1868-1905," *Journal of Economic History* 47:2 (June 1987), 379-90.

55. Goldsmith, *A Study of Saving.*

56. Edwin Perkins, *American Public Finance and Financial Services, 1700-1815* (Columbus, OH, 1994). J. Owen Stalson, *Marketing Life Insurance: Its History in America* (Bryn Mawr, PA, 1969 [1942]).

57. Raymond W. Goldsmith, *Financial Intermediaries in the American Economy since 1900* (Princeton, NJ, 1958), 64-65, 95.

CHAPTER 2

1. Edward Chase Kirkland, *Industry Comes of Age: Business, Labor, and Public Policy 1860-1897* (New York, 1962), 7-10; Robert Sobel, *The Big Board: A History of the New York Stock Market* (New York, 1965).

2. Quoted in Ray Ginger, *Age of Excess: The United States from 1877 to 1914* (New York, 1965), 165-66.

3. Ginger, *Age of Excess,* 171.

4. John D. Hicks, "The Origin and Early History of the Farmers' Alliance in Minnesota," *Mississippi Valley Historical Review* 9:3 (December 1922), 207.

5. Lawrence Goodwyn, *Democratic Promise: The Populist Moment in America* (New York, 1976), 574, appendices A, B. Jeremy Atack and Peter Passell, *A New Economic View of American History,* second edition (New York, 1994), 408-11.

6. Atack and Passell, *A New View,* 511.

7. A good description of the development of futures trading is found in William Cronon, *Nature's Metropolis: Chicago and the Great West* (New York, 1991), 120-32. See also Kenneth Lipartito, "The New York Cotton Exchange and the Development of the Cotton Futures Market," *Business History Review* 57:1 (Spring, 1983), 50-72.

8. Gretchen Ritter, *Goldbugs and Greenbacks: The Antimonopoly Tradition and the Politics of Finance in America* (Cambridge, 1997), 199, 205.

9. Ritter, *Goldbugs and Greenbacks,* 92.

10. Cedric B. Cowling, *Populists, Plungers and Progressives: A Social History of Stock and Commodity Speculation, 1890-1936* (Princeton, NJ, 1965), 7.

11. It is for this reason that corporations held a special, and dangerous, place in Populist economics. No mere legal fiction or financial shell, corporations were viewed as the concrete, legal embodiment of this economy of endless desire. Unlike personal enterprises, corporations could grow and expand without limit. The venerable tradition of free labor saw labor as a person, not a thing to be bought and sold in the market. Corporations negated these limits. They were never reined in by the natural cycle of birth and death that governed the lives and wants of individuals. Their sole purpose was to increase wealth, and they, unlike individuals, could hold and concentrate wealth in perpetuity. So, like the speculator or dealer in paper values, corporations too seemed to have severed the link between labor, production, and the social good. Rural critics of railroad combines or big business operators frequently expressed specific grievances about high prices or unfair competition. That modern historians have trouble documenting such abuses only shows how deep the antimonopolist rhetoric went. Corporations were, by their nature, such a

suspect entity that antimonopolists believed they *had* to be acquiring their position by unfair means.

12. Milton Friedman and Anna J. Schwartz, *A Monetary History of the United States, 1867-1960* (Princeton, NJ, 1963), 122; Raymond W. Goldsmith, *Financial Intermediaries in the American Economy since 1900* (Princeton, NJ, 1958), 56-59.

13. Jeffrey G. Williamson, "Late Nineteenth Century Economic Retardation: A Neoclassical Analysis," *Journal of Economic History* 33:3 (September 1973), 581-607; Thomas Cochran, "The Paradox of American Economic Growth," *Journal of American History* 61:4 (March 1975), 925-42.

14. Atack and Passell, *A New Economic View,* 457-58.

15. Atack and Passell, *A New Economic View,* 402-26. For western farmers at noncompetitive points, likely in newly settled regions, monopoly rates may have been high.

16. Ritter, *Goldbugs and Greenbacks,* 8.

17. Ritter, *Goldbugs and Greenbacks,* 1. William H. Harvey, *Coin's Financial School* (Cambridge, MA, 1963 [1894]). A million copies in 1894 is roughly equivalent to 4 million in sales today.

18. Although the "losers" in this struggle, the antimonopolist farmers, have generally been seen as reformers, historians have ignored or misapprehended the more conservative Corporatists, who also had ideals of reform. For exceptions, see James Livingston, *Origins of the Federal Reserve System: Money, Class and Corporate Capitalism, 1890-1913* (Ithaca, NY, 1986).

19. Eugene White, *The Regulation and Reform of the American Banking System, 1900-1920* (Princeton, NJ, 1983). Goldsmith, *Financial Intermediaries,* 92-93.

20. Sobel, *The Big Board.*

21. George David Smith and Richard Sylla, "Capital Markets," in *Encyclopedia of the United States in the Twentieth Century* vol. III (New York, 1996), 1214. Preferred stocks of corporations paid a better 7 percent and offered greater security than common stocks, but in general small savers still avoided the stock market.

22. Investors Syndicate, *20 Questions Answered and a Plan of the Investors Syndicate of Minnesota,* n.d., filed in National Archives, RG 28, Records of the Post Office Department, Bureau of Chief Inspector.

23. Investors Syndicate, *20 Questions Answered.*

24. Andrew Carnegie, *The Gospel of Wealth* (Bedford, MA, 1998 [1889]).

25. Sylla and Smith, "Capital Markets."

26. Henrietta Larson, *Jay Cooke, Private Banker* (Cambridge, MA, 1968 [1936]), quotation, p. 364.

27. J. Owen Stalson, *Marketing Life Insurance; Its History in America* (Homewood, IL, 1969 [1942]), 454. On Colombian, Letters of John Elliott Tappan (originals at American Express Corporation and copies privately held), Tappan–Washburn, August 21, 1894.

28. Investors Syndicate, *20 Questions Answered.*

29. Stalson, *Marketing Life Insurance,* 319, 496-98.

30. *IDS Broadcaster,* September 1968, "Recollections of a Founder," reprint of 1949 interview with John Elliott Tappan.

31. Tappan–Ben F. Cameron, Jr., October 11, 1917.

32. H. Farnham–Post Master General, January 29, 1897.

33. On problems of the West North Central in particular, see Kenneth Snowden, "Mortgage Rates and American Capital Market Development in the Late Nineteenth Century," *Journal of Economic History* 47:3 (September 1987), 679.

34. On this point of American economic growth, see Thomas Cochran, "The Paradox of American Economic Growth," *Journal of American History* 61:4 (March 1975), 925-42.

35. Hicks, "Farmers' Alliance in Minnesota," 205.

36. Snowden, "Mortgage Rates," 679, 681.

37. Atack and Passell, *A New Economic View,* 402-26.

38. Goodwyn, *Democratic Promise,* 565-70.

39. Margaret G. Myers, *The New York Money Market, Volume 1: Origins and Development* (New York, 1931), 234.

40. Kenneth Snowden, "Building and Loan Associations in the U.S., 1880-1893: The Origins of Localization in the Residential Mortgage Market," *Research in Economics* 51 (1997), 227-50. Leo Grebler, David Blank, and Louis Winnick, *Capital Formation in Residential Real Estate: Trends and Prospects* (Princeton, NJ, 1956), chapter 13.

41. Tappan–C. G. Hillman, June 21, 1915; Minnesota Commerce Department, Securities Division, Investors Syndicate Case file 114.A.12.4 (F), State Archive, Minnesota Historical Society, John Elliott Tappan, Answer to Memorandum, 1921.

42. Kenneth Snowden, "Building and Loan Associations"; also, Snowden, "The Evolution of Interregional Mortgage Lending Channels," in Naomi Lamoreaux and Daniel Raff, eds., *Coordination and Information: Historical Perspectives on the Organization of Enterprise* (Chicago, 1995).

43. Kenneth Snowden, "Building and Loan Associations."

44. The first of the "national" building and loans was started in Minneapolis in 1887. Kenneth Snowden, "The Evolution of Interregional Mortgage Lending Channels," 217-19.

45. Chester Destler, "Western Radicalism: 1865-1901: Concepts and Origins," *Mississippi Valley Historical Review* 31:3 (1944), 335-68. The importance of independence and autonomy to supporters of the Populists can be inferred in Robert Klepper, *The Economic Bases for Agrarian Protest Movements in the United States, 1870-1900* (New York, 1978), who notes that protest movements were correlated with increasing levels of farm tenancy.

46. Investors Syndicate, *Second Annual Statement* (1896).

47. *Investors Syndicate Broadcaster,* n.d.

48. *IDS Broadcaster,* September 1968, "Recollections of a Founder."

49. Tappan–H. R. King, November 30, 1894; Tappan–C. H. Stone, July 13, 1898.

50. Tappan–T. W. Chamberlain, June 1896.

51. Free silver meant returning silver to the nation's money supply, silver that had been removed in the "Crime of '73." By minting and coining silver at the ratio of 16 ounces of silver to 1 ounce of gold, the money supply would have increased. Gold on the open market was actually worth much more than 16 ounces of silver. Populists did not see free silver as the answer to their problems, but in the end backed Bryan and this policy nonetheless.

52. Tappan–T. W. Chamberlin, November 13, 1896.

53. Tappan–Messers. Knacble and Scherer, March 6, 1895.

54. Tappan–W. E. Borland, October 13, 1896.

55. Investors Syndicate, *First Annual Statement* (1895).

CHAPTER 3

1. Carlos Schwantes, *Coxey's Army: An American Odyssey* (Lincoln, NE, 1985), 239.
2. *IDS Broadcaster,* September 1968, "Recollections of a Founder," reprint of 1949 interview with John Elliott Tappan.
3. A point made clearly in Donald L. McMurry, *Coxey's Army: A Study of the Industrial Army Movement of 1894* (Seattle, 1968 [1929]).
4. Coxey's moderation is also evident in his term as mayor of Massillon, Ohio, where he ran on a campaign of municipal ownership of essential public utilities. This sort of "gas and water" socialism was common in the Midwest, often promoted by liberal businessmen turned politicians.
5. McMurry, *Coxey's Army,* 46.
6. Henrietta Larson, *Jay Cooke, Private Banker* (Cambridge, MA, 1968 [1936]), 289.
7. Lawrence Goodwyn, *Democratic Promise: The Populist Moment in America* (New York, 1976), 158-61.
8. Martin Ridge, "Ignatius Donnelly and the Granger Movement in Minnesota," *Mississippi Valley Historical Review* 42:4 (March 1956), 693-709.
9. John D. Hicks, "The Political Career of Ignatius Donnelly," *Mississippi Valley Historical Review* 8:1, 2 (June-September 1921), 80-132; Martin Ridge, *Ignatius Donnelly: The Portrait of a Politician* (Chicago, 1962); David Anderson, *Ignatius Donnelly* (Boston, 1980).
10. McMurry, *Coxey's Army,* 265-66.
11. Letters of John Elliott Tappan (originals at American Express Corporation and copies privately held) Tappan–unknown, January 2, 1897.
12. Tappan–J. J. Bechtold, January 2, 1897.
13. Tappan–W. M. Booth, November 16, 1905.
14. Tappan–George MacDonald, March 7, 1895.
15. Tappan–M. A. Goff, March 21, 1895.
16. Quoted in George David Smith and Richard Sylla, "Capital Markets," in *Encyclopedia of the United States in the Twentieth Century* vol. III (New York, 1996), 1222.
17. Kenneth Lipartito and Paul Miranti, "Professions and Organizations in Twentieth-Century America," *Social Science Quarterly* 79:2 (June 1998), 308-9.
18. Morton Keller, *The Life Insurance Enterprise, 1885-1910: A Study in the Limits of Corporate Power* (Cambridge, MA, 1963), 9.
19. Viviana Zelizer, *Morals and Markets: The Development of Life Insurance in the United States* (New York, 1979); Lawrence Goodheart, *Abolitionist, Actuary, Atheist: Elizur Wright and the Reform Impulse* (Kent, OH, 1990).
20. Keller, *Life Insurance Enterprise,* 3.
21. Roger Ransom and Richard Sutch, "Tontine Insurance and the Armstrong Investigation: A Case of Stifled Innovation," *Journal of Economic History* 47:2 (June 1987), 380.
22. Armstrong Committee, Report, vol. 7, 322-24, quoted in Ransom and Sutch, "Tontine Insurance," 388-89.
23. Even today, it is common wisdom in the investment community that people underestimate risk.
24. J. Owen Stalson, *Marketing Life Insurance: Its History in America* (Homewood, IL, 1969 [1942]), 487

25. Quoted in Lendol Calder, *Financing the American Dream: A Cultural History of Consumer Credit* (Princeton, NJ, 1999), 82-83.

26. Walter Benn Michaels, *The Gold Standard and the Logic of Naturalism: American Literature at the Turn of the Century* (Berkeley, CA, 1987), 223-37.

27. The perspective here, it is important to remember, was not antimarket. Rather, critics of gambling and gambling-like investments sought to protect the market as a source of moral authority, political order, and social stability. Unchecked, self-interest could unleash all sorts of dangers, such as destabilizing frenzies and passions. Properly regulated, self-interest was a tool of the capitalist economy. A moral capitalist economy was sane and rational, not speculative. There were no wild price swings that disrupted natural values. There was no free flow of easy money, which poured into the political system until it undermined virtue and drowned the public interest.

28. In the eighteenth-century Age of Enlightenment, when religion mattered less, American state, local, and even federal governments used lotteries as an alternative to taxes. This practice declined rapidly by the nineteenth century, as all forms of gambling came under attack. There was more than just prudishness or religious fundamentalism at work here, however. When reformers denounced state-run lotteries as immoral, they used the language of mathematics and logic, arguing that, compared to other ways of investing one's money, a lottery ticket was a loser. Ann Fabian, *Card Sharps, Dream Books & Bucket Shops: Gambling in 19th-Century America* (Ithaca, NY, 1990), 116-20.

29. Benn Michaels, "Gold Standard and the Logic of Naturalism," 57-69; Fabian, *Card Sharps, Dream Books & Bucket Shops,* 188-200. The fear of "counterfeits" became almost an obsession of middle-class America at the end of the nineteenth century. Painters, as Michaels (169) has observed, got wind of these fears and incorporated them into their art works. Trompe l'oeil painting enjoyed great popularity. When painters fooled the eye by representing flat objects such as paper money as though they were real, three dimensional ones stuck on a painting, they pushed all the hot buttons of middle-class patrons. Paintings of "forged" money sent the viewer reeling between older notions of the real and genuine, and the newer notions of pure subjectivity and desire. By questioning the natural order of things, good fakery also called into question notions that there was a real economy out there, where money was only the servant of underlying fundamental values. For those still committed to that older concept of economy, nothing could be more provocative. Like farmer charges of "wind wheat" and fictitious commodities, the danger lay in the proximity between the real and its representation, and the potential for conflating the two.

30. Tappan–M. A. Goff, March 21, 1895.

31. Tappan–Headington, October 6, 1894.

32. Keller, *Life Insurance Enterprise,* 62-64, 139-40.

33. See Stalson, *Marketing Life Insurance,* 413-15, 500, on the questions surrounding reserve funds.

34. On assessment companies, see Stalson, *Marketing Life Insurance,* 445-61.

35. Figures from Stalson, *Marketing Life Insurance,* appendices 18, 24, 25.

36. Keller, *Life Insurance Enterprise,* 245-64; Stalson, *Marketing Life Insurance,* 549-59.

37. Quoted in Keller, *Life Insurance Enterprise,* 254.

38. Tappan–M. A. Goff, March 21, 1895.

39. *Chicago Daily Tribune,* March 22, 1896.

40. Ransom and Sutch, "Tontine Insurance," 387.

41. Investors Syndicate, *20 Questions Answered and a Plan of the Investors Syndicate of Minnesota,* n.d., filed in National Archives, RG 28, Records of the Post Office Department, Bureau of Chief Inspector.

42. Tappan–W. D. Guinn, September 26, 1899.

43. Tappan–Unknown, March 17, 1905.

44. Tappan–E. J. Greening, May 8, 1915.

45. Minnesota Commerce Department, Securities Division, Investors Syndicate Case file 114.A.12.4 (F), State Archive, Minnesota Historical Society, John Elliott Tappan, Answer to Memorandum, 1921.

46. Tappan–J. W. Henney, October 8, 1898.

47. United States Securities and Exchange Commission, *Investment Trusts and Investment Companies. Report of the Securities and Exchange Commission, pursuant to section 30 of the Public Utility Holding Company Act of 1935. Companies Issuing Face Amount Installment Certificates* (Washington, DC, 1940), 47-62. These figures are from the late 1920s and early 1930s, and partly reflect the impact of the Depression. Also, the lapsation rate (lapses per amount paid out) was higher during this period (1920s) of rapid growth, since a high percentage of the contracts were from new subscribers, who were not yet due any money. Investors Syndicate still had a lower lapsation rate than most insurance companies, and lower also than its chief competitor, Fidelity Investment Association.

48. Tappan, Answer to Memorandum, 1921.

49. Tappan, Answer to Memorandum, 1921.

50. Tappan–Amil Theimer, May 19, 1904.

51. Tappan–Lee, March 2, 1895.

52. Tappan–E. J. Greening, May 8, 1915.

53. Quoted in Stalson, *Marketing Life Insurance,* 408.

54. Tappan–Max Holtermann, May 7, 1895.

55. Tappan–Fred C. Holt, June 15, 1906.

56. Tappan–T. H. Koerner, November 28, 1896.

57. Tappan–W. F. Borncamp, December 6, 1907.

58. Tappan–T. H. Koerner, November 13, 1896.

59. Tappan–R. Orr, February 18, 1899.

60. Gail Bederman, *Manliness and Civilization: A Cultural History of Gender and Race in the United States, 1800-1917* (Chicago, 1995), 18.

61. Abraham Lincoln, "Speech at New Haven," March 6, 1860.

62. Bederman, *Manliness and Civilization,* 12.

63. Tappan–Mr. C. F. Mackenzie, January 11, 1918.

64. Tappan–R. Orr, February 18, 1899.

65. What follows is drawn from Dora Costa, *The Evolution of Retirement: An American Economic History, 1880-1990* (Chicago, 1998).

66. On pensions and Social Security, see Steven Sass, *The Promise of Private Pensions: The First Hundred Years* (Cambridge, MA, 1997), 88-119.

67. Tappan–R. R. Conwill, May 6, 1895.

68. Tappan–G. M. MacDonald, May 10, 1895

69. Tappan–M. A. Goff, August 24, 1895.

70. Tappan–M. A. Goff, April 7, 1895.

71. Tappan–M. A. Goff, August 24, 1895.

72. Tappan–F. M. Rule, November 8, 1895.

73. Cedric B. Cowling, *Populists, Plungers and Progressives: A Social History of Stock and Commodity Speculation, 1890-1936* (Princeton, NJ, 1965), 14-15

74. Farnham–Postmaster General Wilson, January 29, 1897. Durland Case, see *Evans* v. *US* 153 US 584.

75. Tappan–T. W. Chamberlain, March 15, 1897.

76. Tappan–T. W. Chamberlain, March 15, 1897.

77. Tappan–G. R. Hager, February 10, 1897.

78. Tappan–T. W. Chamberlain, March 15, 1897.

79. Tappan–M. A. Goff, March 29, 1897.

80. Tappan–M. A. Goff, September 1, 1897.

81. Tappan–E. W. Jeffrey, November 21, 1899.

82. Tappan–M. A. Goff, May 7, 1897.

83. Quoted in Calder, *Financing the American Dream,* 87.

84. Tappan–William Wingate Knowles, February 14, 1899.

85. Tappan–C. H. Stone, July 13, 1898.

86. Tappan–J. W. Henney, October 8, 1898.

87. Quoted in E. Anthony Rotundo, *American Manhood: Transformations in Masculinity from the Revolution to the Modern Era* (New York, 1993), 181.

88. Scott Sandage, "Deadbeats, Drunkards, and Dreamers: A Cultural History of Failure in America, 1819-1893," Ph.D. dissertation, Rutgers University, 1995.

89. Quoted in Calder, *Financing the American Dream.*

90. Tappan–F. P. Brown, May 17, 1895.

91. Tappan–H. T. Goodland, January 19, 1903.

92. Tappan–Frank Tappan, May 2, 1895.

93. Tappan–J. W. Henley, October 8, 1898.

94. Tappan–William Wingate Knowles, February 14, 1899.

95. J. W. Earl–Tappan, April 19, 1900.

96. Tappan–Saunders, November 21, 1899.

97. Investors Syndicate, *Second Annual Statement* (1896); Earl–W. L. Finton, July 2, 1900.

98. Earl–unknown client, April 19, 1900.

CHAPTER 4

1. Letters of John Elliott Tappan (originals at American Express Corporation and copies privately held) J. W. Earl–Tappan, November 14, 1901.

2. Earl–Tappan, November 14, 1901.

3. Earl–Tappan, November 15, 1901.

4. Earl–Tappan, November 18, 1901.

5. Earl–Burns McClain, November 21, 1901.

6. Earl–McClain, November 18, 1901.

7. Tappan–Ruth Tappan Dowling, March 11, 1940.

8. Tappan–Mrs. H. Benedict, June 11, 1907.

9. Tappan–Geoffrey Cassen, October 28, 1907.

10. Tappan–Rev. Roberts, October 21, 1907.

11. Tappan–F. P. Borncamp, October 23, 1907.

12. Tappan–Carl Nord, March 1909.

13. Tappan–A. M. Scots, August 31, 1903.

14. Quoted in Lendol Calder, *Financing the American Dream: A Cultural History of Consumer Credit* (Princeton, NJ, 1999), 88

15. Quoted in Alan Olmstead, *New York City Mutual Savings Banks, 1819-1861* (Chapel Hill, NC, 1976), 10.

16. Lance Davis and Peter Payne, "From Benevolence to Business: The Story of Two Savings Banks," *Business History Review* 32:4 (1958), 386-406.

17. Duncan Ross, "Penny Banks in Scotland," paper presented at the Business History Conference, Palo Alto, CA, 2000.

18. Olmstead, *New York City Mutual Savings Banks,* 3-4.

19. George Alter, Claudia Goldin, and Elyce Rotella, *The Savings of Ordinary Americans: The Philadelphia Saving Fund Society in the Mid-Nineteenth Century* (Cambridge, MA, 1992).

20. Raymond W. Goldsmith, *A Study of Saving in the United States* (New York, 1969 [1955]), vol. I, 8-9; vol. III, 182.

21. Alter et. al., *Savings of Ordinary Americans,* 16.

22. Goldsmith, *Study of Savings,* vol. I, 699.

23. Buying secondhand the stock of a corporation—nearly all stock bought and sold on the major exchanges is old, not a new issue—does not constitute true investment, since the funds do not contribute to new capital formation.

24. Goldsmith, *Study of Savings,* vol. I, 309-10.

25. Lawrence Glickman, *A Living Wage: American Workers and the Making of Consumer Society* (Ithaca, NY, 1977); Calder, *Financing the American Dream.*

26. David Hounshell, *From the American System to Mass Production, 1800-1932: The Development of Manufacturing Technology in the United States* (Baltimore, 1984), 189-215.

27. Ronald Kline and Trevor Pinch, "Users as Agents of Technological Change: The Social Construction of the Automobile in the Rural United States," *Technology and Culture* 37:4 (October 1996), 763-95.

28. Warren Belasco, *Americans on the Road: From Autocamp to Motel, 1910-1945* (Cambridge, MA, 1981).

29. On Ford's beliefs, see David Nye, *Henry Ford, Ignorant Idealist* (Port Washington, NY, 1979).

30. Jacob Coxey's answer to the depression of the 1890s had also been good roads.

31. Kenneth Jackson, *Crabgrass Frontier: The Suburbanization of the United States* (New York, 1985).

32. Tappan–Kneut Kneutson, June 8, 1902; April 25, 1902.

33. Tappan–Julia Rand, July 24, 1902; National Archives, RG 49, Bureau of Land Management, Duluth, MN, Homestead Claim of John Elliott Tappan, 1904.

34. Ina Metso, Minerva Balke, and Lorene Ruuska, *The Angora Story* (Angora, MN, 1977), 6.

35. Tappan–M. A. Axelsson, September 22, 1906.

36. *Northland Farmer,* October 5, 1905.

37. *Northland Farmer,* November 30, 1905.

38. Secretary of State, St. Paul, Minnesota, Articles of Incorporation, Northern Livestock and Improvement Company, December 20, 1904.

39. Tappan–unknown, January 11, 1904.

40. Tappan–Emma Meservey, March 27, 1909.

41. *Northland Farmer,* September 4, 1905.

42. Tappan–Schiffer, January 26, 1909.

43. Leonard G. Wilson, "The Historical Riddle of Milk-Borne Scarlet Fever," *Bulletin of the History of Medicine* 60:3 (1986), 321-42

44. Tappan–Sue Quimby, February 5, 1909.

CHAPTER 5

1. On death and dying, see David Stannard, ed., *Death in America* (Philadelphia, 1975); Charles O. Jackson, ed., *Passing: The Vision of Death in America* (Westport, CT, 1977). On funeral practices, see William Henry Kellar and Elisabeth O'Kane, *Service Corporation International: The Creation of the Modern Death Care Industry* (Dallas, 1999).

2. Letters of John Elliott Tappan (originals at American Express Corporation and copies privately held), Tappan–C. Nord, July 20, 1909.

3. Tappan–David Judson, October 1909.

4. Tappan–Charles Featherstone, May 21, 1910.

5. Minnesota Commerce Department, Securities Division, Investors Syndicate Case file 114.A.12.4 (F), State Archive, Minnesota Historical Society, John Elliott Tappan, Answer to Memorandum, 1921.

6. On the "bias" against western cities, see Allan R. Pred, *The Spatial Dynamics of U.S. Urban-Industrial Growth, 1800-1914* (Cambridge, 1966).

7. Kenneth Snowden, "Mortgage Lending and American Urbanization, 1880-1890," *Journal of Economic History* 48:2 (June 1988), 273-85.

8. Tappan, Answer to Memorandum, 1921.

9. Tappan–B. M. Colvin, May 22, 1917; June 6, 1917; Tappan–Financial Department of *Chicago Tribune*, May 22, 1917.

10. Raymond W. Goldsmith, *A Study of Saving in the United States* (New York, 1969 [1955]), vol. I, 98-101.

11. United States Securities and Exchange Commission, *Investment Trusts and Investment Companies. Report of the Securities and Exchange Commission, pursuant to section 30 of the Public Utility Holding Company Act of 1935. Companies Issuing Face Amount Installment Certificates* (Washington, DC, 1940), 41. Figures are from the late 1920s and '30s; no earlier systematic figures on investment patterns are available.

12. Marc Weiss, *The Rise of the Community Builders: The American Real Estate Industry and Urban Land Planning* (New York, 1987).

13. Eric Abrahamson, "Home Ownership, the Building and Loan, and the Transformation of the Republican Ideal in the United States," paper presented at the American Historical Association Meeting, Washington, D.C., 1999, 12-15.

14. Securities and Exchange Commission, *Investment Trusts and Investment Companies,* 40. This deals with a later period, but a period when size and complexity should have produced greater principal-agent problems.

15. Tappan–T. W. Chamberlain, July 8, 1911.

16. Tappan–Kneut Kneutson, April 25, 1902; October 9, 1908.

17. Tappan–Charles Featherstone, November 23, 1909.

18. Tappan–Isaac Peterson, September 15, 1910.

19. Tappan–C. Samuelson, May 21, 1910.

20. Tappan–C. Samuelson, May 21, 1910.

21. Tappan–Wm. B. Walrath and Co., June 22, 1910.

22. Tappan–F. H. Nye, October 24, 1910.

23. Tappan–Caleb Pye, May 12, 1910.
24. Tappan–Charles Featherstone, May 21, 1910.
25. Tappan–Ella Kumm, January 27, 1911.
26. Tappan–T. W. Chamberlain, February 13, 1911.
27. Tappan–J. F. Beyer, June 19, 1913.
28. Tappan–J. J. Lambrecht, January 4, 1913.
29. Tappan–C. H. Guthrie, July 27, 1912.
30. Tappan–Henry Farnham, August 2, 1909.

CHAPTER 6

1. Letters of John Elliott Tappan (originals at American Express Corporation and copies privately held), Tappan–Robert S. Thomas, December 1917.
2. Tappan–J. E. Came, March 10, 1913; March 13, 1913.
3. Tappan–E. M. Pool, January 23, 1899.
4. Tappan–H. T. Goodland, January 19, 1903; Burns McClain-Goodland, January 19, 1903.
5. J. Owen Stalson, *Marketing Life Insurance; Its History in America* (Homewood, IL, 1969 [1942]), 370.
6. Stalson, *Marketing Life Insurance,* 202.
7. McClain–H. T. Goodland, January 19, 1903.
8. Investors Syndicate, *20 Questions Answered and a Plan of the Investors Syndicate of Minnesota,* n.d., filed in National Archives, RG 28, Records of the Post Office Department, Bureau of Chief Inspector.
9. United States Securities and Exchange Commission, *Investment Trusts and Investment Companies. Report of the Securities and Exchange Commission, pursuant to section 30 of the Public Utility Holding Company Act of 1935. Companies Issuing Face Amount Installment Certificates* (Washington, DC, 1940), 18.
10. *IDS Broadcaster,* September 1968, "Recollections of a Founder," reprint of 1949 interview with John Elliott Tappan.
11. On agents in general, see Thomas S. Dicke, *Franchising in America: The Development of a Business Method* (Chapel Hill, NC, 1992).
12. Stalson, *Marketing Life Insurance,* 585-601.
13. Tappan–S. G. Hillman, June 9, 1915.
14. United States Securities and Exchange Commission, *Investment Trusts and Investment Companies* (Philadelphia, 1946), 226.
15. Stalson, *Marketing Life Insurance,* 525-28.
16. On the popularity of load funds in the nineteenth and early twentieth centuries, see United States Securities and Exchange Commission, *Report of the Securities and Exchange Commission on the Public Policy Implications of Investment Company Growth* (Washington, DC, 1966), 7, 22, 247-51.
17. Tappan–Fisk, March 18, 1919.
18. Investors Syndicate, *20 Questions Answered.*
19. Securities and Exchange Commission, *Investment Trusts and Investment Companies: Companies Issuing Face Amount Installment Certificates,* 21.
20. Securities and Exchange Commission, *Investment Trusts and Investment Companies: Companies Issuing Face Amount Installment Certificates,* 24.

21. Roger L. Ransom and Richard Sutch, "Tontine Insurance and the Armstrong Investigation: A Case of Stifled Innovation, 1868-1905," *Journal of Economic History* 47:2 (June 1987), 379-90.
22. Tappan–F. P. Brown, May 17, 1895.
23. Edwin J. Perkins, *Wall Street to Main Street: Charles Merrill and Middle-Class Investors* (Cambridge, MA, 1999), 150-55.
24. Tappan–McClain, March 1, 1902.
25. Tappan–E. R. Roe, January 3, 1917.
26. Tappan–J. J. Lambrecht, January 4, 1913.
27. Tappan–Lambrecht, January 4, 1913.
28. Tappan–T. R. Johnson, May 16, 1918.
29. Tappan–John Goodson, May 24, 1918; Tappan–E. L. Wyatt, May 24, 1918.
30. Tappan–Makepeace, July 9, 1918.
31. Tappan–W. Lambertson, February 7, 1919.
32. Tappan–Grady, November 13, 1918.
33. Pamela Walker Laird, *Advertising Progress: American Business and the Rise of Consumer Marketing* (Baltimore, 1998), notes the change from owner-manager to corporate business and the rise of advertising professionals.
34. Tappan–Public Examiner of Minneapolis, October 29, 1908.
35. Securities and Exchange Commission, *Investment Trusts and Investment Companies: Companies Issuing Face Amount Installment Certificates,* 75; Hugh Bullock, *The Story of Investment Companies* (New York, 1960), 106-7.
36. Minnesota Commerce Department, Securities Division, Investors Syndicate Case file 114.A.12.4 (F), State Archive, Minnesota Historical Society, John Elliott Tappan, Answer to Memorandum, 1921.
37. Tappan, Answer to Memorandum, 1921.
38. Tappan–Mrs. Bessie Pugs, January 15, 1916.
39. Tappan–C. G. Hillman, June 21, 1915.
40. Cedric B. Cowling, *Populists, Plungers and Progressives: A Social History of Stock and Commodity Speculation, 1890-1936* (Princeton, NJ, 1965), 51-64; Vincent P. Carosso, *Investment Banking in America* (Cambridge, MA, 1970), 156-64.
41. Tappan–*Chicago Tribune,* Investors Guide Department, November 1914.
42. Tappan–P. J. Connaughton, March 15, 1915.
43. Tappan–Colvin, April 24, 1917.
44. Tappan–Harriet Gebhardt, November 8, 1913.
45. Tappan–Sen. G. W. Humphrey, August, 1, 1917.
46. Tappan–Pritchett, December 16, 1915.
47. Tappan–McClain, February 14, 1905.
48. Tappan–Harriet Gebhardt, November 8, 1913.
49. Tappan–Petrus Peterson, January 24, 1919.
50. Tappan–Petrus Peterson, January 24, 1919.
51. Tappan–Harry Combs, May 1, 1917.

CHAPTER 7

1. Raymond W. Goldsmith, *A Study of Saving in the United States* vol. I (New York, 1969 [1955]), 146.

2. Morton Keller, *The Life Insurance Enterprise, 1885-1910: A Study in the Limits of Corporate Power* (Cambridge, MA, 1963), 55

3. Letters of John Elliott Tappan (originals at American Express Corporation and copies privately held), Tappan–B. M. Colvin, June 6, 1917.

4. Tappan–Job Nordseth, June 7, 1917.

5. Tappan–Davis, October 1917.

6. Tappan–Hammond Brothers, March 14, 1918.

7. On composition of the Capital Issues Committee, see Vincent P. Carosso, *Investment Banking in America* (Cambridge, MA, 1970), 231.

8. Carosso, *Investment Banking in America,* 156-64, 233-34.

9. Tappan–Charles Ahrens, November 11, 1918.

10. Tappan–Joseph Katz, December 6, 1918.

11. Alfred W. Crosby, *America's Forgotten Pandemic: The Influenza of 1918* (New York, 1989).

12. Crosby, *America's Forgotten Pandemic,* 60-61.

13. Tappan–Arthur Thomas, February 20, 1919.

14. Tappan–Mrs. Ralph O. Edick, January 24, 1919.

15. United States Securities and Exchange Commission, *Investment Trusts and Investment Companies. Report of the Securities and Exchange Commission, pursuant to section 30 of the Public Utility Holding Company Act of 1935. Companies Issuing Face Amount Installment Certificates* (Washington, DC, 1940), 192.

16. Minnesota Commerce Department, Securities Division, Investors Syndicate Case file 114.A.12.4 (F), State Archive, Minnesota Historical Society, John Elliott Tappan, Answer to Memorandum, 1921.

17. Tappan, Answer to Memorandum, 1921.

18. Quoted in *Investing in the Future: A Century of IDS* (Minneapolis, 1994), 58.

19. Tappan–stockholders, August 5, 1918.

20. Cedric B. Cowling, *Populists, Plungers and Progressives: A Social History of Stock and Commodity Speculation, 1890-1936* (Princeton, NJ, 1965), 33-35.

21. Roger L. Ransom and Richard Sutch, "Tontine Insurance and the Armstrong Investigation: A Case of Stifled Innovation, 1868-1905," *Journal of Economic History* 47:2 (June 1987), 379-90.

22. Robert Sobel, *The Big Board: A History of the New York Stock Market* (New York, 1965), 254, 264. But contrast this to Sobel, *The Great Bull Market: Wall Street in the 1920s* (New York, 1968), 74-75, which quotes 3.5 million investors.

23. Goldsmith, *Study of Savings,* vol. I, 719.

24. William Steiner, *Investment Trusts: American Experience* (New York, 1975 [1929]), 39-69.

25. John Fowler, *American Investment Trusts* (New York, 1975 [1928]), 6.

26. Goldsmith, *Study of Savings,* vol. I, 559, 563. On investment trusts more generally, see Steiner, *Investment Trusts: The American Experience.*

27. Sobel, *Big Board,* 267-68.

28. Sobel, *Big Board,* 285-86.

29. Fowler, *American Investment Trusts,* 203.

30. On the way in which America's extensive western movement and development ate up capital and required continual investment in land and land development, see Thomas

Cochran, "The Paradox of American Economic Growth," *Journal of American History* 61:4 (March 1975), 933-34.

31. Such conservatism is not out of step with being a financial innovator. Charles Merrill, who would continue in the tradition of serving the average investor by creating a stock brokerage firm for Main Street, rather than Wall Street, eschewed mutual funds, too, when they came roaring back in the 1950s. Edwin J. Perkins, *Wall Street to Main Street: Charles Merrill and Middle-Class Investors* (Cambridge, 1999).

32. Fowler, *American Investment Trusts,* 6.

33. *IDS Going on 75* (Minneapolis, 1968), 7.

34. Securities and Exchange Commission, *Investment Trusts and Investment Companies: Companies Issuing Face Amount Installment Certificates,* 37-38.

CHAPTER 8

1. Minnesota Commerce Department, Securities Division, Investors Syndicate Case file 114.A.12.4 (F), State Archive, Minnesota Historical Society, John Elliott Tappan, Answer to Memorandum, 1921.

2. David Nye, *Henry Ford, Ignorant Idealist* (Port Washington, NY, 1979), 64-65. Ford was practically obsessed with diet, and spent a good portion of his later life trying to create a more efficient menu manufactured from soybeans. In later life, Tappan sunk his money into a prohibition soft-drink, healthier and safer than alcohol.

3. Letters of John Elliott Tappan (originals at American Express Corporation and copies privately held), Tappan–C. F. MacKenzie, January 11, 1918.

4. Lendol Calder, *Financing the American Dream: A Cultural History of Consumer Credit* (Princeton, NJ, 1999), 191-95.

5. Jackson Lears, "Review of Peter Dobkin Hall, *The Organization of American Culture, 1790-1900*," *American Historical Review* 88:1 (February 1983), 166.

6. Carol Shammas, "A New Look at Long-Term Wealth Inequality in the United States," *American Historical Review* 98:2 (April 1993), 412-31.

7. Felice Bonadio, *A. P. Giannini: Banker of America* (Berkeley, CA, 1994), 301.

8. Edwin J. Perkins, *Wall Street to Main Street: Charles Merrill and Middle-Class Investors* (Cambridge, 1999).

EPILOGUE

1. United States Securities and Exchange Commission, *Investment Trusts and Investment Companies,* Part II (Washington, DC, 1938), 226; also *Investing in the Future: A Century of IDS* (Minneapolis, 1994), 10.

2. United States Securities and Exchange Commission, *Investment Trusts and Investment Companies. Report of the Securities and Exchange Commission, pursuant to section 30 of the Public Utility Holding Company Act of 1935. Companies Issuing Face Amount Installment Certificates* (Washington, DC, 1940), 17.

3. Securities and Exchange Commission, *Investment Trusts and Investment Companies: Companies Issuing Face Amount Installment Certificates,* 23-24. On financial advertising in the early twentieth century, see Daniel Starch, *Principles of Advertising* (Chicago, 1923), 948-73.

4. Robert Sobel, *The Big Board: A History of the New York Stock Market* (New York, 1965), 340.

5. Edwin J. Perkins, *Wall Street to Main Street: Charles Merrill and Middle-Class Investors* (Cambridge, 1999), 9, 142.

6. George David Smith and Richard Sylla, "Capital Markets," in *Encyclopedia of the United States in the Twentieth Century* vol. III (New York, 1996), 1223.

7. Sobel, *Big Board,* 266-67; John T. Flynn, *Investment Trusts Gone Wrong!* (New York, 1975 [1930]).

8. Quoted in Minette E. Drumwright, "IDS Financial Services," Harvard Business School Case # 9-588-044.

Index